Bringing Christ to The Chinese

China-Hong Kong-San Francisco

ii

Bringing Christ To The Chinese

China-Hong Kong-San Francisco

By

Vangina E. Lee
作者: 李永珍

One Spirit Press
Portland, Oregon

Copyrighted 2011 by Vangina (Jean) E. Lee

作者: 李永珍

All rights reserved.
Printed in the USA

ISBN: 978-1-893075-86-3
LCCN: 2011927755

Book Design: Spirit Press. LLC

This book may not be reproduced by electronic or any other means,
which exist now or may yet be developed, without permission of
Spirit Press, except in the case of brief quotations embodied
in critical articles and reviews

One Spirit Press
onespiritpress.com
Portland, Oregon

Forward...vi
Acknowledgment.....vii
Preface: Early Lutheran Beginnings....viii

Chapter 1	God's Call....2
Chapter 2	In His Own Words—Pastor Holt....6
Chapter 3	The Journey—Geraldine Holt....20
Chapter 4	The Mission Field—Lorraine Behling....70
Chapter 5	Seeking the Way....76
Chapter 6	The First Co-Worker—Amy Hau Mui....86
Chapter 7	Immigrants at 606 Jackson Street....94
Chapter 8	Sharing the Gospel....100
Chapter 9	Moving Forward....106
Chapter 10	Dedication of 1725 Washington Street....108
Chapter 11	The First Ten Years—1969–1980....114
Chapter 12	Lives Touched by Pastor Holt....122
Chapter 13	New Ministries....134
Chapter 14	New Co-Workers....148
Chapter 15	20 Years of God's Blessings—1964–1984.....162
Chapter 16	The Church Grew 1980-1990....166
Chapter 17	The First Called Pastor....178
Chapter 18	Calling the Second Pastor....184
Chapter 19	Words of Advice 194
Chapter 20	Ten Years of God's Blessings—1991–2001....198
Chapter 21	Calling the Third Pastor and a D.C.E....206
Chapter 22	A New Century—2001–2010....212
Chapter 23	These are Her Sons—Now 12 Pastors....234
Chapter 24	A Tribute to Rev. Wilbert Victor Holt....256
Chapter 25	The Church 2012....270
Colophon	

Forward

This is the story of how God used His faithful servant, Rev. Dr. Wilbert V. Holt and his wife, Geraldine, to bring the Gospel of Jesus Christ to generations of Chinese people in China, Hong Kong and San Francisco.

He was a co-founder of the Lutheran Church, Hong Kong Synod and first President of Concordia Theological Seminary in Hong Kong.

By the Grace of God and the power of the Holy Spirit, he founded the Lutheran Church of the Holy Spirit in San Francisco. Pastor and Mrs. Holt were influential in encouraging many young people to become pastors and called church workers, thus fulfilling the Great Commission. As of this date, twelve "sons" of this church have been ordained and are serving in Lutheran Churches.

One of Pastor Holt's favorite Bible verses was "Always be prepared to make a defense to anyone who calls you to account for the hope that is in you, yet do it with gentleness and reverence" I Peter 3:15

Acknowledgement

We gratefully acknowledge the prayers, encouragement and assistance of the many individuals who helped to make this book possible. The guidance, articles, shared experiences, and reflections of the many Pastors, called workers, members and friends have made it possible so others might know what God has accomplished through His humble servants, Rev. Dr. Wilbert V. Holt and his wife Geraldine Holt.

We also appreciate the many hours members and friends of the Lutheran Church of the Holy Spirit spent in designing the cover, text and pictures for the book, as well as those who assisted in preparing the pictures for the book. The financial support of members of the church made possible the publishing and printing of this book.

To God be the Glory!

Preface
Early Lutheran Beginnings In China

Excerpts from "Lutherans on the Yangtze"
by Dave Kohl. Available March 2012

To understand the significance and contributions of Rev. Wilbert Holt among Chinese Christians, a few background details should help the reader gain insights for the one hundred years of Missouri Synod presence in Greater China. This is a quick summary of a 350 page book to be released in 2012, "Lutherans on the Yangtze," by David G. Kohl.

Bold faced names are locations of mission activity from 1913-1949.

Two years after the Chinese Revolution of 1911 that ended Imperial rule and established the Republic of China, a lone Lutheran pastor and his family arrived in Shanghai from St. Paul, MN, to begin bringing the Gospel of salvation to Chinese people. He selected **Hankow** 675 miles west on the Yangtze, as his base. The three-city area named WuHan (including **Hanyang** and **Wuchang**) was central China's major north-south railroad and east-west water hub. There were experienced Lutheran missions of other Synods nearby.

Rev. Edward Arndt, also a professor of science and mathematics at Concordia College in St. Paul, had not found sufficient interest or support within the his Synod to finance his dreams of work in China. He formed a mission society and gathered the support of about 700 pastors via its newsletter and sales of a book of his sermons. During his first four years, the "Arndt Mission" was able to recruit only one Seminarian, Erhardt Riedel from Springfield, IL, to help with evangelism in Hankow.

In 1917, the year before Wilbert Holt was born in Illinois, this self-supporting small mission was assumed by the Evangelical Lutheran Synod of Missouri, Ohio and other States (ELMOOS) (The name was changed to the Lutheran Church Missouri Synod on its centennial in 1947). World War was raging in Europe. Seventy-five percent of German Lutheran congregations in America transitioned to using English. The Synod was in financial straits, but hesitatingly added China to its foreign mission work, begun in India in 1895.

With Synodical support, recent seminary graduates, many with new brides, were commissioned to the China Mission. Expansion beyond Hankow in the early 1920s established upriver operations in **Shashi** and **Ichang**, 1100 river miles west, close to today's Yangtze Three Gorges Dam. A third opportunity in the isolated city of **Shihnan** was discovered, where no other Christian work was being done. Shihnan, later re-named **Enshih**, was a 75 mile walk along a rutted trail crossing three valleys from the Yangtze.

Evangelism among the working class of these cities took several forms. Waitang, or open street ministry, was preaching done on street corners and in tea shops, with messages spoken by missionaries still learning the local Hupeh dialect of Mandarin. Usually, a translator was necessary. Women who had accepted Jesus were known as 'Bible Women" and could talk and witness to Chinese women, since it was socially unacceptable for men to talk publicly with women. Bible women often made house visits, working with mothers and children.

God was referred to as *shang-ti* (Supreme Lord) or *shen* (a god with a name). Roman Catholics used *Tien Chu* (Lord of Heaven). Because of difficulties in finding a most acceptable term for God, both *shang-ti* and *shen* Bibles and literature were in print. After years of on-going heated debate, Synod theologians determined to use shang-ti, but it allows *shen*.

Missionaries, native evangelists and Bible women distributed printed tracts and Bible "portions", usually the Gospel of John. Reading in China was becoming much more common with the introduction of simplified vernacular language known as *beiwah*. Several other missionary societies printed these small books, and Arndt had also brought a small printing press with him to do similar work, which was distinctly Missouri Synod. This literature was usually not given gratis, but sold at the cheapest cost for the smallest coin, otherwise the impoverished locals often used them to line their cloth shoes.

There were also colporteurs, itinerant men who walked from village to village, selling Bible portions, tracts, and occasional complete testaments to publicize the Gospel. Once the common Chinese learned to read, they proved to be voracious readers, and seemed to be constantly seeking reading materials.

Missionaries also rented small shopfronts, to function as makeshift chapels. Opening the doors and playing a portable reed organ and/or singing loudly would attract a curious crowd, who were then invited inside to sit on benches and hear the foreigner talk about the love of Jesus *He Su).*

Culturally, it was very difficult for a Chinese person to become a Christian. Generations of tradition were grounded in Taoist, Confucian, and Buddhist beliefs - which are commonly termed "Chinese Folk Religion." Buddhism was an imported religion from India, Taoism espoused the philosophy of Lao Tzu from the 5th century BCE, and Confucian thought structured society into ascending levels of loyalty and duty to parent, family, clan, state, and Emperor. Each individual had a duty to honor their ancestors through daily ritual incense burning and a food offering. Many traditions centered on appeasing un-happy, hungry or evil spirits or ghosts.

A person's descendants were expected to honor and revere the ancestors going back many generations. If a person accepted Jesus and became a believing Christian, the family was devastated, angry, even hostile, upset that they would no longer practice these filial duties, and leaving parents without eternal honor. Victorian missionaries had labeled this practice as "ancestor worship", and insisted that converts completely abandon the practice, even though it could be seen as a variation of the fourth commandment to honor one's parents.

Education has always been a major component of Lutheranism, holding that each believer makes his own informed decision to accept Christ and grow in the Faith. Arndt had established a school within months of arriving in **Hankow**, and missionaries, converts, and evangelists opened at least ten schools and four chapels throughout Hankow's native quarter. There had been no tradition of universal or public education in China, but by the late 1920s, all schools were forbidden to teach religion. With the goal of establishing a Concordia Seminary in China, the Mission rented two upper rooms for a Bible School in which to train evangelists.

Schools and chapels grew in **Shashi** and **Ichang**. At **Enshih,** a middle school for girls and an orphanage was operating by 1924. With the arrival of two American nurses, a clinic was also opened, eventually becoming a midwifery school and small hospital.

Two additional stations were opened, both in Szechuan province. **Wanhsien**, was started in 1922. The walled city was a Treaty

Port about 50 miles upriver from the Yangtze Gorge. **Kweifu**, farther east on the north bank, but within the Gorge, was opened by a pair of missionaries in 1923.

Missionaries held annual conferences downriver at **Kuling**, at a 4000 foot altitude in the Lushan mountains of Kiangsi. These were times to rejuvenate, pray, make decisions, write, and relax. Four stone houses had been financed by donations from the Walther League. For families, it was the highlight of their year. Foreigners of many occupations and nationalities summered amidst the clouds and cool air of the scenic mountain retreat.

Synod had established a Board for Foreign Missions in 1917. The Director for 35 years was Frederick Brand, followed by Otto H. Schmidt. In addition to administrative, teaching, and worship duties, missionaries were held strictly accountable for every cent of scarce mission dollars.

Civil war in 1926-7, major floods in 1931 and 1935, the Japanese occupation of eastern China in 1937 with the "Rape of Nanking," and the bombing of Pearl Harbor in late 1941 all contributed to lack of stability or growth for the mission. From 1937-45, the stations at Hankow, Shashi and Ichang were under Japanese rule. Enshih and Kweifu were severely bombed. Only Wanhsien remained beyond the fray. Concordia Seminary moved there in 1938, the orphanage and schools continued at this base in "Free China." **Chungking**, the wartime capital further upriver, became the final city added to the Mission with a Hankow graduate as local pastor. **Kunming**, where the Flying Tigers had operated in Yunnan province, also first appears in Synodical history in 1944, primarily as chaplaincy for the military.

Because of the 1937 Japanese occupation, several missionaries had left China, and five families moved south to the relative safety of British Hong Kong by 1938. Three adults and nine children were still there when Hong Kong fell on Dec 25, 1941. They were interred as civilian POWs in Stanley Camp for 8 months. In July 1942 they were repatriated aboard the international mercy ship *SS Gripsholm*. Three other Mainland families under house arrest were returned aboard the same sailing to New York, August 25.

Over 30 years, 58 missionaries and their families had evangelized, educated, worshipped, healed, and parented in the name of the Lord. The China mission appeared to be closed.

Student Wilbert Holt graduated from Springfield Seminary in January, 1945, after two years of vicarage as a teacher in California and Dean of Boys at Synod's Addison, Illinois orphanage. The Matron and nurse of that orphanage was Geraldine Bierwirth, whom he would marry in March. The Synod decided to send missionaries into China as soon as victory was declared, and Holt was among several men called to that field. They attended Mission School at the St. Louis Seminary, taught by Elmer Zimmermann, a Synodical China missionary from 1928-42. Zimmermann had been among 25 missionaries, wives and children interred as POWs by the Japanese in China, repatriated in August 1942 aboard the *SS Gripsholm*, under auspices of the International Red Cross.

With the end of war in 1945, the seminarians and wives were first able to obtain passage to China in Fall 1946, seven men aboard the *SS Marine Lynx* from San Francisco to Shanghai; Holts and Martha Boss sailed aboard the *SS Santa Paula* to Karachi, then overland via Bombay to Chungking. It had required 2 months of travel from New York to their assigned station at Enshih.

The story continues in Rev. Holt's own words.....

Listening to The Lutheran Hour
Broadcast out of the Philipines

Yangtze Gorge, the only way to Enshih

4 Seminary Professors and
two Chinese Graduates

Missionary Wives at Kuling

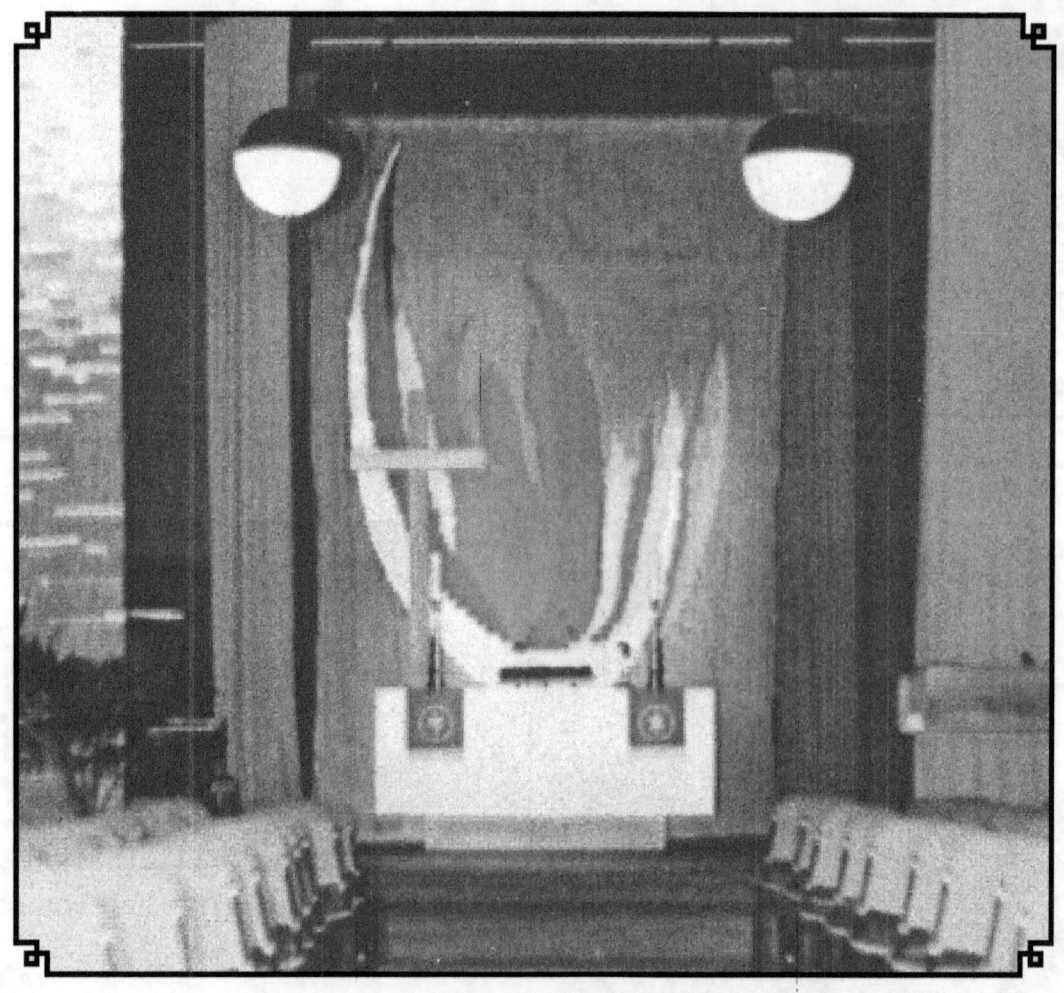

Sanctuary of the Lutheran Church of The Holy Spirit at 1725 Washington Street, San Francisco, CA.

"Be filled with the Spirit, addressing one another in psalms and hymns and spiritual songs, singing and making melody to the Lord with all your heart, always and for everything giving thanks in the name of our Lord Jesus Christ to God the Father." Ephesians 5: 18-20   RSV

God's Call

"Always be prepared to make a defense to anyone who calls you to account for the hope that is in you, yet do it with gentleness and reverence"

1 Peter 3:15 RS

Wilbert V. Holt Seminarian

Chapter One

God's Call

Rev. Holt served two years of internship before graduating from Concordia. For a year he served as Dean of Boys at the Lutheran Child Welfare Association of Addison, Illinois, where he met his future bride, Geraldine Bierworth, who was the matron of the Institution.

His second year of internship was spent in canvassing and helping to organize a Lutheran congregation in Colton, California.

When he graduated from Seminary in January 1945, he received two calls: 1) To China, 2) The Colton Church extended him a personal call. Rev. Holt and Geraldine Bierworth were married in Addison, Illinois on February 10, 1945. After much prayer and soul searching, he accepted the call to China.

The Second World War was still going strong and so there was no way to go to China at that time. The Mission Board sent them to the mission school at St. Louis Seminary in the meantime. When the war ended, the Mission Board gave permission in November, 1945. Rev. and Mrs. Holt sailed to China, where their field of work was Enshih, Hupeh, in West China.

During the war in China, Rev. Holt was cut off from his station while on an evangelistic tour. He left Chung King the day before it fell to the Communists in 1949 and arrived in Hong Kong in November 1949.

During those dark days of 1949 and 1950, one to five thousand refugees poured into Hong Kong each day. Rev. Holt, together with other members of the China Mission, Gertrude Simon, Martha Boss, and Lorraine Behling began the work of the Missouri Synod in Hong Kong.

He had been a Missionary for 16 years and was one of the founders of the Lutheran Church Hong Kong and first president of the Concordia Theological Seminary in Hong Kong.

In 1962, Rev. Holt and his family said farewell to Hong Kong and returned to the United States. Geraldine had developed a tropical illness, Sprue, and she received treatment at the Tropical Medication Center in Louisiana for about one year. The family moved to San Francisco in the summer of 1963.

The Holts have six sons: Paul, John, Joel, Daniel, Jim and David. Rev. Holt was the founder of the Lutheran Church of the Holy Spirit in San Francisco in 1964 and was active in its ministry until his death in August 2003.

DIPLOMA OF VOCATION

for

China

In the name of the Holy Trinity, God the Father, Son, and Holy Ghost. Amen.

The BOARD OF FOREIGN MISSIONS OF THE EVANGELICAL LUTHERAN SYNOD OF MISSOURI, OHIO, AND OTHER STATES, exercising the authority which God has vested in His Church on earth and by said Synod is vested in the aforementioned Board, have decided to call

the Reverend Wilbert Moeltje

of Elmhurst, Illinois

to be a missionary among the heathen in China

BY THIS CALL YOU ARE AUTHORIZED AND OBLIGATED as a preacher and teacher of the Gospel of Jesus Christ: —

To proclaim the Word of God in its full truth and purity as recorded in the Canonical Writings of the Old and New Testaments and as professed in the Confessional Writings of the Evangelical Lutheran Church, the Book of Concord of A. D. 1580; and

To administer the Holy Sacraments in accordance with their divine institution.

IT IS EXPECTED OF YOU: —

That by the gracious help of God you will execute your high calling with all fidelity and self-sacrifice and will show Christ to young and old among the heathen as the only Savior of the fallen human race;

That as a shepherd and curate of souls you will discharge the functions of your office in an evangelical manner among those who have been gathered to Christ, paying especial attention to the Christian education of the youth;

That you will walk among men in a consistently Christian manner, adorning the doctrine of God, our Savior, in all things, thereby commending the Gospel of Jesus Christ to the conscience of every one;

And, as God is a God of peace and good order, the Board pledges you at all times to observe and cultivate true brotherly and friendly relations with your colaborers, being intent upon keeping the unity of the Spirit in the bond of peace; also to cooperate conscientiously with the Board by complying with, and carrying out, the rules now existing, and such as may from time to time be formulated, for the regulation and advancement of our Foreign Missions enterprise.

ON THE OTHER HAND, we, THE BOARD OF FOREIGN MISSIONS, will at all times be mindful of our duty and responsibility to advance the cause of our Foreign Missions to our best ability and to provide faithfully for the decent maintenance of yourself and family, as the conditions in China and in the homeland demand and permit.

God, our Savior, who bought also the heathen with His precious blood and commanded us to preach the Gospel unto them, make you willing and joyous to His service: to go out into heathen lands as His Messenger of Peace!

May He bless you and make you a blessing unto many according to the riches of His grace! Amen.

In the name and by authority of THE BOARD OF FOREIGN MISSIONS OF THE EVANGELICAL LUTHERAN SYNOD OF MISSOURI, OHIO, AND OTHER STATES: —

O. H. Schmidt
(Director and General Secretary.)
Executive Secretary

Saint Louis, Missouri.

Date: January 10, 1945.

God's Call   Chapter One

"Thus making it my ambition to preach the Gospel, not where Christ has already been named, lest I build on another man's foundation, but as it is written, "They shall see who have never been told of him, and they shall understand who have never heard of him"

Romans 15: 20 RSV

Pastor Wilbert V. Holt

Chapter Two

In His Own Words
Pastor Wilbert V. Holt

I was raised in a Christian family. It was a home filled with love. I had 2 brothers and 3 sisters. My sister Lydia was 4 years older than I. A very pretty young lady, she was a great Christian, very moral and took her faith seriously.

It was a very sheltered world in which we grew up. The doors were never locked and the keys were left in the car. There were about 14,000 people in the little town where we lived. Most of the people worked in the city of Chicago and took the train to and from work. It was a town where many German and English families lived. In those days it was not unusual for towns to be either Jewish, Italian or German. It was a time of much prejudice. There was only one Chinese family in our town. They had a laundry. We did not have much contact with them.

I was raised in a very conservative world. It was a time of deep depression and poverty in America. In the 1930's there was a great need to show compassion. Many hobos got off the train a few blocks from our house. My mother always gave them food to eat, bread and jam or coffee.

I have fond memories of my mother rocking me to sleep and singing. She loved music. I was greatly influenced by strong Lutheran families and the teachers in the parochial schools we attended. I was also influenced greatly by my mother and older sister.

I had a French/English friend. He never went to church but we went fishing often. We liked things of nature. I never got him to be a Christian and I was so frustrated because I wanted to help him become a Christian. The last year in High School I had another friend whom I admired greatly. He left to study for the ministry and I knew he wanted to share his faith with others. Another great influence was my pastor. He was a real scholar. He was an older pastor at that church. I admired his enthusiasm in preaching. My mother and I would take the train to attend evening services—it was about a 10 mile ride. At night we waited for the train about 9 p.m. but it was a very secure world. Waiting in the dark for the train gave me a lot of time to think. It was so dark but we were not afraid.

After graduating from high school I worked for about 3 years. The family needed money. I worked in a grocery store, and in a sewing machine factory. I left in the morning in the dark and came home in the dark. One day my mother said - "Why don't you just go to school, working doesn't help us that much". But my uncle didn't agree with that. So I got a job at $17 a week at Safeway. Then I worked in a shoe store. I sold Fuller Brushes for several years. It was very interesting and was good training for me.

It was my uncle who decided we should change our name from Hoeltje to Holt so it would be easier for people to pronounce our name.

My mother wanted me to go to the Springfield seminary. Later I went to Concordia Seminary in St. Louis for 2 years and then Evangelical Lutheran Seminary for 2 more years. I was given two vicarages. The first was as Dean of Boys at an Orphanage in Addison, Illinois. There I met Geraldine Bierworth who was Matron of that orphanage. We soon became serious about spending our life together.

My second vicarage was to Colton, California. In those days many people were moving to California. I was sent to start a church there.

After graduating from the seminary, I received two calls. One to St. John Lutheran church which I had started in Colton. There were about 16,000 people in Colton and 16 churches already established there. The other call was to China.

I considered the reasons for my choice. I was interested in missions. I had volunteered at the seminary to go to Africa but they said 'we need someone tougher than you.' I talked to Geri and her attitude was 'I will go wherever you go.' She was a nurse and the most ideal person to be my mate as a missionary.

Then I applied to go to China. I actually got the vision to go to China the day I received the call to China. I realized that to go where the church was needed most was my motivation.

World War II was not over when I graduated, so I went back to the seminary to prepare. At the St. Louis seminary, I learned the missionary methods, basic Chinese language and what to do on the mission field from Rev. Zimmermann, a former China missionary. From February to November we studied until things opened up and we could leave for the China field.

Finally we got tickets on a Caribbean Cruiser which was going to pick up soldiers from India. Deaconess Martha Boss was also traveling with us. The Santa Paula was a small ship. It was in the fall, and the Atlantic ocean was stormy. The ship had no ballast. They were afraid it would break into two. The sea was so rough, suitcases flew from one side of the room to the other. People were so sick.

We sailed through Gibraltar, the Suez Canal and on the Indian ocean until we landed in Karachi. Then we took a railroad car across India to Calcutta. We lost half of our baggage. There was another missionary fellow with us. We wanted to see the sights, especially the Taj Mahal, but there was so much political turmoil. We were always changing trains because India had many different sizes of rails.

Our tickets had been prepared for us and the trip planned but it certainly was not a nice time to travel. There were riots among the political groups and you never knew what would happen. On Christmas day, we had to stay in an American barracks in Calcutta because the riots were so bad. We lost half of our luggage and it took 6 months for another missionary in Calcutta to help us find it again.

The city trams in India do not stop—you have to jump off and keep running. Martha Boss didn't run and she fell and broke her arm. We were delayed about a month while we got her fixed up.

From Calcutta we had to fly over 'the hump' (Burma) on Jan 3, 1946. Just 37 pounds of luggage was the limit. It was hot in India but Geri and Martha put on their heaviest coats, several layers of them, and we got on the plane and flew into Chungking in the small plane. We stayed in Chungking for a couple of days.

Rev. Paul Martens met us and drove us to his mission station. He knew the country and the language. They were really great people! He helped us go down the Yangtze River to Wanhsien.

Then we had a 5 day walk—75 miles

over the mountains—to Enshih. Coolies carried our luggage. Martha Boss was carried in a bamboo chair by coolies because she had a bad leg infection. From time to time she was Geri's patient—especially when she had such infections. Mrs. Holt walked sometimes and then got a ride in a bamboo chair sometimes too. Sometimes things didn't make sense, like when Martha broke her arm in Calcutta or got her leg infection.

My passage soon became: "Be content with what you have"! Each day we lived on two bowls of rice, staying at farm houses along the way. Most Chinese people had never seen white people so they came over to compare our arms and hands. Ours was light; theirs the color of leather. We were like pied pipers. People followed us wherever we went. I never will forget one 8-year old boy who was just petrified when he saw us - and broke into tears.

God was really alive in our lives. We were always conscious of His presence. We remembered the Bible verse "Be content with what you have". No matter where or in what situation, we remembered this verse as it is so easy to get discouraged and frustrated when you see the poverty of the people and the misery they endured. We arrived at Enshih in Hupei province, our station, in 1946 and I would stay there until November 1949.

Our station in Enshih was established 20 years before. It had about 300 members there. My job was to be in charge of the hospital, the orphanage, and a training school for native nurses. In September 1946, the war-weary missionary, Gilbert Wenger, who had been there before us, needed a furlough, so he went back to the states. He had stayed about half a year to help us get settled.

There were 30 orphans at our station and about 50 people in the hospital and some young women training to be nurses. There was a lot of tuberculosis. It was a small operation on top of a mountain. The station was not part of the Enshih congregation, but we went down to the church every Sunday for services.

At first I studied Chinese (Mandarin) about five hours a day for two years. One teacher was from Peking—the other man was from the local community and his accent was different. People were good to us. The Chinese doctor and head nurse were really great. Dr. Y. C. Ch'en spoke some English and was very gifted. He prayed before each operation. There were about 10 nurses in training. Geri Holt was the anesthetic nurse. Martha Boss was head nurse at the hospital—this was her calling. The fine pastor from the church would come to visit patients. He was a good story teller and very warm. People liked him and he told stories that were Christian and Non Christian.

We had lots of workers to help—water carriers, gardeners, two farmers to plant crops, a cowboy to take care of livestock, a gate man, and a buyer to go into the city to purchase food for us. It was a very warm family.

It was a good start for us!

We talked to people if they spoke English. There were two men at the radio station. One was a Catholic, the other I baptized. He was the first convert at the station. It was a big farm community. About 15,000 people lived there. We visited people on their farms, walked down rice patties, and got bit by dogs. It took three years before I could speak Mandarin.

In May, 1948, 35 people were baptized—it was a great day! It was a time of release from fear and filled with joy! Some were farmers, others masons, household servants and farmers' wives. People respected the missionaries. They saw the courage of the missionaries. We would meet on certain days and just talk. The real helpers were the mission workers. I have said many times, pre-evangelism is very important. People must be prepared for the Gospel—to see people living their life as examples of the Gospel. We were out among the people everyday. Sometimes we went pigeon shouting outside the compound. We were invited to church dinners and became acquainted with people from the city.

We were in a part of the country where war had not come to yet, but the change came very fast in early 1949. I took two trips to Hankow by truck. It was very hard to travel as there was no filling stations and we had to carry 50 gallon cans of gas in the truck. I brought medicine valued at $1000 dollars to Hankow. I slept outside and felt very safe. There were missions along the way to take us in.

It took the Communists a long time to get to Chungking.

I got to know a General who stayed at our hospital. He said we should leave before they came to our city. I went with Rev. Chang to an evangelist meeting in Chungking. It was decided in October that what we should do was to travel up and down the Yangtze River, encouraging the missionaries there in time of persecution. We visited churches, held evangelistic meetings and encouraged people to make the most of the days. Trust in the Lord! It was a fast trip, only lasting one week.

The trip was rewarding and helpful. You could see the fear and anxiety in members of the congregations. All were small congregations but the Pastors were mature people. I don't know what happened to the congregations at Chungking and Wanhsien—they had a lot of courage. We were prevented from going to Wanhsien coming back, as the area had already been lost to the Communists. When we arrived in Chungking we learned our station at Enshih had been lost to the Communists and we could not go back. We stayed in Chungking for a short while and a couple weeks later we heard Chungking would soon be under seize. The day I left, Nov 29, we could hear the guns in the background. Gertrude Simon was with me. Chinese Pastors in Chung King were very fearful.

Mrs. Holt and Paul had left China eleven months before I did. The consulate told her to leave so they flew to America. I felt very disconsorted when left alone in China.

When we knew we had to close the Enshih station, church members took the 30 orphan children into their own families. A long time teacher had 4 children of his own but he took one more, saying 'I can divide the rice into 5 portions.' They were fine people. A deep love for each other!

Before the communists came, we took money that had been sent to keep the station going and buried it in the ground in the garden the night we left. The Mission Board had told the pilot of the "St. Paul," a Lutheran Federation plane, to pick up Gertrude Simon and me, with medicine and supplies. So the two of us got out of Chungking at the last moment to Hong Kong. It was the last trip out of Chung King for that little airplane. Just before I left I ordained an evangelist, Mr Liu, as a Chinese pastor. I later heard that Rev. Liu, was arrested because he would not compromise. I felt very very bad. But I've found out that he still lives there today as a pastor. He serves under the 3 Self-Help church rules of the PRC government.

Martha Boss and Lorraine Behling had gone to Chengtu to study. They were also rescued one week later and arrived in Hong Kong, on Dec 5.

Our church never expected us to go to Hong Kong. But in 1949, it was the only way out! People thought Hong Kong would fall too and this was the argument between the missionaries and mission board in America. Can you imagine 50 years later China took back Hong Kong—our church in Hong Kong was nearly 50 years old!

The mission board wanted us to go to New Guinea and forget Hong Kong. We saw the mission in Hong Kong. It was rough! 5,000 people per day poured into Hong Kong. People suffered. They had only the clothes on their backs! I felt a great responsibility for these people. They filled the sidewalks with lean-to shacks, even the neighboring hills with tarpaulin or tar-paper shacks.

How to get in touch with God's will at such a time?! We saw the mission in Hong Kong. We could speak Mandarin. The four of us pleaded with the Mission Board to see the mission field in Hong Kong. Finally the mission board saw there was a mission in Hong Kong. and gave approval for us to stay when they saw that the Communists did not take over Hong Kong. We all lived by faith! Later they did see what we could do.

First thing was to find a place to live. We found the Basil Mission House (on Tai Po Road) where 50 missionaries, of all denominations, lived. They had come from all over China. Many left and went back to the states.

Having no money for church rental, we found a private school (Houng Kong College) where they let us use a room off the street to teach English to refugees and we used this room for Sunday services. On March 26, 1950 the first regular public worship service of the Lutheran Church—Missouri Synod's Hong Kong Mission was held in the Houng Kong college. Martha Boss and Lorraine Behling were also teachers at the school.

Amy Mui's husband, Jason, was one of the first persons we got to know. He was a basketball star and his father was a professor at this college. They allowed me to do campus ministry.

The refugee ministry helped people find work. Young Christians...just anybody... was involved. I preached anywhere. I liked to preach. There was a young man, Paul Chang, he brought me to several Evangelical churches.

They were very conservative. For example, Paul would say, 'I want to introduce you to a church over here' and then he would say 'I want Rev. Holt to preach here.' He was like an assistant to find preachers. There was no time to prepare a sermon, you were just told—preach! He was a good interpreter—a kind of "bridge" person. A mixed blessing! A very special person!

My wife and young Paul came to join me after 6 months. We decided to stay. We saw the potential. We did things like using loud speakers on the street. People could talk to me easily—anywhere. We tried everything! Once there was a wall with nothing on it. We painted a picture of Jesus on it—it didn't cost much. No one had any money but this picture drew a lot of people for street evangelism.

There were other Lutheran missionaries there from LCA, whose mission was to the sailors in the port. Many soldiers came to see me and talk with me. One said, "Everyday when I saw that picture it told me to talk to you!" God gave us a lot of people to help tell the Gospel. I am amazed how God provided. We just clung to the Bible verse - "I will never leave you or forsake you". We found what we needed, for what we had to do! We knew this was our mission field!

Everyone wanted to talk about food. The Lutheran World Federation was busy in that area too. They were the agency through which American World Relief was sent to Hong Kong. Since we did not have a church building, we were not involved with LWF and food as other Lutheran church were. Then we rented a place at 232 TaiPo Road and we began formal work. It was the main street, up from Nathan Road—not a bad beginning for us. We continued to use the Houng Kong college for church services. With 5,000 refugees coming into the Colony each day, it increased the people living in Hong Kong from 700,000 to 1.5 million in 10 months.

The British government was most cooperative. They built high rises and on the top of each, charities were allowed to begin schools, clubs, and churches. Some people made money on these schools. There was a great need for schools for the refugee children.

Then our church began schools. We got land from the government and subsidies. The British were very open and happy with the missionaries who helped the refugees. I was not involved with the schools but my job was to teach the Word and preach there. It took a while for the church to get permits.

Gertrude Simon decided she wanted to move out among the refugees at Rennie's Mill camp. It didn't take much money to do anything in those days. We decided to stay in the city. So our family moved into the Basil Mission house. The first family we met was the Lau family (John Lau now worships at Zion Lutheran, SF) John was one of the first boys I baptized. His father and mother were both Christians. His father was a builder and he helped to build many of our churches and schools. Later, John was my first interpreter in San Francisco at 606 Jackson Street.

This was a time of great opportunity! Refugees asked deep questions, they wanted to know what happened after death. They were searching for answers and had so many questions about this great calamity that had overtaken them. They said 'if you people had come to us in China we would not have listened to you'. Life in China was filled with a web of religious life, filled with superstitions, even demon worship, for them to become Christians would be to break into their religious webs.

Now they had no money...nothing...only the clothes on their back. They slept in doorways, on mats. Now they heard about the true God. People became satisfied because Jesus could give them an answer and a hope. Many people gave up in despair and jumped into Hong Kong harbor. The British government and many others helped as much as possible to find jobs and create home industries.

What a shock! The doctor said 'you must relax.' You have Tuberculosis! In the midst of this busy time, he said 'you must take one year of bed rest so you can get well and serve the Lord for many years.' I wanted to get well but why God are you asking me to leave? I know you want me to be here. I talked to God—"everything is going great here. How can you send me to the showers in the middle of the game?"

I felt I really didn't know why? I still don't know why it happened. But I was obedient. It took me 3 months to calm down and at the end of 1950, we left Hong Kong for the Wheatridge Sanitarium in Colorado. It was such a great disappointment—leaving Hong Kong was like having a door slammed in my face!

In the meantime, Rev. Herbert Hinz, a former LCMS China missionary, had made a trip to San Francisco to see if any Chinese work could be started there. The people told him, there is already good Chinese work being done there—get lost!

Then he was sent back to Hong Kong to take my place while I was recuperating from TB in the States. He was a very stable missionary and the Mission Board realized now the potential in Hong Kong. He started the Lutheran Hour in Hong Kong. He found interpreters for it and special speakers. He did a good job.

So in 1951 I had absolute bed rest at the Sanatorium for one year. The experience of being in isolation gave me an opportunity to pray and study the word. I was not sick, but just had to lie down all the time. This gave me an opportunity for deep prayer and study of the word. Prayer and reading was something I never had enough time for before. If you ever want to do anything for the Kingdom of God, you must spend time alone with Christ. Being confined to bed was not easy for me. I had a roommate from Latvia and we became good friends.

Mrs. Holt visited me every week. She had a lot of strength. She never complained about any situation. This was a nice environment for her to renew relationships with some old friends. She stayed with these friends. During this time our second son, John, was born in Colorado.

One day in 1951, the Wheatridge chaplain said to me, 'I want to share something with you, but I want you to go to our worship service first.' Afterwards he said. 'I am sorry to tell you your brother has been killed in Korea.' That really shook me up! He tried to comfort me. My younger brother had been killed at the age of 23! This was a lot to bear.

It was interesting that people Geri had worked with at the Orphanage in Addison, Illinois - Ruby and her husband Jacob - were Social Workers in Denver. They were the couple who she knew before we were married. Now they gave Geri and the boys a good family life and friendship, all provided by God in His plan. They had two children and we had two children. I did not have to worry about their lives. God did provide! Our Lord provided everything they needed during the year I had to take time off! That was great!

I just needed to be alone and pray. It was not convenient, but it was what I needed to get well. Time at the Sanatorium was not wasted, but I did not think it was appropriate. Somethings in life we really don't want to do. We have thousands of thoughts each day but how many of them are really about God! We need to have time alone with God each day!

After I was dismissed from the Sanitarium, the Mission Board wanted to be sure I had recovered. They sent me to the Seminary for further training. It was good training for what I was to do later in Hong Kong. The family moved to St Louis while I studied how to do training of evangelists in the future. It was wonderful and just what I needed for the future. Time went fast! I knew that I would return to Hong Kong! There are many blessings in life in God's plan. It was not a wasted two years but a very blessed two years! After almost four years I was pronounced a cured man!

John was born in early 1952 and Joel was born near the end of 1952 while we were at the seminary. We returned to Hong Kong at the beginning of 1953 with 3 children.

The work in Hong Kong had expanded quite a bit. There were established churches working with Chinese people. We had great teachers who were principals of High Schools. Many language schools were set up.

When I think of the work in Hong Kong I think of the dreams of the many people who were our workers. Basic Bible schools were started by evangelists who were real loving people. Evangelists were assistants to the missionaries. They all had dreams to help people in Hong Kong.

Martha Boss often went to Rennie's Mill where Gertrude Simon had started the work. Martha was a strong woman. Always smiling! There they had asked General Chiang Kai Shek for a grant to let his soldiers help build up the area. When I saw the school that Gertrude Simon and Martha Boss had named after the Savior rather than someone's name, I was so thankful. It was a long distance between Kowloon where we were and Rennie's Mill so we seldom got together. There was also a Tuberculosis Sanatorium called Haven of Hope, which Martha Boss helped for a while.

Mrs. Holt took care of our family which continued to grow. She was also involved in the blind work. The Colonial government also got involved in that work.

My focus was training of evangelists and local pastors. I helped them prepare every week for preaching of their sermons on the weekend. There were many people and many missionaries to train. We had one person among them that did not like Chinese people. He didn't do much—I never knew how he could be sent out to Hong Kong as a missionary since he was from a very different generation. He had to leave.

We started the seminary when evangelism got to a growth where deeper study was necessary. We had general education, classes in speaking, history, and doctrine, and then finally the training of Pastors - in four years. No, it takes a life time to train a pastor but it was a good beginning. Classes were conducted in Mandarin—the text was in English and translated into Chinese.

It was a real job to start the seminary and took awhile before it was accredited. Afterwards, the person was sent to America for training at the seminary there. All the evangelists understood Mandarin. In January 1959 the Mission Board approved the establishment of the Hong Kong Concordia Seminary. I was the first president. I also preached every Sunday myself to Missionaries and teachers in English.

Now they even have a Seminary building. Government was very generous and gave us land. In fact, I wish our American government had a more perfect attitude towards the church. Here we have to keep the government out of the church, which is our real problem.

Schools were a big big thing. We always maintained our relationship with the Houng Kong college where we got our first start. Geri continued her work with the blind. She and some members of the church would go out among refugees to find and identify any blind persons there. A blind school was started with funds from friends. There were teachers from our churches, and some of the churches had a sizable number of blind or deaf persons among them.

They also set up a classroom so the deaf could learn sign language. Some churches used a variety of Chinese dialects to relate to special groups of people.

In Hong Kong, there were many things for us to learn:

1. Greatness of faith is the #1 priority. Worship, time for God, study of the Word, and prayer are most important.

2. In times of turmoil and danger or persecution, this is when the church is purified and the church is made strong.

3. From our own experience we learned that when the church becomes strong, there is a tendency for things to hurt people—like too much authority or money. St. Paul says "they seek their own things, not those of Jesus Christ".

4. When people desire to have their own way - too much power, love of money, selfishness and contempt - this makes serving God of very minimal value.

5. Love your God with all your heart and soul, this is a great commandment but if they forget Him, then they are not of much use.

By 1962, the Seminary in Hong Kong was going well. Then Mrs. Holt got the Sprue, which keeps the body from assimilating food. The Doctor in Hong Kong said she would have to leave that country as she could not live in this climate. If she went to America, she could be cured but could not return to Hong Kong. So in 1962 we returned to America. We received calls to many places. There were many interesting calls but they were just not the right one for me.

In 1963 I was called to begin the work among Chinese in San Francisco. Here again God provided. I was commissioned at St John's Lutheran Church in San Francisco on September 29, 1963, by Circuit Counselor Rev. Herbert Schroeder.

I met up with the first person I had baptized in Hong Kong, John Lau. They were members of Zion Lutheran Church when we arrived but they said 'we will help you get started!'

Other congregations were very interested in helping us get started. Fifty Lutheran men helped us renovate the property at 606 Jackson Street into a nice chapel. The CNH District was very interested in Chinese work. The LWML provided $4000 to begin mission work. More than fifty local Lutherans provided us with teachers, reading room attendants and many other helpers. The time was right! God provided the right people.

A young man, Henry Lai, a teacher in the Hawaiian Islands came to us and was engaged as a youth worker for 3 years. Sometimes he was my interpreter too. I spent the first 5 months learning Cantonese. A change of dialects was difficult.

Editor's Note: In a letter to friends on January 4th, 1967, Pastor Holt wrote: "It was a pleasant and profitable year for the Holts, although in November Geri had extensive repair surgery and is doing fine now. Our eldest son, Paul, 19, is in his second year of college at Oakland. John attends a public high school—a junior - and Joel is a freshman at St Paulus Lutheran Jr. High, where Daniel is an eighth grader. James is in sixth grade and David a fifth-grader at Zion Lutheran School.

Our Chinatown church is now three years old. We have lost our store-front lease, so we must find new quarters before March 3, 1967. The congregation numbers about Eighty baptized souls and about forty confirmed souls. We are considering beginning the Lutheran Hour in Chinese in 1967. Chinese immigrants continue to come to San Francisco by thousands, so already there are perhaps 45,000 in San Francisco.

We pray that the Lord will grant you each a full measure of the Holy Spirit, so that you may have the peace, the faith, the love, the joy, the power to witness to the Message of Reconciliation in the year of grace, 1967."

God continued to provide. Amy Mui came to visit us in SF, representing the Lutheran World Federation as a fund raiser. I invited her to interpret one Sunday and was very much impressed by her ability to do simultaneous translating. Amy was hired as a secretary and later as a Parish worker.

We did canvassing in the Chinatown area. Most people worked during the day so we contacted mainly seniors and young people. Then we started youth programs, we had play days, had children with drums walking in the streets to attract other children. We had day by day reading room open for drop ins. There were volunteers who taught English. It was a meeting place for older people. It took awhile to get those in between—when they had a day off.

Things were going quite well! It was a very friendly atmosphere. Other churches were conscious of a need for an ethnic Chinese church. They had been talking about it for many years. They were helpful!

Our first Divine Worship service was held on March 26, 1964 and the Lutheran Church of the Holy Spirit began. There were probably 60 people at that service, including guests from other churches. My personal feeling was—there is potential here! It is just a matter of time!

The first lady to join was Mrs. Lau. She was a very troubled lady, filled with fear after seeing her parents killed by the Communists. When she got to hear the message of Jesus, it had a healing effect on her. She read the Bible, began to believe. She had just dropped into the chapel, but found Jesus could give her peace. Some people asked her why she wanted to join a white man's church. There was a lot of prejudice but the prayers of God's people prevailed.

As the church grew, more children came. They liked to come there. We had Bible clubs and English classes. It was truly a family place. Then we had retreats. They were cheap and transportation was free. Jason Mui, introduced us to a bus driver who drove us to retreats all over the area, using the bus from Trinity Lutheran Church in San Rafael. We had what we needed! God always provided!

As I said, history shows that God has always provided whatever we needed. In 1969 until 1981, Deaconess Carol Halter, just returned from Hong Kong and Renee's Mill, was our English youth leader.

It is true today, as it was from the beginning, build a foundation to win young people before 14 years of age, then 85% of them will become Christians.

Don't give up! The church must be friendly. Most churches are closed door churches. Meet people, sit down talk with them. It is not a Sunday only thing!

We were a mission church for 10 years before we became self - supporting. We had only 2 workers, and we were very realistic. When Carol came she was a volunteer for 10 years. John Lau was a volunteer also. God will provide - just use all the facilities available to you!

Then the rent became prohibitive. One day Amy and I were visiting an elderly lady and there was a realtor there also. He asked, "Is there anything I can do to help you?" Again God provided. This realtor found a place that had been a dance studio, a theater, and then a temporary church for the First Presbyterian church on Van Ness and Clay, while they were building their new church. There had been a fire in the building and it had been condemned. It had to be sold. The time was right! The realtor told us to hurry up and buy it as lots of people were interested.

Again God provided! The LWML at their 25th Silver anniversary, provided $100,000 from their mite box money for the down payment. We had a new church home! From March 25, 1964 to November 1969—5 years, many, many wonderful things happened.

My thoughts about the Lutheran Church of the Holy Spirit - First, to me, Pentecost is neglected so many times in our churches. It is not as inspiring as it needs to be. Jesus had to leave, otherwise the Holy Spirit could not come. In our lives, the Holy Spirit is often neglected, as well as in our teaching. The Word and the Spirit comes thru the Word—Jesus Christ is Lord!

The Holy Spirit is not a priority in the Christian church. This is why we chose the "Lutheran Church of the Holy Spirit" for our name—so the Holy Spirit could be our priority!

I've found that there were only 2 or 3 congregations among 6000 churches that use the Holy Spirit in their name. The Holy Spirit has been working in our congregation.

Secondly, we still have not learned the need of prayer. Jesus says, "Pray the Lord of the Harvest to send forth workers in the Harvest field". For one whole year I could only pray! I know the value and importance of prayer! I trust the Lord to provide people to serve with me in mission work. I know the value of need for workers and the Lord provided such for establishing the Lutheran Church of the Holy Spirit.

It was the prayer of many, many people that Chinese work would be established. Pastor Riche always prayed for our work. The laity had concern for the need and 100 people responded to build the church at 606 Jackson Street. That store front was a vision! Mission work means being a friend to people. You must be a friend and totally care about the person.

Third, trust in God to provide! This is what the church needs! Pray for workers. You know the story—how God provided Amy Mui, a dynamic evangelist with the gift of evangelism. We praise God for her.

After 5 years another gift—Deaconess Carol Halter, in the States temporarily, asking if there was a need for someone from Hong Kong to help out. For 11 years Amy and Carol went in parallel work to the youth.

Another gifted person was Pastor C C Wang, from the Tao Fong Shan outreach to Buddhists in Hong Kong. He was a deep scholar who lead 200 monks to become Christians and many of them are pastors today. He called and said he would like to come to San Francisco to help. What shall we say? The Lord continued to bless us!

Later a relative of Amy Mui, who was studying for the ministry in an Alliance Church, said one day, 'I need to become a Lutheran pastor.' He was convicted as a teenager. He went to the Concordia Seminary and was qualified as a Lutheran Pastor. We called him in 1983 to be assistant pastor at Lutheran Church of the Holy Spirit. He stayed 6 years until he felt called to return to Hong Kong.

Another young man from the English group was influenced by Carol. That was Terry Chan, who also became a pastor. He was called by Lutheran Church of the Holy Spirit later on. God has always provided qualified people. Pray to the Lord of the Harvest to send people.

Praise God during the years our church has produced many teachers, workers and pastors. Truly the Holy Spirit has called many into His service. It is important for the Christian churches to pray, otherwise they will suffer for lack of workers.

Fourth, when we began the Chinese Lutheran Hour, God provided us with dramas from Hong Kong in Cantonese adaptable to our work. Parish Worker Amy was articulate in proclaiming Christ on the radio. She became a speaker on the additional half hour of the program. This was another great God given provision for our church. At that time Mrs. Lau would cook dinners and the young people would serve the dinners, with proceeds supporting the Chinese Lutheran Hour. We must keep praying!

Just like the Lord sent out 2 by 2, it is important to realize all the gifts a congregation has, and they must be convinced that the church is the body of Jesus Christ. This means we need every member. We do not say 'we don't need an eye or an ear'. Every member has a gift from God—it is important to look at the members and recognize their gifts.

Regard all members highly. Utilize every person's gifts. Share the gifts you have—know what gifts you have! Always be ready to share what great gifts God has given to you. Are you well equipped? Are you ready to use or share with other people?

The congregation is the Body of Christ, it is not just a congregation but a part of the Body of Christ with a super abundance of Holy Spirit's gifts.

Ask ourselves—do we have special resources to share with other congregations? Are you adequately sharing your gifts with other congregations? We must realize we have a responsibility to share our gifts with other congregations. How can we work together? How do we do outreach to the community? I feel strongly about this—it is so easy to be selfish! We need to pray about this.

Sixth, make your homes reflect Christian hospitality. Make joy and peace of God's Spirit the atmosphere of your home. Fill your home with love and use of the Word of God. It is vital if you want to be people who share.

Marriage is a great witness of God in our lives. It is vital to show that your home is different from that of the world. This is important when reaching out to the world around us that Jesus Christ is the head of the family. Families have special gifts to be used in evangelism. Lutherans should always be ready to share our gifts with others.

Number seven, I learned in China that the message of Jesus Christ can change lives—educated or uneducated—there is no difference. It is the basic need of all people. There is pride, greed and selfishness in all people. Intelligent people can be the most vicious. The nicest people sometimes resist God's grace.

When a sinner is without God, he begins to see what he is missing without God. Under the family of God there is a message for all sinners. The Word of God can change people.

To reach Chinese people we must realize they are part of the race of God. Many pictures form a Chinese character. Early Chinese all worshiped one God. Only when the great wall was built (before Christ) they added more idols to their emperor worship.

Finally, it is vital people need to get to know the Bible. Recognize the God of the Bible and how he reveals himself. How wonderful it is that the prophets preserved for us that God is a faithful God. God spoke through the prophets to reveal that God took a human life so he could take our place—that is Christianity.

Christianity stands out as a fact—it is a message of reconciliation, forgiven people with lives forever changed. The heart of the Bible is the reconciliation through Jesus Christ.

May God continue to grant His Holy Spirit to our church!

About a year before Pastor Holt met his Lord in 2003, he recorded his life story and his experienced observations in bringing Christ to the Chinese. His comments have been edited for clarity and historic detail.

China Bound Missionaries at Concordia Seminary in St Louis

Mother Hoeltje

Sister Lydia Holt

Pastor Holt's Family in Illinois

I am with you and will watch over you wherever you go"

Joshua 1:9 RSV

Geraldine Holt, R.N.

Chapter Three

The Journey
Geraldine Holt

Wilbert Holt arrived at LCWA in June of 1942 for one year vicarage from Springfield Seminary to serve as dean of boys and in charge of daily devotions for the staff and children. Wilbert Holt was a very special person who truly loved the Lord Jesus and he was always carrying his Bible, reading, studying and sharing it with everyone. We did a lot of talking together, sharing our faith and dreams. Soon we realized we were in love and meant to share our life together.

Wilbert vicared another year in Colton, CA where he started a church. He returned to the Seminary and graduated in January of 1945. He received two calls. 1) To China, 2) The Colton Church extended him a personal call. We were married in Addison, IL on February 10, 1945. After much prayer and soul searching, he accepted the call to China. The second world war was still going strong and there was no way to go to China. The Mission Board told us to go to the mission school at St. Louis Seminary in the meantime. I was in the first class of coeds at the Seminary.

When the war ended, the Mission Board told us to prepare for departure. So, we got passports and started to shop and pack for a seven year stay in Kumning, China.

We said our farewell to Wilbert's family in the Chicago area and went on to my family in Buffalo. It was hard to part and say "God be with you till we meet again in seven years, God willing." The Mission Board called my home in Buffalo and told us to proceed to New York City where we were booked for passage to India on an Army transport leaving for India on Nov. 14,

On Our Way

None of us had ever been to New York City before, and we had two days to sight-see the city. The Mission Board had made reservations for us to stay at the YWCA. We embarked from NYC on Nov. 14, 1945. What a cold day it was! The SS Santa Paula was a Caribbean Cruiser converted into a troop ship—enroute to India to bring World War II soldiers back home to the USA and in time for Christmas.

We boarded and had our baggage put in our state rooms. Wilbert and I had an officer's cabin with four bunks, a lavatory, sink with cold ocean water. Martha was assigned a bunk in the hospital unit with three other ladies. The hospital had hot water in the bathroom so we were able to take a bath when we visited Martha. Ed Kraft was in another officer's cabin for single men. We had an early supper and went out on deck to say good-bye to the Statue of Liberty and our homeland. It was too cold to stay out on deck and the ship was beginning to rock and roll. So we all went to bed and got rocked to sleep.

By morning, we were all seasick and couldn't get out of our bunks. So we stayed in bed all day. The second day, the ship was still rocking and rolling, but we managed to climb up to the dining room. The passengers all sat on both sides of one long table. Every time the ship rolled, the plates and cups would slide way to the other side of the table and we soon learned to hang on to our plates and cups and try to eat something before it spilled off the table onto our laps or the floor. The waiters had to bring up trays of food from the kitchen down under some place. They often had to hang on to the railings trying to walk about and up and down the stairs. We bundled ourselves up and tried to sit in a deck chair that was roped to the railing. We looked out over the ocean waves. The ship was rolling so much that now you see the ocean waves, and now you don't—now you see the sky and now you don't. Martha said that their baggage was rolling back and forth across their hospital room, keeping them awake at night. So they got up and put the baggage in the bathtub. For two weeks we bobbed across the Atlantic like a cork. The waves were huge and crashed over the decks.

Then we entered the Mediterranean Sea. What a change from the wild green waters of the Atlantic to the calm beautiful blue sea. It was Thanksgiving and my husband got permission from the captain to hold a service in the lounge. We had much to thank the Lord for.

Days later, at Port Said, Egypt, many small boats full of wares, drew up to our boat. The store keepers yelling "Buy cheap—buy cheap". They threw ropes up to the passengers and attached small baskets bearing their wares. My husband bought a pair of camel hide slippers which a year later grew hair in our dark, hot, and humid closet in Enshih, China and frightened me half to death when I touched them rummaging around in the bottom of the closet.

The trip through the Suez Canal was very interesting. December 5, 1945, our voyage ended after 21 days at sea.

India

On Dec 15, we landed at Karachi, Pakistan. That same day, a thousand or so Pilgrims arrived on the way to Mecca. So, the inns were full and there was no room for four missionaries. Finally our baggage carrier found an old Indian Hotel that would accommodate us. They gave my husband and me a room and tried to put Martha Boss and Ed Kraft into one room. Ed tried to explain the situation to the desk clerk that they needed one more room. But was a 'no go' situation. So, Martha and I ended up in one room and my husband and Ed in the other room.

At that time, the Caste System was in effect in India. In the morning, they brought fruit, nuts and tea to our room. So we called the men to join us. We tried to find out when we could go to the dining room. They kept saying "no" to us. Finally they said they could make a meal for us at 6:00 p.m. We had to go to the train station to get tickets to Bombay, and we ate wherever we could buy something.

At 6:00 p.m. we went to find the dining room. When we looked in the room they told us was our dining room, they were still painting the walls. They said they would call us when our meal was ready. Finally at 8:00 p.m. we were called. There was a table with four chairs in the middle of the room. It had a white sheet on top. We sat down and a tall man came in wearing a white turban and long white coat over white pants. He was barefoot but he was wearing white canvas gloves. He served our meal of soup, curried rice, lamb, nuts, fresh fruit, tea and cakes. It was delicious!

The next day, we went to the station with our baggage. One man carried our two foot lockers, two suit cases, two duffle bags on his head! Martha and Ed each had a carrier for their baggage. When we finally found our train compartment, it was jammed full of people and we couldn't get in.

The train was about to start when a kind Brahman (a member of the highest Hindu caste) opened his compartment door and invited us to come aboard. He was traveling with his daughter. He explained and shared many cultural differences of the caste system, political unrest and personal experiences. Missionary Holt was able to talk to him about the life of Jesus Christ. The Brahman was very attentive. We thanked God for this man's kindness to us and an opportunity to "sow the seed" of the Gospel.

Every hundred miles or so, the gage of the railroad track changes and everyone leaves the train with their baggage and catches another train going in their direction. By the time we arrived in Bombay, we had lost half our baggage.

We stayed at a Mission Guest House and the manager said she would help us put a lost luggage check on our missing pieces. We thanked God for this restful guest house. We had a little time for sight-seeing at Hanging Gardens and a tour of the city and to attend worship services in an Anglican Church.

At this time, Ed Kraft left our group to go south to his assigned station in India. Martha Boss, Missionary Holt and I departed Bombay for Calcutta via train. The manager of the guest house promised to send on our baggage if found.

This part of the trip was hot, dry, and dusty through the desert. Our coach was like a box car with open slats and a long wooden bench along the sides. When the train stopped in the middle of nowhere, a group of begging children came along side our train coach and smiled, danced, and sang, "Pistol Packing Mama". There were taught to sing and dance by the American GI's. The train stopped at many stations and we were able to buy food and drink. There were palm trees in the desert and we saw many monkeys.

By the time we arrived in Calcutta, we were covered with dust and sand. We couldn't even get a comb through our hair! We were besieged by beggars (the lowest caste). We wanted to help, but there was no way to help.

We finally were able to hire a horse carriage to take us and our baggage to the Basel Mission House. It was truly a "home away from home". They were very friendly and helpful. My husband and I were given a large, very comfortable room, across the street and on the edge of Wellington Square.

Every night there were riots in the Square, yelling and fighting, burning rickshaws etc. The people against the police (British authority). India wanted to be free of British rule and do away with the Caste system. We had daily devotions and prayers. We had so much to thank God for—food, clothing, housing, new friends, protection, and good health.

One of our new friends was Chaplain Wenger stationed at the U.S. Army base outside Calcutta. He was a brother of Missionary Gilbert Wenger stationed in Enshih, Hupeh, China. He was very helpful to us and drove us out to the base a few times for dinner and church services. One evening, after dinner, the army closed the base because of riots in the city and we had to spend the night at the base. They had to clear out an officer's sleeping quarters so we would have a place to stay the night.

It was getting close to Christmas but the only signs of it were large "XMAS SALE" in shop windows. We had frequent thoughts of home, family, and Christmas celebrations.

One day, we were out getting our passports checked and trying to find a way into China. We were on a tram car that just "slowed down" at the stops so one had to jump off and run to keep from falling over. Martha jumped off but did not run along and so she fell over and broke her arm.

We got a taxi and went out to the Army Base where they X-rayed her arm. But when they saw the elbow was broken in pieces and would necessitate surgery, they said they could not operate on a US civilian. So we went back to Calcutta and found an English surgeon. When Missionary Holt asked if he was qualified to do this kind of surgery, he became very upset with us and did not want to help us but Missionary Holt told him he was personally responsible for Martha and he didn't know anything about English medical practices.

The doctor calmed down and decided to help us. He made arrangements for Martha to go to the hospital and he told the surgery nurse to hire a servant from the Caste system that would cook for Martha, do her laundry, bathe and care for her in the hospital. So Martha had her surgery and ended up with a cast on her right arm from the shoulder to the finger tips. Martha was in the hospital over Christmas.

My husband and I went to Christmas Eve services at the Army camp and joined the soldiers from the services as they caroled outside the Army Hospital windows and around some of the barracks. We were not the only ones homesick for Christmas! Our prayers became more fervent for India and China—for telling everyone about Christ the Savior of us all.

While waiting for Martha to be discharged from the hospital and the doctor's care, we had time to explore Calcutta.

Looking up, there were many vultures sitting on top of the buildings waiting for the dead bodies to be put up on high platforms to be absorbed by the Sun god. But it seemed the vultures got there first. We visited the burning-gats where the dead bodies were placed on a pyre and torched by a close family member. There was considerable wailing and moaning and sobbing for the dead. Sometimes a wife would throw herself on the burning husband's body and die with him. Such tragedy. Our hearts burned with zeal to go on with great task of preaching the Gospel to a dying, sin sick world without hope.

Calcutta is the largest city in India. The population well over 2,000,000 in 1945. It sits on the east bank of the Hooghly Distributary of the sacred Ganges. Calcutta extends over a surface of 40 square miles. The Ganges River is a special place for bathing, prayers, and meditation. Some dead bodies are placed on flower decked rafts and floated down the river.

Cows roam the streets and eat whatever pleases them from the vegetable stands until the merchant gently slaps them and turns them away. The cow is divine in her own right and is generally revered as the representative of mother earth. Many animals, plants, and natural objects are sacred in varying degrees. Monkeys, tree squirrels, and snakes, the many rooted Banyan and the Pivopal, two of the largest trees of India are sacred—also wild basil. We would have liked to visit our Lutheran Mission in Southern India, but our travels did not allow such a side trip.

Martha was given permission to travel from her doctor. He said it would be better for her to leave the cast on for another week.

We were able to get a flight on "Flying Tigers of China Airlines" into China over the "Hump" (Himalayas) Jan 3, 1946. However we were limited to 65 lbs. of baggage but we could carry a lap robe and wear as much clothing as we could. We had to weight in at noon the day before our flight. We stayed up most of the night trying to fit our belongings into one suitcase and one duffle bag. We decided to each carry a double wool blanket and into the fold of them we packed typewriter ribbons, shoe polish, toothpaste, and a few books.

I wore a pair of boots over my shoes and three skirts, two sweaters, and two coats. One was Martha's because she could only wear one over her big cast. We thanked God—for the lost trunk because it would have taken more hours to try to decided what to take into China.

We finally were dressed and ready to depart for "weighing in" at the airport. All sensible people take a siesta but we had to go out and try to find a taxi. We were finally able to hire an open air horse carriage.

There we three sat—the hot sun shining down on us and people stopped and stared. Only mad dogs and Englishmen go out in the heat of noonday, but here were three Americans dressed for a blizzard—out for a carriage ride in the hot sun.

At the airport, Martha's bags were weighed first. When they weighted her second bag, they told her she was three pounds over the limit, so she took out one pair of shoes and put them in the bag off the scales. The worker just stood there with his mouth open but he just waved Martha on. Our bags were left at the airport but we had to wear everything back to the Mission House and wear it the next morning on our flight out of India.

We left one foot locker full of books and things we could not take with us with Chaplain Wenger. He thought he could get it on a flight out of Kumning Army Base in the near future. On January 3, 1946, we flew out of Calcutta, India

Into China

January 3, 1946 we are "off to the wild blue yonder". The airplane had "bucket seats" along the 2 sides. There were "peek-hole" windows above the seats the length of the plane. If one could turn around and look out, one might see the Himalayas or get a glimpse of China. We had so many coats and clothes on that we could not look around, but tried to see something out the windows on the other side of the plane.

My husband and I were getting ready to get off the plane in Kumning. We were saying our goodbyes to Martha and saying a prayer for our mission work in China, for our protection, for our loved one's back home and for our church's worldwide mission work.

When the plane touched down in Kumning—my husband was handed a telegram from the Mission Board in St Louis telling him to stay on the plane to Chung King and proceed to Enshih, Hupeh, with Martha Boss. The Mission Board thought my husband could work with the U.S. Soldiers stationed in Kumning and start Chinese mission work as he was able.

However, the Army closed the Base and the U.S. Soldiers returned to America. So the Mission Board did not want to start a new mission station so far afield from the established mission stations.

Our passports were stamped, the necessary visas were granted and tickets purchased for continuing the flight to Chung King. My husband and I had mixed emotions about the change in plans. We had prepared ourselves for living in Kumning. During World War II, Kumning received many refugees from eastern China and became a Chinese military base. It was also of great importance as the transport terminus for the Burma Road and for cargo flown over the "Hump" by U.S. Air forces. The streets were paved, there were modern-style buildings and stores. The city had electric light and power. There was a French-built railway from Haiphong 530 miles away. Kumning is the seat of Yunnan University and also has a medical college and institute of technology. The population was 700,000. Four institutions of higher learning moved into the city during the war.

There was an opportunity for mission work in Kumning. But it was not in God's timing for us to start our church's mission here. So—we turned our thoughts toward Enshih and started once more on our way. We landed at Chung King Airport and were greeted most enthusiastically by missionaries Paul Martens and Olive Green, two well seasoned "China Hands". They did the Chinese translating for us to get through customs.

Chung King was the war time capital of China from 1938–1945. Extensive damage was caused by Japanese bombing from 1938 to 1941. The city became a U.S. Air Base 1944 and 1945. Beginning in 1938 many coastal industries and down river Chinese moved to Chung King to escape the Japanese. Chung King is a Yangtze River port, high above the river and the airport, we climbed hundreds of stairs to the city and our hotel. We were very cold—chilled to the bone—in this cold, damp climate after living in hot India for a month. We were happy to have all the extra clothes on and we slept in most of them trying to stay warm.

We didn't visit our Chinese Pastor and mission in Chung King as we arrived late in the afternoon and the next day we spent repacking and preparing for our down river trip to Wanshien. We just couldn't get warm in Chung King. We went to bed early because it was too dark in our room to read or write. We had to use our flashlight because the electric light bulb was too dim. We used our hot water bottle to try to warm up our bed.

We had to be at the river side by 7:00 a.m. Missionary Martens hired a water taxi to take us out to the river streamer which was anchored in the middle of the river. Oliver Green bought 1 dozen hard boiled eggs. When we arrived at the river steamer we had to climb up a ladder to get on board. A collie was hired to give Martha a "Piggy Back" up the ladder because she had the cast on her right arm and no way could she climb aboard. When we got to our state room it was already occupied by eight persons and their baggage and we were five more. We compared tickets and we were all assigned the same stateroom. The other eight roommates gave up three bunks. They had five bunks. We piled our baggage on the bunks and our sleeping bags on top of the baggage. We had no place to sit but on the bunks.

The decks were filled with people and their baggage. They were mostly refugees returning to their pre-war homes down river. It was impossible to walk on deck without stepping on someone so we spent two days and a night mostly lying down on top of our baggage. Miss Olive Green was very kind to share her hard boiled eggs with us. We did manage to get a bowl of noodles in the dining room.

When the steamer anchored at Wanshien, our getting off-place, Martha said, "I don't think I can walk". I said, "I don't think I can walk either". She said she was not kidding and that something was wrong with her leg. She pulled up her slacks and showed us a large red swollen area on her leg. A coolie was hired to carry her down the ladder to a "water taxi" (a small row boat) which took us and our baggage to shore. Coolies were hired to carry our baggage to the mission compound. Martha was carried in a sedan chair. The rest of us walked miles to the compound.

Olive Green said it was good to be home. This was where she would live and work. She knew the Christians and they gave her a big welcome celebration with tea and cakes, flowers, welcome streamer, banners and long speeches. They were all excited and curious about the rest of us. They also recognized Missionary Martens. We all were made comfortable at the mission compound.

The next day I said, "the first thing we have to do is to get Martha to a doctor or hospital where she can get her leg taken care of and the cast taken off her arm." Miss Green said, "There is no doctor here nor a hospital. We will take care of Martha." So being a nurse I was given the task of caring for Martha's infection on her leg. When I examined it there were red streaks running out of the center of the red area. Martha and I decided to try hot wet soaks.

I asked Missionary Martens to get some kind of tools to help us get the hard plaster cast off Martha's arm. It took us half a day to cut, break and pry open the cast. We used a hammer, chisel, cleaver, saw, pliers and a lot of physical force to free Martha's arm from the cast. What an ordeal for Martha. When the cast was finally off, Martha's arm just hung down limp. She could not raise it up so we put the arm in a sling. Meanwhile we kept soaking Martha' huge infection on her leg.

Martha became discouraged and said she would be of no use at the hospital. She said she should have gone to Germany where she knew the language and could have worked with the German Deaconesses. We all encouraged Martha and told her God had great plans for her life in China. We told her that her arm would soon be activated back to its full strength and that her leg infection would be healed. We prayed together for God's healing.

Miss Olive Green told us many Mission stories and about the orphanage we would find at Enshih. She told us how she and her faithful workers moved the children from Enshih.

The smaller children were carried in a basket tied to each side of a shoulder bar by coolies. Some of the older children walked. It was a long trip and took 3 weeks. She told us how they all prayed daily for God's protection and the well being of the children entrusted to their care. They also told us about the many faithful Chinese staff and Christians. Missionary Martens told us about the hospital in Enshih, the doctor, Dr. Chen, his wife and the midwife and nurses (graduates and students). About the church and Pastor Chen and Bible woman, Mrs. Ma, about the school and faithful teachers. Missionary Martens was anxious to get started on the last leg of the journey.

We were all concerned about Martha's infected leg. We decided to use "cupping" procedure. We heated up some bottles and jars. We applied oil to Martha's leg and cautiously placed the hot bottles and jars one after another to the elevated red area of the leg. Nothing happened, every hour we tried again to no avail. The next day we decided to make a small cross cut in to the area and do more "cupping", praying we would do no harm to her leg. Soon the infection started to drain and we applied more heat and made a deeper opening and sponged it out with green soap solution. I had provided myself with a "Visiting Nurses' Bag" and I had a few instruments, medications and bandages that a doctor friend, formerly in the U.S. Army, suggested I take along. So I was able to treat Martha's infection.

Missionary Martens informed us we would leave the next morning. I asked, "how are we going"? He said, " it will take about a week—roughly 150 miles. We will walk. Martha will be carried on a bamboo chair. Coolies will carry the gear. There will be one extra bamboo chair with 2 coolies for whoever wants or needs a ride. We will take our meals at our rest stops and stay in "Chinese Hotels" at night. We would sleep on our own cots in sleeping bags. After our evening meal and devotions, we retired early for a good night's sleep.

We were up at the "crack of dawn". After morning devotions, breakfast and treating Martha's leg, we said our good-byes to Olive Green and the faithful workers and staff of Wanshien.

On Our Way to
Enshih, Hupeh

It was winter and cold. Martha was bundled into her chair which the coolies picked up on poles and carried on their shoulders. They sang a rhythm as the load swayed from side to side. On flat surfaces, they would run. I wanted to keep up with them but I soon was outdistanced so I walked with the men.

Missionary Martens taught us how to tell time in Chinese. The scenery was farm land country. The main highway was a slab stone pathway. I didn't see any restaurants or hotels.

After two hours, the coolies put Martha down and they ran into a nearby field to relieve themselves. We helped Martha out of the chair to stretch her legs. We all sat down by the roadside. The coolies changed places and we were again on our way. After about one hour they put Martha down again near a small shack in an open field and pointed to it.

When I came up to Martha, she said it must be the "out house" and the pigs' house. There was no door on it, so we took a blanket to hold up over the doorway. The coolies got all excited and started to yell and run to the farmhouse. The farmers in the field all came running towards the pig house.

Martha came out and I rolled up the blanket and said no way was I going in there. Martha got back into her chair and I gave her the blanket to hold. We wanted the coolies to go on, but they were all excited and yelling to the farmers. By this time, Missionary Martens and my husband arrived on the scene. When the coolies told Missionary Martens what was going on, he roared with laughter.

I wanted to know what was so funny. He said they told him we stole a pig and had it in the blanket. They said one of the ladies went in and got a pig and the other lady rolled it up in the blanket, so we had to unroll the blanket and show them that there was no pig. Missionary Martens told them we were modest ladies and needed privacy in the pig house. He suggested we stop for a bowl of noodles. So we walked over to the farm house and the farmer was happy to cook for us.

He picked up a dirty rag from the floor and dusted off little stools and "buck horses" for us to sit on. Then he got out some bowls and dusted them with this same dirty rag. He made noodles and gave us all chopsticks and bowls filled with noodles. We did not know how to use chopsticks. We were very hungry and cold. We just held the bowl up to our mouths, held the chopsticks together and pushed the noodles into our mouths. He served us hot water to drink.

Again we were on our way. I rode a few hours in the bamboo chair as did Martha. The scenery was beautiful and the swaying motion of the carriers made me drowsy and I had a catnap. At the rest stop we were able to purchase peanuts and oranges and have tea.

At 4:00 p.m., we stopped at a farm with a large barn like wooden structure. That was our hotel for the night. We set up cots and sleeping bags. A meal was prepared for us. Rice, soy bean curd, green vegetables and a polima (yellow, round, thick skin citrus fruit like a grapefruit).

Afte supper, we had evening devotions. After prayers, I changed Martha's dressing on her leg. The coolies told the inn keeper I was a doctor from America going to the hospital in Enshih. Word got around the country side and the people carried their sick into our hotel barn. Missionary Martens would tell me what they were complaining about, so they thought he was a doctor too. I would treat them as best I could, always praying I would do them no harm. They had all kinds of chest pains, infected sores, rashes. I used a lot of soap and water and clean bandages. They brought babies with infected eyes, etc. I had a few medicines in my nursing bag: sulfa drugs, aspirin, and boric acid. We took care of everyone and Missionary Martens told them about Jesus. I spent most of the night in prayer. I was happy to be on the way the next morning.

We started to climb and go around mountains. The scenery was very beautiful. The farmers had terraced the land all the way up the mountains. The fields were flooded and when the sun shone on them, they reflected the scenery like a thousand mirrors. There were many different kids of song birds. What a wonderful trip the Lord was giving us.

Coolies, farmers, men, women and children were coming and going on this official path. Everyone walking and carrying loads of wood, mail, grain, vegetables, live pigs and chickens, cloth, garments, oil , etc. At every rest stop, there was gambling of some sort among the coolies and trades people. There were many little shrines along the way with incense, red papers filled with Chinese words, and pinwheels to ward off evil spirits.

Many people were filled with wonder when they set their eyes on us. The children were frightened of us and covered their eyes and looked through their parted fingers. Some people and children called us "foreign devils". All were amazed when we blew our nose in a handkerchief and put it in our pocket and saved it. They blew their nose with their hand and threw it to the ground. The farm houses were made of mud, with wooden doors, oiled paper covering the windows for it was a cold winter. The roofs were made of tile.

We walked about 15–20 miles a day, stopping at farm houses for most meals. There were a few small towns along the way where there were restaurants where we could get a fuller meal of rice, bamboo shoots, bean sprouts, vegetables, and meat (fish, pork or chicken). They made steamed buns and sweet lotus seeds and tea. Some mornings we had eggs and hot cooked wheat cereal or rice gruel.

At night the farm barns or inns had no electricity. For light, a lighted wick was placed in a dish of oil. This gave a very small light. Sometimes they gave us a candle in a paper lantern.

We carried our own "wash basin". Sometimes we were able to get some warm water to bathe with, but mostly it was cold stream or well water. We had to be careful not to rub our eyes or wash them because there was so much trachoma (a chronic contagious form of conjunctivitis) We mostly wore the same clothes every day. We did change our socks.

Sometimes it rained a fine mist, and sometimes the pathway was slippery and muddy. But for the most part, the weather was good for the long hike. Some of the pathway was perilous—only room for one person going around, up high, on the mountain. One dare not slip or look around. I never did like the hanging suspension bridges—only one way traffic—sometimes a board or two was missing.

Every evening we had a neighborhood clinic. Martha's leg infection improved but her right arm remained useless. We all did a lot of praying along the way.

There were rumors of bandits, wild animal attacks and landslides, but the Lord protected us from all harm and danger. Finally, after a week's trek we arrived at Enshih—tired, dirty, hungry and our feet hurt—but thank God we were home in China at last. Somewhere along the way, we crossed over from Szechwan to Hupeh—probably on a suspension bridge.

Enshih, Hupeh

What a trip! What an experience! Two months and six days! Thanks and praise to our Heavenly Father for daily providing us with all of our needs, for protection from all harm and danger, and for good health.

Hupeh is a province in China and is in the heart of agricultural China. Enshih is surrounded (in the distance) by mountain ranges. The farmers grew sweet potatoes, greens, corn, soy beans and other vegetables. Also grown were rice, tea, and tobacco. There were at least three crops growing in the same field at the same time. They rotated crops and had vegetables growing all year long. Summers were hot and humid. Winters were relatively mild.

Enshih was a walled city on the Ching River. Our Lutheran Mission compound was on a hill, across the river, overlooking the city. The Lutheran Church was in the city. A pagoda was on the next hill over a Buddhist tower with a peaceful symbolism to the country side. When we climbed up to the mission compound, we noticed from the city many sticks of incense and red and gold papers with Chinese lettering stuck into the earth to ward off evil spirits. Almost every acre of farm field had a mound where family members were buried.

In every open door, one could see a mirror. If by chance an evil spirit should wander in the door, it would see itself and would be frighten by its own image and flee out the door. We could also see red wooden altars hanging on the walls inside the homes, with red candles, incense and a bowl of fruit or other food.

Our hearts were moved with compassion as we could see the idolatry and superstition that held these people captive. I prayed in my heart for the Holy Spirit's power to help our mission staff to witness for Jesus Christ and set these people free.

At our compound gate our arrival was announced by the old gate keeper. Everyone stopped what they were doing and joined in one big welcome! So many happy voices and faces. Missionary Wenger was indeed happy to see us—for now it meant he would soon be able to leave on furlough to USA to be reunited with his family and bring them back to China. His wife Elsie, and 3 children, Kathleen, Geraldine and Timothy were in America for the duration of the 2nd World War.

We received a lot of hugs and kisses—dirty as we were. They were all so thankful to God for bringing us safely to them.

They were all concerned about Martha's condition and offered all kinds of help. The student nurses helped Martha get settled in our home. There were two houses, made of stone, with wooden floors and glass windows and tile roofs built for the missionary families about 1925. My husband and I shared one with Martha Boss. The Wengers lived in the other house. There were two bedrooms, a living room and entrance room, a dining room, a study and a kitchen with a wood burning stove. The bathroom had a wooden bathtub and a wooden cabinet for towels and wash basins and other toiletries, a wall mirror and a pail of water with a dipper, a floor drain and commode with a large earthen ware bucket inside. The toilet paper was brown "grass" paper. Everyday the farmer came and emptied the content of the bucket. We cautioned him not to use it on our vegetable garden.

The cook prepared a delicious meal for us while he was heating large pails of water for our baths and shampoos. It took awhile to heat the water on the wood stove. There was a well in our back yard that supplied our cooking and drinking water. Our water for bathing and washing clothes came from the river. The well water had to be strained and boiled for use.

We had no electricity. We used kerosene lamps when kerosene was available, but ordinarily we used candles for light. They were mostly made of grease and would melt down very fast in a pool of grease. We used our flashlights when we could get batteries. Outside, at night, we used a paper lantern with a candle inside and carried it on a stick. After we ate and the bath water was hot, we took a bath in our wooden tub and washed our hair.

Martha's infected leg was very much better. The student nurses came to our home everyday to massage Martha's arm. Martha was determined to get her arm working. Every day she added a dipper full of water to a heavy pail and she would hold it in her right hand for 15 minutes. She gradually got her arm down.

Rev. Wenger told us that the doctor left with his family to go to his pre-war home down river to get his mother and bring her to live with them in Enshih. There were two capable midwives to run the hospital and clinic along with the student nurses.

After two days in our new home, I became very sick. I had terrible stomach pain, diarrhea, and vomiting. I couldn't eat. I became weak and had a 103 degrees fever. My husband gave me "stomach powders" that the doctor had prescribed for the clinic patients.

Everyone was concerned and prayed for God's mercy and healing. I was bedridden for a week. They gave me sips of boiled water, tea, then rice gruel with ginger; and chicken broth with ginger. By the second week I was well again. How we thanked and praised God for my healing! Many missionaries, their wives, their children got sick and died (and were buried in China) because of lack of medicine and medical care.

Missionary Martens left Enshih to go down river and to USA on furlough and to find a wife, God willing.

We started our language study of five hours a day with a language teacher. He was very patient with us and taught us to speak, write and read Mandarin Chinese—the national language of China. The local people spoke a local dialect.

We soon had two teachers come to our house five hours a day. My husband needed more Bible terms and reading. So he studied alone with both teachers and Martha and I studied together with both teachers. We drilled and drilled tones. Many Chinese words sound the same, but the tone gives the meaning. We soon discovered that you didn't have to be a Lily Pons, but it sure would have helped.

Martha had a German accent which went with her English and now with her Chinese. Martha got a lady teacher—the sister of one of our male teachers. Martha studied medical terms with her. She was a part-time teacher. So Martha continued to study some of the time with me. I wanted more household terms as I was in charge of our household and had to be able to talk to the servant boy we hired to be our cook and housekeeper.

Martha had a birthday the end of January. We had a birthday cake, chicken, rice and vegetable dinner. We gave her little gifts that we bought in the city. We hung a long string of firecrackers on a tree outside our front door and had the cook set them off. That became a birthday celebration tradition.

Martha's leg was completely healed and her arm was beginning to look and act normal. She combed and braided her own hair. She still had the student nurses come to massage her arm. She started to teach English medical terms to the student nurses and they all developed Martha's German accent.

There was a college and a high school that moved into the Enshih area. During the war years, to avoid interruption of the education process, some of the students found their way to our compound and would rap on our door in the late afternoon or on Saturday.

They wanted to try some English conversation with us and we wanted to try our Chinese with them. After a few visits they could see they were not getting any English feedback. We tried to give them some English and Chinese Bible stories. One student always came to our bathroom door. I always thought it was the farmer come to empty our pot. The student always called me "sir". I called him "girl student'". I told him I thought he was the farmer. He asked me how the country bumpkin was.

The college had a music department and we were often invited to special programs of classical Chinese music played on Chinese instruments. They also had a Chinese chorus. We went a few times and the program lasted several hours. So, we had a good indoctrination to Chinese music. The college moved back to its pre-war location after the school term ended in the Summer of 1946.

Orphanage

The orphanage was a part of the Mission compound. Mrs. Ma, the Bible woman was in charge of the orphanage. The building was large, two-story with tile roof and wooden floors and stairs. The windows were covered with "oiled paper" in the winter and "rice paper" in the summer. The Mission workers, professional and laborers, ate two meals a day at the orphanage. To tell you about the type of children we had at the orphanage, we look at the case histories showing how the children came to be there.

Wang Nan was a "slave girl" of a family in Enshih. She was well treated by the family. On the day of the bombing of Enshih, June 7, 1939, the home of the family was completely burned out. The occupants fled to safety, this girl being a cripple managed to shift thru the mob, was directed to Yang Wan (the Chinese name of our mission) by Deaconess Gertrude Simon. The crippled condition was the result of TB or Rickets.

Chu Hsio was found in front of the gate at "Yang Wah" sickly. Her mother died soon after her birth. The father was an opium addict. Her first wet nurse gave her opium. She had chronic conjunctivitis, Trachoma.

Ming Shen—The parents are unknown when she was left on the steps of our city orphanage. She was in a very poor physical condition. Full of boils and had Trachoma.

Mei Yuin—The mother, a cripple, was deserted by her husband, and no longer able to handle the child or support him. The child was unable to walk at 4 years old, legs too weak

Lo Ta—She was thrown in front of our city orphanage. She was formerly supported and cared for by the nuns of De Wang Tzu Temple until they were unable to care for her.

Sung Hsai—Left on the doorsteps of the orphanage in 1938. She had scurvy and rickets.

Fu Cheng—Born 7-25-38 and left on the doorsteps of the orphanage. She had scabies and conjunctivitis.

Fu Hsui—Mother was blind, father dead, very poor. Admitted 1941 with trachoma.

Sui Yuin—Found at the compound gate. Left there perhaps by her mother the same day she left our hospital.

Fu Ming was found at the gate by Dr. Chen. He was placed in the hospital for several weeks and then brought to the orphanage. He was admitted 1941 and had trachoma and scabies.

Fu Tsan—Admitted 1941. Found at the clinic. Had beriberi, unable to walk at 3 years.

San Yan—Child of a refugee. Mother died a year before. Father working, has 2 other children.

Fu Kwang—Found in the large rice bin at the orphanage. Trachoma, chronic conjunctivitis and scabies.

Tso Yin—admitted 2-9-42. Foundling and later discovered that his mother is living. A refugee threw the child in front of our gate so that she could be a nurse to another child of means. Had trachoma and scabies.

Ming Yin—admitted 1942. Foundling and later found out that his mother was formerly in the refugee camp. Threw the child in our field in order to be nursemaid to some other child. No way of giving the child back.

When we arrived in 1946, most of the children were well. There were 30 children, most of them girls, unwanted, since everyone in China wants a boy and not a girl. Most of the people were poor farmers, who work the land and pay rent to wealthy land owners in far away eastern cities.

The orphans went to the Lutheran School which was also on our mission compound. Some of the orphans could be trained to be nurses' aides or nurses. They were all taught embroidery and knitting and basket weaving, etc. The ones who were able also helped out in the kitchen, helped the farmer and laundry women. I went down to the orphanage every day. I saw that there was little time for play and also noted that they had no toys, especially the little ones. The older ones had a Ping-Pong set but no balls. I wrote to my friends at the orphanage in Addison, IL where my husband and I formerly worked. I asked them if they could send some toys and balls for our orphans. They sent many boxes of toys and ball for many happy hours of play.

The orphans had morning and evening devotions and prayers and catechism instruction and Bible stories. They were baptized and confirmed in the faith. They could sing all the hymns. They wore long padded garments in the winter and skirts and blouses in the summer. Their shoes were made of cotton material and hand sewn by the orphanage staff and older girls. In rainy weather they went barefooted so as not to ruin their cotton shoes. The shoes were made of black cotton uppers with a strap and button fastener. The linings were white cotton. The soles were several layers of strong coarse white cotton, with an in between layer of pieces of old cloth, starched and dried and pasted on a board to dry and cut to shoe size and sewn between the layers of new cloth.

Every Sunday all the orphans went to the church in the city. The older ones walked and the little ones were carried in baskets swinging from a carrying pole. Mrs. Ma the Bible woman, played the church organ. She ushered the women to their seats and tried to keep them quiet. The Pastor told everyone to come after their morning meal. People ate at all different times and their arrival at church varied. When we arrived from our hill the service began. The seats were bucks—no backs—and it was hard to sit on these seats for 1½ hours or more. The Pastor was always updating the sermon for the new arrivals.

The Lutheran Mission— Enshih, Hupeh, Chin

The hospital consisted of two mud wall buildings (one one-story, and one two-story) with wooden floors and Chinese tile roofs. The windows were covered with oiled paper to keep out the cold and rain. The water supply was carried from the river by water carriers and emptied into large earthenware containers stored outside the hospital. Drinking water must be strained and boiled.

There was an outside toilet. There was no central heating. On cold mornings, a charcoal fire was started in an open pan. The patients wore their own padded garments and are covered with a cotton padded quilt.

The nightlight is in the form of a bowl of oil with a string wick which gives off ½ inch of flame of light. For nighttime emergency operations or deliveries, kerosene lamps are used. But was very expensive as the kerosene is hauled in over the Burma Road.

The laundry is taken to the river by wash women, who beat it on the rocks with a stick. After it is washed it is spread out on the grass covered beach to dry. In rainy weather, it is hung on bamboo poles over charcoal fire to dry. It is hung inside where there is space or in a drying shed.

The kitchen is small and puts out gruel for breakfast, and rice, vegetables, bean curd for lunch and dinner. The patients' visitors bring food—already prepared from home or bring a small fire pot and cook it outside. Often they bring sweet potatoes, noodles, live chickens, eggs, dried smoked fish, and ducks. This food is stored under the patients' beds or hung in fishnet bags suspended on the walls or on the beds.

We were in need of all kinds of equipment. Martha and I wrote to friends and relatives in the U.S.A. For instruments, stainless steel basins, bed pans, towels, wash cloths, diapers, baby gowns, layettes, medicine, bandages, and money. Martha bought local coarse cotton cloth and had it made into sheets for over the straw mattresses. Martha and I were anxious to help out at the hospital. It was cold and damp outside and inside the hospital. We wore heavy sweaters over our white uniforms. My school's nursing cap was white with a black band and Martha's was plain white. We decided to pass medicines. We numbered the charts and beds as we could not read the Chinese numbers and names. We poured out a tray of medicine and passed it out. Whoever was in bed #1 got the medicine ordered on chartt#1. The medicine bottles were labeled in English and Chinese.

The Chinese are very polite and proper. As I approached the 3rd patient, he waved his hand for "no". I said this is what is ordered for you and it will make you feel better. He tried to avoid taking it but I insisted. Finally he took it. I was quite pleased with myself for being of some use at the hospital.

Later that day, I saw a strange thing take place at the hospital. A visitor arrived, all tired out from climbing our hill from the city. The patient got out of bed and insisted that the visitor rest in the bed. The visitor climbed into bed and the patient went outside for awhile. In a "flash back", I remembered the patient who didn't want to take the medication. I wondered if I insisted a visitor take a patient's medication. I prayed all the more fervently for help and wisdom in all of our nursing care of the patients.

In the Spring, the doctor and his family returned. The hospital was soon filled to capacity. Martha and the doctor set up the nurses' training classes and programs. The doctor was pleased with the medicine and supplies that we brought along from America. Martha gave him catalogs so he could see what was available and choose what he needed and we would try to find friends in America to pay for an order. He wanted to do more operations and he wanted Martha and I to help out. He said he needed someone to administer chloroform to anesthetize the patients for surgery. I volunteered saying it was used in some "home deliveries" when I was a student nurse on "home calls."

The operation room was painted white and had a wooden table. The patient often brought his friends or relatives to watch the whole procedure. The patient was helped up on the table, The tray of instruments were sterilized in a "pressure cooker". The gowns, caps, masks, sutures, cotton balls, dressings, sheets, and gloves were "baked in our oven". The doctor's wife was his assistant; Martha and the surgical nurse were standing by. I had the mask and chloroform ready.

Before every operation, the doctor had a prayer asking God in His mercy and for Jesus' sake to heal the patient and give success to the surgery so that God would be glorified and the patient would know that God healed him. He prayed for wisdom for himself and for blessings on the staff to do their very best work as unto Jesus, so that everything done at the hospital would be done to the honor and glory of the Triune God. We then prayed the Lord's prayer and the operation would begin. After a few drops of chloroform the patient's arms and legs were secured to the table. I never knew what stage the patient was in so the doctor or his wife had to motion to me to give more or hold back.

Because the doctor was trained in western medicine and practiced the same, and because he was from another place in China, he was not always trusted by the patients. That is why he allowed visitors and relatives into the operating room. And because I was a foreigner, they did not trust me. Many patients refused the anesthetic because there were afraid they would end up in a foreign spirit world and would be unable to communicate and get back into the Chinese spirit world.

Anything that was removed from a patient was sent home in a basket with a relative. There were many rumors about the doctor using the removed parts to make medicine. So, the parts were sent home and the family usually sold them to the Chinese medicine men. Immediately after the operation, the patient sat up and bowed to the doctor and staff, and thanked the doctor and the staff.

The doctor was a very fine surgeon and his fame spread for many miles. Many of the sick were carried for miles to our hospital after all else failed in their locale.

During one operation, I became very weak and perspiring and had to put my head down. After the operation, the doctor took me to the clinic and tested my blood and he told me I had malaria and gave me quinine and told me to put up a mosquito net around the bed. My husband also got malaria and we had frequent bouts with it throughout our stay in Enshih.

The clinic was in the basement of our home and our back yard was the waiting room. Our elderly gateman was the clinic registrar. He sat at the gate, smoking a long pipe. Being an old man, he had already purchased his coffin which took up a large part of his room. He would give a number to each patient entering the compound gate.

Not all entering were clinic patients, some came for the Pastor's Bible stories and to see the Bible Story on the Concordia Picture Roll. Sometimes a professional Chinese storyteller would be in the audience and add the Bible Story to his repertoire. Mrs. Ma, the Chinese Bible woman, would also talk with the patients in our backyard. Sometimes the doctor's family would sing hymns for the crowd in our backyard.

Quite often a recovered patient would return with a long string of firecrackers and a professional orator. The firecrackers would be set off to get everyone's attention. Then the orator would deliver a speech extolling the doctor's skills. The doctor would come out to take a bow and tell the people his gifts of healing came from the Lord Jesus Christ and to thank God for the healing. When it rained the people did not come to the clinic but would send a family member for renewal of a prescription. The pharmacy was a part of the clinic and the doctor's wife was the pharmacist.

On Mondays, our laundry day, many people would come to our back yard and sit under our drying poles and try to figure out who wore what and how you wore it. Our servant spoke with authority on these matters. After our laundry was finished, he washed his own clothes in our soap water and then sold the soap water to whoever had a bucket to carry it in. Many times people would come around to our front yard and lay on our grass or pick our flowers or peek in our windows. We were celebrities, foreigners, sometimes foreign devils, but we tried to be friendly.

Holidays

Soon after our arrival in Enshih, we celebrated our first wedding anniversary and our first Chinese New Year in February 1946.

For our wedding anniversary, we cut off some early peach, apple and cherry blossoms. Our cook made a nice cake and a chicken dinner for Rev. Wenger, Martha, my husband and me. We had a special decoration on our wedding cake, the text of Ps. 37:3–6, and we sang our wedding song "O Perfect Love" and "Let Us Ever Walk with Jesus. We told Martha and Rev. Wenger about our wedding at St Paul's Lutheran Church in Addison, IL We had all the 250 children and staff members of the Luther Child Welfare Association invited to our wedding. One little orphan girl sang a solo, "O Perfect Love". The snow was deep. The bridesmaids left in a car from the orphanage and got stuck in the snow.

The minister from the LCWA was driving me in a car behind the bridesmaids. He gave them a push out with his car and they drove off to the church. Our car was now held fast by the snow. I don't drive so I was no help. The minister had to get out and push the car and steer at the same time. It took over ½ hour for us to get out of the snow and to the church. The minister walked me down the aisle in his soaking wet shoes and pant legs. He delivered the sermon and the local Pastor had the marriage ceremony.

The war (World War II) was still on. Because of gas rationing and shortage of film, we had to drive into the next town to the photographer's studio for our wedding pictures. We drove back to the LCWA for our reception. My husband's brother-in-law was a baker, and he baked a huge wedding cake and pan wedding cake for the children. A happy memory.

For Chinese New Year, our cook left for two weeks to go back to his family in the mountains. Everyone was busy preparing for the New Year. Need to get haircuts before the price doubled, so everyone had very short hair. All debts must be paid so everyone needed money. New clothes and shoes had to be made. Sweet cakes and gluttonous rice were prepared. Gifts, oranges, flowers and red envelopes were prepared. The house had to be thoroughly cleaned. The kitchen god's mouth was smeared with honey so only sweet words would come out of his mouth when he reported on the family when he visited the heavenly spirits. Candles, incense, firecrackers were purchased and red paper doorposts had to be printed. Colorful lanterns in various shapes of animals, butterflies, birds, fish and flowers had to be made.

It was a happy time of the year. All businesses and work stopped for two weeks while the people visited, played mahjong and checkers, hired storytellers, shadow puppet shows, magicians, and musicians. The traveling opera show came to town. The ancestors were worshiped. The evil spirits were scared off with firecrackers. The wells were sealed up. There was a lantern parade at night. We were visited by the staff families, Pastor's family, orphans, church members, etc! We served tea, cookies, oranges, peanuts and played games like passing a ring on a string, button-button who has the button musical chairs, charades, singing, etc. I started my first fire in the wood stove and cooked my first meal on it. I surprised everyone by starting a fire so quickly. I had a secret way—I threw in a greasy candle or two and had a blazing fire in short order.

We had to buy our staples well before Chinese New Years before prices doubled and then all shops and business were closed for two weeks of celebrations. We bought and stored one month supply of firewood, charcoal, oil, candles and grass paper.

Our food pantry had good supply of rice, sugar, tea, soy sauce, peanuts, ground wheat, flour, eggs, oranges and cooking oil. We had no refrigeration. We used a "wind box" and hung some perishable food down the well. We asked the hospital cook to buy our daily meat, fish or chicken. I never had killed or de-feathered a chicken and I never cleaned a fish.

When we went to the market, usually after Church on Sunday, we had to take a basket and bottles for oil and sauce. The storekeepers had no bags. Most things like rice, flour, sugar could be wrapped in brown grass paper and tied with strong grass bands. The meat was hung out on racks in the street with mangy dogs close by. There were flies about in all seasons. When one purchased a piece of meat, the butcher would make a hole in the corner and lace a grass string thru the meat so one could carry it on one finger and have the dogs jumping and yelping trying to get at it. I laid our meat on grass paper in the market basket. The meat was always pork or dog. We hoped we bought pork.

We got most of our vegetables from our compound farm, paying our fair share into the farmer's pay and seed money, etc. All fruit and vegetables had to be eaten in their season. We did some home canning but we were happy to receive food packages from family and friends in America. We asked for coffee, canned milk, milk powder, canned fruits, dried fruits, raisins, dates, canned beef, salmon, tuna fish, cake mixes, etc.

In March before the college moved away, the physical education teacher invited us to Kite Festival Day when prayers could be written on paper and sent up to heaven by kite. Not all kites carried prayers. There were many competitions to show off the skills of the kite fliers. With prizes of 1st, 2nd and 3rd place ribbons. There were competitions for the first kite flying 50 feet in the air, competitions for small, medium, large kites, kite wars with the kite string having no more than three razors blades attached to fight a war with 7, 15, and 21 kites to see who bring down the most kites. There was also judging of the most beautiful kite. The festival lasted all day. We were given an opportunity to talk about our prayer life and our "direct line" to our Heavenly Father and how we received this most precious gift.

April—We celebrated Easter. The fruit trees were in bloom and the flowers in our garden. We thanked God for His creation and gave witness as often as we could. We colored eggs with food coloring from our family food box from America. We treated the orphans to an egg hung on our front lawn. I planted some small seeds in eggshells for the orphans to watch and care for a tiny plant. We made paper crosses and had our deaf writer write some Easter Bible messages on each one to give out along the walk to church.

We made some fudge bunnies for our own Easter nests. Martha made excellent fudge. She had the nurses make crosses for the patients at the hospital and clinic. They also made paper lilies with the Easter message attached. We asked God for His Holy Spirit to bless our message and enable us to speak His word correctly so that many could be brought to faith in Christ Jesus—the Savior of the world.

There is so much to be done in China. What a harvest field we are in. God used us to extend His kingdom of Grace. Isaiah 55:11, "My word will accomplish what I desire and achieve the purpose for which I sent it."

Funerals—When a family member dies, the family hires a special person who can find the best place for the grave site and the best day for the funeral. Sometimes this takes weeks on end. Many times the coffin is already purchased and is kept in the home. The coffins are made of fine wood and treated with oil and lacquered. The corpse is dressed in new clothes and a coin is placed between the lips and on the eyes. Yards, of new materials (silk and wood) are laid on the corpse. A live chicken is tied on the coffin so the spirit of the dead can go into the chicken and stay warm.

When the gravesite is arranged and the day set, the mourners don white robes and white hoods and follow the funeral arranger. The coffin is carried on poles by four men. Wailers are hired plus a funeral band of musicians. Priests and friends follow also. The grave is shallow and the earth is piled up into a mound. Red candles and incense are lighted and stuck into the ground. Paper clothes, houses, money and sedan chairs, boats are burned on the grave so the dead will have a wealthy life in the spirit world. Pinwheels and mirrors are placed on the grave to chase away evil spirits. Firecrackers are shot off to also scare away evil spirits. Much money is spent on funerals and a lifetime is spent paying off the debts.

Ching Ming Festival—During this Spring festival, families would make a trip to the family graves to sweep and clean the grave sites and offer food to the spirits of the ancestors—a good family outing.

There is also a festival when the spirits of the drowned are honored and tamales made of special glutinous rice and red bean mixture is wrapped in large leaves and steamed. They are thrown in the river for the spirits of the dead and also eaten by the living on this festival day. There are "dragon boat races" which take the entire day to determine the winner. At night, there are riverboat parties with colored paper lanterns and music. A very enjoyable day.

In the Spring, Summer and Fall when the full moon lights up the sky, we had lawn parties for the student nurses and orphans. We played games outside on our front lawn, Farmer in the dell, Mouse and cat, Two deep, Here comes a blue bird thru my window, Hide and seek, London Bridge, etc. We served cookies, tea, fruit in season and peanuts.

These parties lasted several hours. Also had a lot of singing and drama acting. We always ended with a devotion and prayers.

End of April, 1946

We finally received a letter from my family in U.S.A. The first word I had from them since we left home in Nov. 1945. It was full of amazing news. My parents moved from Buffalo, NY to retire in Oklahoma City. They wanted to be near my older sister and her family with three grand-daughters. My younger sister remained in Buffalo, NY and had her wedding planned for July 1946. I had to face up to the fact that I no longer had my home in Buffalo.

The Journey   Chapter Three

A variety shop in Enshih just received their first shipment of supplies since the war ended. I bought some yellow cotton material to make a ruffle-like drape for the dining room window. It framed the top and sides of our casement windows. The cost was $8 US currency. We also purchased a bar of soap (akin to Red Lifeboy) for $1 US. I was impressed with the cost and decided to ask our friends to send some soap and material for a dress in our "care" packages. I thought our dining room looked very cheerful with the yellow ruffle and I was pleased with it until my language teacher said, '"What a waste of money and material!" The material could have made clothes for five little children. Every time I looked at the ruffle, I thought, "Was it really worth it?"

Our cherry trees had bloomed and we had cherry pie. We also were able to can some, thanks to former missionaries for the jars and for our friends in America for sending fruit jar rubber, sealing lids and rings. We also were enjoying peas and strawberries from the garden.

Many Chinese people are suffering with malaria this month. Most of our days are still devoted to language study. My language teacher gave me a Chinese name: Ho (last name) Chieh Yin (first). All winter I stood too close to the fireplaces and burned the hem line off the back of three wool skirts, so the tailor is trying to reweave the burned areas. He is very clever. I gave him some cotton material that came in a "care package" from family members back home in USA and a picture of a dress from a USA magazine. He looked me over from all sides and made a few notes in his notebook and departed. The men tailors do not take female measurements. He returned in a week with my dress which fitted perfectly to my size. Instead of two big collar like tabs on the front neckline, he inserted the contrasting tabs. Interesting. He was very pleased that he could make American women's dresses.

In June we canned peas, string beans and cherries, and had a lot of nice strawberries and so we made strawberry jam. It's very warm and humid inside and outside and with cooking on the wood stove, ironing, boiling water, it gets hotter and hotter. We had the outside shutters and eaves painted. There were about 10 painters looking in our windows for two weeks. They painted with rags instead of brushes. They painted like that in India too.

We had a lot of snakes around—black and brown ones about five feet long. Coming back from the orphanage, I almost stepped on a few sleeping or sunning themselves on the pathway steps.

The mosquitoes were out to get us and give us malaria. We slept under nets but they got in with us. It got harder and harder to walk to church every Sunday in the heat of Summer. The sun was hot, the flies were on everybody and everything. We had to watch our step going down the stone step pathway to the city. Every home had their door open to the pathway and frequently a pan of waste water was thrown out onto the pathway. The children were naked. The men wore shorts and the women wore pants and Chinese tops.

The dogs were mangy. Their hairy coats hanging in patches on their backs. Many children and adults had infected scalps (tinea) and scabies and infected eyes. It was not a pleasant sight. There was a lot of human and animal excreta along the pathway and many unpleasant odors. The pathway was busy as it was a main artery of travel. Everything was carried by humans. We all had to wait at the river for the long narrow boat which was poled back and forth across the river by one or two men, depending on the depth and flow of the water. The passengers all stood up. All the loads were taken on board. It was a short walk to the church from the river.

We always rested up at the Pastor's house, next door to the church. His wife always felt my stomach—looking for new life. She also admired my silk stockings and lifted my skirt so she could tell all the women what I wore underneath. She said my feet were bigger than her husband's. She made me a pair of cloth shoes and told everyone how expensive they were to make because of my large feet. I never dared to wear them because of the cost. Instead I wrote and asked my mother to send me some sensible walking shoes. After being refreshed by a drink of hot water, we went into the church and sat on the buck pews with our knees touching the back of the people in the pew in front of us.

The Bible woman played the organ. We never did recognize the hymn melody, but we sang along with English words of prayer and praise. We did not understand the sermon but we prayed for the Pastor and people in and out of the church. Many people followed us into the church from curiosity. The church was long established and had 200 members or so. We know that the Lord's word never returns void. Church was over in the heat of the day. It was too hot to wear a sun hat so Martha and I used beautiful parasols.

The children always saw us first and ran on ahead to announce our coming, shouting out in Chinese, "Here come the Americans" — sometimes calling us "Foreign Devils". Everyone came out of their houses to see us and smile and wave. We always felt like celebrities. We prayed a blessing on all the people. It was slow walking up the hill to our compound. I always wished for a cold drink along the way, but when we arrived home, it was always warm or hot tea or water.

On Sunday afternoons I was always homesick. I missed my family and friends. We had a windup phonograph and many classical records in our living room. I would wind it up and put on a record and open the window. Outside the window was a beautiful pink and lavender bush, and as soon as the music floated out the window, all kinds of birds flew to the bush and sang their hearts out. It was wonderful concert and how I thanked God for this special blessing. Then I was able to write some letters to family and friends in the good old USA.

It was time for the Ministers' Conference in Hankow. My husband left with Missionary Wenger who would leave for USA furlough after the conference and bring his dear wife and children back to Enshih. Our Chinese Pastor Chen would also go to the conference and return to Enshih with my husband. That left Martha Boss and me alone in the mission house. But we had plenty of Chinese staff living on the compound. I really had to admire the single women workers who came out to serve on the foreign mission fields. They really loved the Lord Jesus and the souls of the heathen. Everywhere we went we heard stories about Gertrude Simon and her horse. She rode all over the countryside visiting and caring for the sick on their farms or in the jails. She taught hymns and told Bible stories. After the war, Gertrude was sent to Batung and worked in the mission station there.

1946 Rolls On

Martha Boss continued to work and teach at the hospital. I continued to keep busy at home and visited the orphanage every day. I spent enjoyable time playing with the children, spraying heads and bedding with D.D.T. for head and body lice. All the staff wanted to borrow the spray for personal use. I wrote a letter off to USA for more D.D.T.

I missed my dear husband away in Hankow for the conference and daily prayed for his safe return. When he returned he had many stories and greetings to share. We thanked God for his safe return and for all his experiences. He had mentioned about going out street preaching with Missionary Albert Ziegler. They would stop at a busy cross road or in tea house sand Missionary Ziegleer would get out his violin and play and sing hymns until he had a good audience and then he would begin to preach and teach about the beautiful Savior Jesus Christ. His messages of love were always well received.

I recalled being invited by Missionary Ziegler's wife (while we were students in the Mission School at Concordia Seminary in St Louis) for lunch at their apartment in the Mission House and went with her to a Ladies' Aid meeting where she was going to give a China Mission talk. When I arrived at their apartment, there was Mrs. Ziegler calling out the door to one of the many missionary children playing outside. She was baking bread and sweet rolls and each child was baking a sweet roll in her oven—about a dozen kids! I was so impressed to see this woman—a busy mother going calmly about her busy schedule of baking, making lunch for her family and an invited guest, and going out for a mission talk

I remember the delicious sweet rolls, but most all, her talk at Ladies' Aid about her and her children's internment in a Japanese prison of war camp in Hankow, China. Her husband was away on a missionary trip and he was never interned and was able to return to America while his family was interned in a POW camp until the war was over. Mrs. Ziegler was put in charge of the women and children and kitchen at the camp. She recalled many a "tongue lashing" by the commandant but the physical lashing was given to her personal officer in charge of her camp work and in her presence. She prayed for mercy for her adversary. The Lord supplied their every need and was their Great Protector. Her story appeared in "The Saturday Evening Post", 1945. I prayed to God that my faith would be strong enough to see me through whatever life experiences would come to me as a missionary's wife.

The inflation of Chinese currency continued. There were rumors of Communistic trouble in another province, but all is peaceful in Enshih. Wilbert started an instruction class for Baptism among the laborers of our mission station.

The Summer is past and the Fall rains have arrived and my thoughts turn homeward as the holidays approach. Dr. O.H. Schmidt from the Mission Board in St. Louis was here for Thanksgiving (escorted by Missionary Herb Hinz). We saved our best canned foods from America for his visit. We had chicken instead of turkey, but we were able to come up with all the trimmings. Dr. Schmidt felt we ate as well in China as we did in America.

The local governor invited Dr. Schmidt and us to come for dinner at his home. He sent chairs and carriers to our compound along with an official escort. We were served a very tasty Chinese feast. Afterward, the governor wanted to call a photographer to come and take a picture, but Dr Schmidt said it was not necessary as he had some pictures of himself and he gave an autographed photo of himself to the governor.

We in turn invited the Governor to our mission compound home for dinner. We did not send a chair or escort as the governor had his own official chair and carriers and escort. We served a family style American dinner where the bowls of food are passed and everyone serves himself. The bowl of potatoes was offered by our cook to the governor who proceeded to empty the whole bowl onto his plate and he did the same with the gravy. The cook looked on in utter amazement—then hurried into the kitchen a brought a big plate of bread for the rest of us. The cook took it upon himself to serve the governor with 3 pieces of chicken and 3 spoonfuls of vegetables. The cook also brought in a slice of cake on each plate for dessert. It was a very special meal that we will never forget. We sent a tin full of homemade cookies and 3 tins of fruit home with the governor. We also presented him with a Chinese/English Bible. His chair carriers and escort men ate their meal with our staff at the orphanage.

December —all the mountains surrounding us are covered with snow. What a beautiful sight. Our hill isn't cold enough for snow. We just have rain. Everyone is wearing his padded garment and knit hat.

Christmas 1946
The big question—How to celebrate Christmas? We had to have a tree, so we ordered one from the wood cutters. We had no decorations so we made some paper ones— stars and chains. We painted egg shells. We had saved the tin lids and cut out stars and pasted on nativity scenes. We made some popcorn chains. We left some white and painted some red with food colors from U.S.A. The tree was very pretty. We gave some money to the Chinese Pastor for decorating the church for Christmas. The orphans and most of the staff from our compound caroled on our way to the church in the city where we joined the members in caroling up and down the city streets. We returned to the church with most of the city's population. There stood a huge tree in the front of the church with lighted candles. In front of the chancel was a bamboo framework from floor to ceiling and from one side to the other. It was covered with white paper

on which was drawn a huge nativity scene with bats, fish, turtles and rabbits painted around the edges. The whole scene was lit up by candles secured to the bamboo frame. It was truly a sight to behold.

The church was packed with people and many more jammed in so we were squeezed in on all sides. It became very warm and noisy, so the Pastor ordered the windows to be removed and soon every window was a complete wall of faces of the people standing outside and holding up others to see and hear what the celebration was all about. For all the singing we couldn't hear the organ. The whole crowd was singing their hearts out to God, the Son. Every once in a while someone would yell out "Fire!" and an elder would "smother out" the fire on a tree branch and replace another lighted candle. The shadow of a man crawling around on a scaffolding replacing candles could be seen.

The Sunday School children acted out the Christmas story of the Savior's Birth. The Pastor preached and my husband read the Christmas story from the Bible in Chinese. You could have heard a pin drop in the quietness of the huge crowd of people. After the service which lasted two hours, it was like a "three-ring-circus" with putting out fires on the tree and replacing candles on the facade and tree and all the people "hot and loud" like a Chinese celebration should truly be. We carried lit candles " prayer lanterns on our way home across the river and up the mountain, caroling our way home.

At home, we had tea and sandwiches and cookies and prayed for God's blessings on Christmas celebrations around the world. We just go into bed with lights out when the carolers came and sang by our window. We got out of bed and opened the window to see the doctor's family. We invited them in for tea and cookies. After about half hour, they left and we went back to bed. Soon we heard more caroling at the front door. We got up again and it was the orphans and "coolie" staff. We invited them in and gave them tea, cookies, and peanut candy. After they admired our tree, they left and we went back to bed.

Soon there was more caroling and we got up again to welcome the nurses and teachers. More tea, cookies and peanuts were served. We had no more water to boil and no more cups. We kept washing cups but could not keep up with it all. Finally we fell into bed and slept a few hours.

On Christmas day, we were all tired out and went quietly down the hill to church. We brought some cookies and a chicken and some oranges for the Pastor's family. The Pastor's mother gave me her "wedding slippers". They were so tiny as she had bound feet. This was a very special gift to me. I didn't want to accept them but the Pastor said she really wanted me to have them as I always admired their cloth shoes. So I reluctantly accepted them with much thanks. It was a most treasured gift.

Our co-workers at the Lutheran Child Welfare Association in Addison, IL had sent boxes of stuffed animals, dolls, coloring books, crayons, jump ropes, marbles, balls, puzzles, yards of cotton cloth and yarn for making sweaters. These were given to the orphans on Christmas Day.

We had many visitors from the city church. All admired our tree. We served tea, orange slices, peanuts and cookies. There was little time for thoughts of our homes and families in U.S.A.

Welcome 1947
Every Sunday the Pastor's wife felt my abdomen and informed the ladies of the congregation, "No baby."

We are still learning the language and Chinese ways of thinking. Chinese is the most inaccurate language, although the most interesting and the most difficult. Our idea of knowing things exactly is a puzzle to the Chinese mind. Why anyone would want to know exactly how many people lived in a village is beyond them. If you asked about this, you would probably get the answer—"a few hundreds or several hundreds" or "not a few". If you asked someone's name, even then, you can't be sure that you can absolutely identify a fellow, for he has many names—one which he is given at birth, another when he enters school, another when he is baptized, another which friends and his wife may use. Married women often use their maiden name.

With weights, the same variety prevails. One always has to ask whether they are thinking in terms of old or new Chinese pound. With forms of politeness, everyone knows everyone else is just putting on "face". At a feast where there will be perhaps a dozen or more different dishes, the host will apologize that there is nothing to eat. People are always telling each other what a great work the addressed person is doing or how brilliant the addressed person is. But then, everyone knows it's all form and no one takes the flattery seriously.

The inflation is getting out of hand. The exchange is $3500 Chinese dollars to $1 U.S. Money. Salt is five pounds for $2900. Tea is $1000 a pound. Rice is $100 a pound. Egg are $100 for one. We have a few cows but no calves so no milk. We are making soy bean milk. In time we will get to like it—I hope!

March 1947

Word has spread around the countryside—the pumpkin put in our bed at the Moon Festival last fall worked for the foreigners! We tell them "God heard our prayers and in His own time and way, He will bless us with a child." We are all happy and I will continue to be examined by the Chinese Pastor's wife who will keep the congregation informed as to the progress of this pregnancy. All I know is I am very sick most of the days. They said I am not pregnant, but I know I am!

May 1947

We have a lot of company these days. The Wengers arrived by plane and the plane was impounded by the airport officials because they did not have permission to land. The airport belongs to the Chinese Army. So we have the three fellows which make up the plane crew with us. One fellow is from Germany, and the other two from the U.S. It is so nice to have a family next door.

The Wengers have three children, two girls (9 and 6) and a boy (4). What joy and happiness they brought into our lives. Now it was much more meaningful to celebrate the American holidays.

The airplane "St Paul" belongs to the Lutheran World Federation. It was impounded for two weeks. The crew hiked down to the airfield everyday to check the plane out. They enjoyed their time with us but they were anxious to be on their way out of Enshih.

In August Wilbert had to leave on another trip to Hankow. He left Enshih by bus (really a big truck). After a two-day trip through the mountains he arrived at Patung on the Yangtze. The water of the Yangtze was very high and none of the streamers were stopping at Patung. The next day, they stayed in Putung looking for another way to get to Ichang. Their party consisted of a language teacher, a Chinese student returning to school and a little 8 year old orphan girl who was going to her adoptive home in Hankow. Finally they found a tow boat which towed two junks. The next day about 100 miles from Patung, the tow boat hit a whirlpool and the junk which Wilbert's party was on was thrown against a rock and a large piece of the bottom of the junk was torn out. Ten minutes later it sank. No one was drowned but many people lost all their baggage. Wilbert was able to stay on the sinking boat long enough to save half of their baggage. There was a time when all three boats were in danger of sinking but they finally cut the sinking junk loose. We are certainly thankful to God that no lives were lost for so few of the Chinese are prepared to meet their God.

I did not find out about the sinking of junk until my husband returned to Enshih about the middle of September. Everyone knew about the sinking because a message was sent to the city but staff did not want me to be upset and anxious in my pregnant condition. I had word that they arrived safely in Hankow and I was not anxious about their trip home. "What you don't know does not hurt you"

1947 was drawing to a close. The inflation is still rising and we all take a large bag filled with money whenever we go anywhere. The exchange is 77,000 Chinese dollars to one US dollar. I still walk down the mountain to church but we hire a chair and I am carried back up the mountain.

The other day Wilbert and I were doing our usual walk after Chinese language classes. We always stop and talk to anyone we meet along the narrow footpaths between the farm fields. There was a farmer working his field close to the path. So we stopped and greeted him in Chinese and asked a few questions about his farm. His dog came running and stood beside him. We talked to him about Jesus. He was polite and tried to understand our proper Mandarin. The farmers speak a local dialect which is hard on our ears and understanding. We said "God bless you and we hope to see you again soon." As we were leaving I accidentally stepped off the narrow path onto his field but his dog came up from behind and bit me high up in my leg. The farmer tried to call the dog back but he kept a close watch on us to see that we stayed on the footpath. He was a real guard dog. It is said that Chinese dogs do not like the smell of foreigners and usually bit them as they pass by. Our doctor insisted on me taking 14 rabies injections. They are given in the abdomen, it is quiet uncomfortable. That dog gave me a new fear of dogs and I do not enjoy the walks in the countryside or through the village on the way down the mountain.

We received boxes of baby clothes, blankets, cloth diapers, and rubber pants from our families and friends in America. I want to dress our baby as we do in America. The mothers do not use diapers. The babies and children wear pants with the crotch seam open and the child is held in a squat position and the mother makes a "hissing" sound to encourage urination and stool evacuation. When they go visiting the family dog is taken along to clean up the voidings, etc. We do not have a dog.

Our faithful Chinese Bible woman was happy to receive the colored Bible story pictures on the primary Sunday School leaflets sent by friends in America. She said it makes it much easier to tell the stories to the woman and children in the hospital and orphans.

I have been working at the hospital two hours a day supervising our new student nurses. I can't get into my uniforms so I wear operating room gowns. They are more my size.

Everyday we have more and more poor folks at our door. They cannot afford to buy cloth for clothes and so their clothes are ragged and have many patches. We received about 100 bags of clothing from the Lutheran World Federation. The local government gave us the use of a large meeting hall for sorting and distributing the clothing. We are thankful for this gift but we need many more bags of warm clothing. I feel so sorry for the poor farmers dressed in rags in this cold, damp time of the year. Most people have to stay home and indoors because they do not have enough clothes to wear to be outdoors.

Most of the carriers stay warm while they carry their load of wood, etc. to he market place, but with the inflation many of them do not have enough money to buy another load to carry and so they freeze along the way. We give most of our money to feed and clothe the hungry and naked who daily come to our door for help. We are eating spinach and carrots from the garden. The tangerines are starting to get ripe and we had a few already plus a fruit that is something like a grapefruit.

We are all prepared for our baby which we expect any day. My husband called the carpenter to come to our home and he made a very nice cabinet for the baby supplies and clothes and a cute little bed with shelf below to hold a warm brick or hot water bottle to keep the new little one warm. The carpenter and our Chinese staff found this very strange. They keep their babies in their bed right next to them or if they are not in bed, the baby is completely covered up. I'm so surprised they don't suffocate.

December 22
Christmas is almost here. Our tree is up and trimmed with paper angels. We made a manger scene with cardboard figures and animals. So now we can tell the Christmas story to all who enter our home.

December 23
The last day of school and there was a Christmas party for the school children. Every child received a ball. George Albright from Addison, Illinois collected over 100 balls and sent

them to us along with toys for the orphans. In the evening the school children had their Christmas program at the school. The school is only a short walk from our home so the Wengers, Martha, my husband and I attended. My husband gave a Christmas devotion. We prayed that God would bless the message and the children's witness. The children acted out the nativity story. After the program we invited the Wengers over for our Christmas exchange and refreshments.

December 24

There was caroling in the city in the afternoon. The Wenger children received their gifts in the late afternoon and Martha, my husband and I went over to their home to watch the children open their gifts. It is so good to have the Wenger family here to share holidays and events.

The children's program was given again in the evening at the church. I stayed at home with the Wenger children. After church, the orphans received their presents from George Albright. The orphans were so very happy with their presents from America. We gave the nurses and teachers and staff some religious mirrors, puzzles, key chains and luminous crosses which Deaconess Nanke sent from America.

December 25

5:00a.m. The orphans came and caroled to us. 6:00a.m. The nurses and hospital staff came and caroled. We had many guests coming all through breakfast. All of our Christians caroled outside on our porch before coming in. There was a church service in the city. I stayed at home with Timothy Wenger who was ill. In the late afternoon there was a Christmas dinner at the orphanage which I attended. My husband had a Christmas sermonette. After dinner the orphans had entertainment and singing of all the carols. We thank God that our Mission is serving all the needs of the Christian community, the city and countryside.

December 26, our Red Letter Day

6:00 a.m.—Awoke with a big pain. My husband told the cook to boil water and call the doctor. The cook ran to wake up the doctor. The doctor told the cook to call the midwife and get the delivery table up from the hospital. Everything and everyone in place. No pain activity. There was a church service up on our hill at the school so we had many visitors coming for tea and spreading the news. I had invited the Wengers over for a Christmas dinner at 6:30 p.m. And our cook went right ahead preparing the chicken, etc. and I went along with the pains.

At 6:00 p.m. Our son, Paul, was born. He was so hungry when he was born, he just cried and cried. So Mrs. Wenger gave him 1-1/2 oz. of water from a bottle and everyone was amazed that he could suckle. He weights 7-1/2 lbs. The Wenger children came over to see their "cousin". Little Geraldine Wenger whispered to me, "I guess my prayers were good for you, too." She was praying for a "little brother" or better still—twins!" for her mother who is expecting #4 in the summer.

The cook announced the supper but Mrs. Wenger had their cook prepare supper. She thought naturally we would call the supper off. So my husband invited the doctor, midwife, Mrs. Wenger (who also helped) and Martha Boss to supper.

My husband had a special Thanksgiving devotion after the supper. Everyone was so thankful for our baby boy. Martha saw to it that the delivery table was properly washed and sent back to the hospital. My husband and I were so thrilled with God's gift to us—a beautiful healthy baby boy. We prayed for God's guidance in caring for this precious life entrusted to us. We couldn't sleep, we just marveled at our special blessing. We stayed up all night making sure our baby was warm and comfortable.

December 27

We had many visitors and the nurses had a pageant in the afternoon so many of the Christians from the city also visited us.

December 28

Everyone went to Church in he morning and the nurses gave their pageant again in the evening so we had more visitors.

December 29
There was a feast at the hospital and Wilbert again had the devotion.

December 30
The pre-school orphans came to our home for their party. Wilbert entertained them and showed them his son.

December 31
The older orphans had their party at our home. Wilbert entertained them and also showed off his son. There was church in the evening.

January 1, 1948
Church in the morning and a feast at noon in the city. Supper at the Wengers. They sent a tray over for me. And so it went! Wilbert had little time to spend with Paul and me, with guests to entertain, services in the city and devotions to prepare but gradually our life is returning to normal. Our Paul is a very wonderful baby and hungry all the time. His hair is very light blond. His eyes are blue. He was given several pairs of Chinese embroidered shoes, three Chinese hats and Chinese embroidered bibs. I stayed mostly in bed for two weeks trying to keep warm and adjust to baby Paul's schedule. I'm thankful to friends and relatives who sent warm baby clothes before Paul was born. I'm thankful for all the kind care of Dr. Chen, and the midwife who assisted me at the birth of our son. We thank God for providing for all our needs.

April–May, 1948
Our darling baby has given us hours of pleasure and days of joy. He has blond hair and blue eyes, and a strong little body. He cries, coos, sleeps, eats, laughs, smiles, plays with his fingers, holds his head erect, follows moving objects—just like other babies—only it's different, you know, when it's your own. When its your own, the pattern of thinking is cut on a bias.

Little Paul has created quiet a stir with the countryside. Word has gotten around that the "foreigners" have gotten a baby boy but he is a "little old man" with white hair. So every day travelers and "carriers" rap at our door and ask if they can see our little old man.

They are just thrilled when they see him smile and laugh and wave his arms around and make happy sounds. We tell them, "He is just a baby and a precious gift from God."

Spring is truly beautiful in China. It is a sight to behold to see all the fruit trees in bloom against the mountains in the background. However Spring passes quickly and the cherries are green on the trees. Our peas are about ready for eating and canning. Our carrots, lettuce, spinach and cauliflower are ready.

Our neighbors, the Wengers, are expecting a baby next month (their 4th child) God willing.

The inflation is running wild. Shopkeepers do not even want to sell their goods, because by the time they are able to receive new stock, the money will have become so inflated that they cannot pay for it. No one saves money, everyone saves things. Even banks have Tung oil and tea as their capital, and one often must give the bank several days to liquefy such stocks. The people who suffer the most are the ones at the bottom of the economic ladder: coolies, farmers, tradesmen, the poor, and the old who are without family connections.

August 1948
The Wengers new baby is a boy and that brought a lot of celebration to the Mission Family. We thank and praise God for the children He has given us and we ask Him for wisdom in training our children in the way they should go and grow.

Our son has had malaria and worms, and he is just seven months old. He stands up all the time; he hates to sit down. He crawls and climbs all over. He walks around his playpen and bed holding onto the rails. He stands up in high chair and he almost toppled out a number of times. I can hardly hold him—he jumps and climbs all over me. In his bath, he slaps the water with both hands. It's just like trying to hold a fish. I can hardly change his diaper—he always crawls away. He had his first haircut last month and looks like a "real boy". His daddy wants everyone to know he is a boy.

He does not like to be alone. He jabbers all day long and hates to sleep. He wakes about 3:30 a.m. And talks loudly and plays until about 5:30 a.m. when I finally get out of the bed and give him a bottle. He won't go back to sleep until after his bath at 9:00 a.m. He then sleeps until 11:00a.m. at the most. I try to give him an afternoon nap but he just cries most of the time. I usually have him in bed by 7:30 p.m. and I wake him at 11:00 p.m. when I go to bed and give him a bottle. He usually goes right back to sleep. All the Chinese people like to play with him and he always cries when they go. He makes them all feel like they are his best friend.

He eats a lot of cereal oatmeal—Farina or wheat. We were able to get some canned vegetable baby food sent in from Shanghai. I also prepared tomatoes from our garden, peaches and pears which we can buy. He enjoys toast, cookies, water and his milk. I prepare a formula from powdered milk.

He is covered with heat rash. He has very sensitive skin. He is getting his whooping cough shots. He has two lower teeth. He enjoys being outside. His daddy carries him on long walks around the mission compound. He tries to sing with the birds.

We had a lot of rain and that always brings mold and mildew. Our clothes are a mess. Martha Boss and Dr. Chen are busy making plans for building a larger hospital. Two nurses arrived from U.S.A. Miss Norma Lenshau and Miss Heidi Mueller. We thank God for their safe trip and also for adding to our medical staff so the medical outreach will be more fully expanded.

1948

The peaceful calm and routine life of the city and surrounding country side has suddenly become unsettled. Rumors of the success of the Communist troops overtaking more cities and provinces in the north are reaching our countryside. The Nationalist Army is drafting soldiers in our area. All the young men have fled the area or are in hiding. The recruitment army arrived with chains and handcuffs and they will seize a young farmer or "carrier" and handcuff him to the chain of recruits—what an inhumane way to build up the army. Some parents are able to come up with a sizable bribe and buy back their son from the recruitment chain gang.

The soldiers are chopping down our bamboo to make cots for the soldiers. Our language teacher said to let them take our bamboos. Better they take yours than the poor farmers. They also take our vegetables to feed the Army troops in our area. After all, they are protecting us and the city.

Norma Lenshau, one of the American nurses became ill and had to return to the USA for treatment. Rev. Wenger accompanied her to Hankow where she would be able to return to USA with furloughing missionaries.

We received a letter from the US consulate advising the women and children to leave the country as soon as they could make travel arrangements. They said that they could not promise us protection or evacuation but they would do what they could to evacuate all US citizens if there was a complete takeover by the Communists. My husband and Rev. Wenger decided to send their wives and children home to the USA as soon as arrangements could be made. We did not want to leave our husbands and we did not want to stay in China with our children and have no way of escape. It was a heavy, sad time for our Christian community in Enshih. It was a time for prayer and strengthening of faith. We comforted each other with God's promises.

October 1948

My heart is heavy as I realize that our little son and I will return to the USA. The Lutheran Federation airplane, The St Paul, has been chartered by our church to bring the missionaries' families out of interior China to Shanghai.

Mrs. Wenger and four children, Paul and I will try to get bookings on a ship from Shanghai to the USA. Martha Boss decided to stay on in Enshih with Rev. Wenger and my husband.

She will later go to Chentu and enroll in Chinese language study until this civil war is over. We all pray it will be a short time.

God's ways are not our ways. Just as we are getting "a handle" on the language, the Lord is shutting the door on China—Foreign Mission work. Our dear Chinese Christians will be on their own with no American funds. We ask for the Holy Spirit's power to evangelize China. We ask God's forgiveness where we missed opportunities and for our human frailties in not grasping the urgency of our times. We are packing, as we must go immediately to the airfield when the plane comes for us.

October passed—no plane. We are happy to have more time together. November—We were able to celebrate my husband's birthday and I am thankful for this extra time together so that he can see how little Paul is developing. Paul is trying so hard to walk alone. He goes for walks with daddy—hanging on to his trouser legs. It is becoming more and more difficult for me when I think of leaving my husband here in this land of uncertainties. I pray God our separation will not be long.

Thanksgiving—we have so much to be thankful for. We cherish every celebration we can still share as a family.

The inflation is very difficult for our Chinese workers. They are caught up with the changing times and wonder how they will survive. We are all praying more. We have so many questions without answers.

November has past—no plane! We are into winter. Paul is walking by himself. Thank God for that. He is quite a load to carry. Some of our Chinese friends knitted sweaters for Paul. I had some corduroy cloth from USA so the tailor made some overalls for Paul.

We are preparing for Christmas. It isn't the same joyfulness. Mrs. Wenger is getting anxious for her husband's return with the plane. We know that all things work together for good to them that love and trust God. The joy of Christmas is hope.

We thank and praise God for His wonderful gift of a Savior to save us from our sins. "And the angel said unto them, Fear not, for, behold I bring you good tidings of great joy, which shall be to all people" Luke 2:10.

The day after Christmas Paul has his first birthday—I thank God he can have it in China. The Chinese here hate to see the little fellow go. They all like him and like to play with him.

The other day, they taught him to answer the question, "How old are you" by putting up one finger and saying "one" in Chinese. He sings when they ask him to, claps his hands and is have a tough time deciding whether the world speaks English or Chinese, but he seems to understand either, but most of his sounds seem Chinese to us.

December has past—no plane! For the last months we have been expecting the plane. The plane has been delayed these many days due to a typhoon in the Hong Kong area, and the waiting for and replacing of two new motors and bad weather conditions in China.

January 1949

On the 10th of January the plane came in and down to the airport we went, with one suitcase and a blanket. Mrs. Wenger gave me her spring coat to wear when we traveled home in USA. Parting is so hard but my heart goes out to my husband who will return to our empty home in Enshih. I have Paul to comfort me. We know God will take care of us and help us through these trying times.

Shanghai

Strange noises and smells—lots of people. We arrived at the Palace Hotel and we (Paul and I) have a large room connecting with Elsie Wenger (and children) The windows are huge overlooking the harbor—filled with ships and boats from around the world—all shapes and sizes and kinds—whistles and bells and steamship blasts—sounding almost constantly. The U.S. Government gave us a notice on arrival to the effect that when we heard a marine whistle, we were to go to the lobby with one suitcase and one blanket and wait to be taken aboard a U.S. Navy ship going to America.

At that time in history—there were no airliners or ships leaving Shanghai for the U.S. The Communists were nearing Nanking and Shanghai would be next. Mrs. Wenger and I were concerned with the children's and our own safety. I was constantly opening the door to the hallway to see if we were being rescued. Rev. Paul Martens and the bell boys said, "Don't be concerned—we will call you when it is time to go."

My son, Paul, was right by my side and would not leave me out of his sight. He was amazed at the running water and the big bath tub. When I flushed the toilet, he shivered and shook.

He was overcome by it all. He was interested in looking out the window at the ships. What a change for him from the quiet, peaceful countryside of Enshih. He was not a happy little toddler. He missed and looked for "Ba-Ba" (Father). He did not want to eat the hotel food or baby food from jars.

Everyday Paul Martens would take one of us to the American consulate for passport check. After three days of this and accompanying his wife and twins, and Elsie Wenger and four children, Paul and I went to the dining room. The bell boy said, "We expect 'Big Tip' from American with three wives and seven children.

After a few days, we were becoming more relaxed. I spent one happy day with Rev. Paul Kryling and his wife, Susie. They took me shopping for jade earrings for my mother-in-law and I bought a beautiful red Chinese embroidered jacket to wear when I would give "mission talks" in America. We ate in a floating restaurant on the river.

The next morning, I happened to look out the window and saw to my disbelief our American Navy ships sailing out of the harbor to the ocean. It seemed we were going to be stranded in Shanghai—possibly interned. Needless to say, we prayed more fervently for a way home to America. It was too late to try to get back to Enshih.

Everyday was the same—no American ships in the harbor and none scheduled to come to Shanghai. The Communists were not advancing and there seemed to be a lull in the war. Northwest Airlines informed the U.S. Consulate that they would apply for "flight clearance" from Shanghai to Seattle. Rev. Paul Martens then wired the board for permission for Mrs. Wenger and children and Paul and me to fly home. This permission was granted. Rev. Martens and wife and babies were to go to Hong Kong. Rev. Paul Kryling and wife were sent to Japan.

We were happy to be on our way home at last. Northwest flew from Shanghai to the Aleutians. We landed in a blizzard and were taken off the plane by bus to an army canteen for breakfast. The blast of cold air took our breath away as we made our way down the steps of the plane to the bus. "What a cold, chilling ride. We were not dressed properly for the freezing weather.

When we arrived at Anchorage, it was the same story—out into the blizzard of ice and snow—into a cold terminal. We walked around in a cold daze—Paul had burped up all over me on the plane, and I could hardly stand the smell myself and he had diarrhea all over his cloth diaper and rubber pants and overalls. I tried to clean us both up in the rest room, but we didn't have access to our clean clothes. So we had to endure the pungent odor of ourselves all the way to Seattle.

We finally got a taxicab to take us from the airport to the hotel. Mrs. Wenger and children in back and Paul and I with the driver, who opened his window all the way to the hotel. I tried to tell him about our trip, but he was not interested. He was just anxious to get us to the hotel.

When we arrived at the hotel, the only accommodations they had for two mothers and five children was the bridal suite. A wonderful view and two bathrooms—a living room two bedrooms and a kitchen.

First thing we did was bathe the children and put them to bed. I tried to wash out our soiled clothes and hang them up to dry after rolling them in towels. I bathed and washed my hair. We thanked God for a safe flight and providing us with such wonderful accommodations. We had an early flight next morning to San Francisco so we didn't get much sleep but we have clean clothes.

When we arrived in San Francisco, Elise and children were met by a Pastor and his wife. Their husbands were classmates so they went home with them and onto Missouri. Paul and I went to the Travelers' Hotel and the Rev. D. Brohm visited us and offered assistance with our train tickets to San Diego. Paul and I were both sick—fever, chills, upset stomach, diarrhea, etc. We spent a day and night in bed at the hotel. We were worn out, exhausted and probably had malaria. But we were able to get out bed, pack and get downstairs to the lobby and on the bus to Oakland for a train to San Diego. The train trip was relaxing and as we didn't eat, we were not sick or having diarrhea, only weak in the knees.

In San Diego, our dear friend, Rev. Vic Hermann met us and took charge of our baggage, etc. and took us to his home. His wife, Lucy, and sons welcomed us and my mother-in-law came from Chicago to accompany us to her home.

We thanked God for these friends with open hearts and home and a dear loving and concerned mother-in-law. After a few days rest, good home cooked meal, loving tender care, and a trip to the world famous San Diego Zoo, we were on our way to Oklahoma City where we stayed with my parents, my sister, her husband and their four children. My parents were overjoyed to see their grandson, Paul, and to see me after four long years of separation. I was always very attached to my mother and I could hardly pull away and move to my mother-in-law's home in Elmhurst, Illinois. My parents bought me a warm winter coat, hat, scarf, mittens, shoes, goulashes, hat, and snow jacket, ski pants, mittens and goulashes for Paul.

Elmhurst, Illinois—1949

February—Paul and I are settled in the Holt family home. The home is large and sits on ½ acres of land. The household consists of Mom and Dad Holt, one of my husband's younger brothers, his wife and six months old baby boy and my husband's youngest sister, a teenage high school student. There is a bedroom for Paul and I. Dad Holt works in Chicago. He leaves home early in the morning by train. He works a job and a half and returns home late at night. Mom drives him to the train station in the morning and picks him up at the station at night.

The brother and wife both work in a nearby town. They have a car and drive to work. Mom Hoeltje takes care of the baby, cooks, bakes, cleans and does the laundry and shopping. I helped Mom Hoeltje with her tasks as best I can.

I take Paul outside every day. I walk to town with Paul in the stroller or sled. We bring home a few groceries, toy cars, books etc. I try to have Paul take a nap after lunch.

Mom Hoeltje sells "Highlights for Children" and "Fuller Brushes". Everyone calls on the phone all day long or stops by for coffee and homemade coffee cake. She also "caters" for private parties and at the "country club". She does all the baking and cooking at home. She also sews, making dresses and skirts for the family and friends. She works circles around me.

My husband sent a telegram from China for our Fourth Anniversary telling of his love and how he misses little Paul and me. It makes me cry. I pray, "Lord Jesus help us bear the separation and please bring us together again soon. Thank you. Amen." I read Paul a Bible story everyday and sing "Jesus loves me" and "I am Jesus' little lamb". We pray for daddy's protection and guidance and health, etc. I pray often during the day because my thoughts are of China and my husband.

My husband comes from a very large family. He has 50 first cousins—mostly in the Chicago area. We are getting to know his aunts and uncles and many of these cousins. Everyone is very kind to us. My husband's older sister and husband and two sons live in a nearby town and so we see them quite often.

I made some friends at Immanuel Church and I have given some "Mission Talks" at LWML societies in the District. This helps me to be less lonesome for my husband and the mission work in Enshih. I call the Mission Board in St Louis to hear about any news they might have received from China. They said my husband wants half of his salary to be sent to me in the U.S.A. I read in the newspaper that Shanghai had fallen to the Communists. They are gaining more and more of China.

Paul passed a long pink worm which I found very much alive in his diaper. I promptly flushed it down the toilet and called the doctor for an appointment. She was very interested in our life's story and she told me Paul appeared bored. She said he is too much with adults and needs to play with little children. I went back home with worm medicine and tried to figure out where to find playmates for little Paul. I played cars with him, my brother-in-law played with him, read to him and took him for walks, runs and etc., but I knew he missed his Daddy's love because I did and I was bored too.

Waiting in the U.S.A.
February 10, 1949 was our 4th Wedding anniversary. It is hard to be separated from my husband and it is hard for Paul to be separated from his daddy. We received a telegram of love from Enshih, Hupeh, China.

I am kept busy lecturing around in the Northern Illinois District and English District LWML Societies. It helps to keep from getting homesick for China. I am prayerfully considering a job offer from the Lutheran Children's Friends Society of Minneapolis, MN to be "Housemother" in their new unit for troubled teen-age girls. Rev. Glabe felt it would be good for the girls to have Paul as a little brother. The job would also be good for me. It is a challenge and I would be serving a branch of the Church at large.

I decided to take the job so Paul and I prepared to move to Minneapolis. We traveled by train from Chicago to Minneapolis where we were met by the social worker from LCFS and driven to our new home. We had a lovely place to live. The grounds were beautiful.
The staff was so kind and caring and helpful. We enjoyed the work. Paul made himself right at home with the girls. I thanked God for this job and asked for His guidance in my role as "Housemother". We had daily devotions and attended a church within walking distance. Many times, on my day off, I would lecture on China Missions in the St. Paul Minneapolis area LWML Societies. The girls went to school during the day and had to help in the kitchen and with the housework along with getting their school homework done. I had time to care for Paul and keep our room clean and laundry done.

I prayed every day for my husband's health and protection and his work in China. My heart and love went out to him. We didn't know where he was or what he was doing, but we trusted God to do His will and take care of him and bring us together again. The news from China was growing more alarming by the day. The Communists were taking over large areas of China. Many people were trying to leave the country. I wondered what would become of our church's work in China.

My mother came to visit Paul and I during the summer. She enjoyed talking to the girls and they loved her and called her "Grandma". I did my best to try to help the girls adjust to life and solve their many problems. As 1949 was drawing to a close, I had word that my husband was coming out of China and going to Hong Kong. I resigned from my job and Paul and I moved back to Elmhurst, Illinois to my husband's family home.

**News from Hong Kong
or What Next?**
My husband writes from Hong Kong that all have arrived safely from China mainland via The St Paul (Lutheran World Federation Plane on its last two flights out of China). Gertrude Simon and my husband out of Chung King and Martha Boss and Lorraine Behling out of Chandu.

The Board of Foreign Mission has assigned them all to other mission fields. My husband is to go to Africa! However, thousands of Mandarin speaking refugees are pouring into Hong Kong daily. This presents a new God-given opportunity to the church.

The four former China missionaries have found living quarters at the Basel Mission Home in Kowloon, Hong Kong. They immediately got involved in Mission work. Street preaching, going to refugee camps to preach and serve how they can. There is so much to do. They wrote to the Board of Foreign Missions asking permission to stay in Hong Kong and work among the refugees. Their request was granted but they were not to rent any facility for a church. Dr. O.H. Schmidt would be out soon to evaluate the situation.

My husband and teacher Lorraine Behling started to teach English Bible classes (Scriptures is a required subject in all colleges and government approved schools). One of the colleges where they taught allowed them to use a classroom for Sunday morning worship services. They also taught English to the staff at a nearby hotel and were given permission to use a small room on the roof for Bible classes. This room had an open doorway and open windows, so when the wind blew, it was "hang on to everything!"

Martha Boss found a young friend who worked in a mortuary and he was able to round up some friends who wanted to study English Bible and he was able to get permission to have these classes held at the funeral parlor.

The Lord is good and always provides a way for every opportunity. Gertrude Simon went to the border daily, and as the refuges came from China into Hong Kong, she welcomed them. She smiled and told them to thank God for a safe place. She walked with them and taught them songs along the way. Soon she had many smiling and singing.

Back home in Elmhurst, how I prayed to know the Lord's plan for me and Paul. How soon could we go to Hong Kong and join my husband? I was growing restless and impatient so I decided to visit my sister in Buffalo in March 1950. I asked her to arrange some speaking dates for me while there.

The first thing after Paul and I arrived in Buffalo, a reporter from the newspaper came out for an interview. The photographer took our picture. We dressed up in our Chinese clothes for the picture.

I was surprised to read in the next day's paper above our picture, "Had to Flee China—The Communists drove the couple from Enshih, Hupeh Province a year ago." The article also told about our hospital and its mission work. The article also mentioned I was a Buffalo woman who trained as a nurse in Buffalo City Hospital. It also mentioned that I would speak at the Buffalo Pastors Conference and at Bethany Lutheran Church where I was a former member. After my Buffalo visit, I went back to Elmhurst—to wait!

I again decided to take a trip. This time to Denver to see my dear friends Ruby and Paul Jacobs and their two sons, Peter and Timothy. Ruby and Paul were friends from LCWA, Addison, IL. Paul Jacobs now was a social worker for Wheatridge T.B. Sanitarium Foundation.

It was so good to visit with this dear family. I had a few speaking engagements in the local churches and LWML Societies. More new friends to pray for Hong Kong ministry.

When I got back to Elmhurst, I had a call from Dr. O.H. Schmidt telling me about his visit to Hong Kong. He was very impressed with the work and was very enthusiastic about the opportunities that presented themselves. He said the Mission Board decided to "go ahead" with the mission and establish a center there. Paul and I were to make plans to proceed to Hong Kong. Thank you, Lord Jesus!

California, Here We Come!
The Mission Board sent our tickets. We were booked on the SS General Gordon of the President Lines. We will be in a dormitory stateroom with a dozen or more women and children. It will be an interesting voyage with a stop at Hawaii, Okinawa, Philippines, Japan and finally Hong Kong—Twenty One days!

The Journey Chapter Three

Paul is excited with all the packing and talking about the long train ride from Chicago to San Francisco. The "Big Boat" ride across the ocean to Daddy!

Everyone is happy for us but it is always hard to say good-bye to family and friends. We are going to the other side of the world—a long, long way from home. The good Lord always provides us with "family" wherever we are, wherever we go. We love Him and trust Him and believe His promises. He has opened a door for mission work in Hong Kong and we thank and praise Him for giving us the opportunity to serve Him there.

My brother-in-law, Derald, drove us to the station. On the way, we were "rear-ended" and as it was near to departure time we got a taxis to take us the rest of the way to the station. A "red cap" helped us with our baggage and gave me the track number of our train. I found our berth and proceeded to undress Paul and put on his pajamas. I thought it strange that no one else was in the coach. Could they all be sleeping already?

Soon a porter came by and said, "Ma'am. I don't know where you are going, but this train ain't a going anywhere tonight." I hurriedly got out our ticket and gave it to him. He said, "We can try to catch that train." He ran ahead with our suitcases and I ran after him, carrying Paul. We just stepped on to the train when it started to roll out of the station. We went straight to our berth and settled down with our prayers of thanks to God and asking His divine protection of us as we traveled through the night.

Paul loved the train. We ate breakfast in the dining car and had lunch as it came around in baskets by vendors—sandwiches, milk, fruit and cookies. We had our supper in the dining car (The "meal money" was supplied by family and friends). Paul enjoyed looking out the window—playing with his toy cars, reading his books. We did exercises and singing.

After 3 nights and 2 days, we arrived in San Francisco, and there to greet us were Verna and Karl Steinbeck of the LWML hospice committee. They took us to their lovely comfortable home in Oakland, California. They informed me of a Stevedore strike that had shut down all shipping activities at S.F. Wharf. So we were "on hold" for our sailing date to Hong Kong. Of course we were disappointed—we were so anxious to get to Hong Kong and be a family again. The Lord knows our longing aching hearts.

Verma and Karl Steinbeck are such kind, considerate Christians. They make us feel so welcome. They are so interested in the Lord's mission work. They share their home with two foster girls. They have daily devotions and are very much involved with their Church's programs. Verna is very active in LWML activities and she has set up many speaking opportunities for me so the time passes swiftly.

We have many things to check every day with storage and shipping, tickets, passports, visa's, etc. Karl has taken time to show us the sights and sounds of San Francisco, including a trip over the Golden Gate Bridge and Muir Woods. We also visited his meat company. Paul enjoys the sausage and hot dogs, and every day looks forward to Karl bringing home some sausage and a hot dog for him.

After three weeks delay, the strike is over and we will be on our way. The Steinbecks and the local LWML gave us a farewell party. We thank God for these very special friends. The Lord knows when we need friends and in His own time and way, He seeks them out.

Once again, we are happy to be on our way. The "General Gordon" is truly a "big ship" The Steinbecks came to see us off and help us settle in the dormitory. It is time for them to leave the ship. Paul is upset that they are not going with us, but Karl gave him a package of sausage and hot dogs. I took Paul to the stern area of the ship where the passengers were gathering.

We had some paper streamers to throw down to the Steinbecks who caught them and hung on until the ship sailed and the paper streamers tore away. That made Paul cry and then so did I. We were comforted by a steward who showed us to the dining room where we found our table and full menus to choose from, but Paul ate his hot dog and sausage and milk and cookies. And so to bed and rocked to sleep

NOTE: The following is transcribed from a Little Red Diary written day by day about life in 1950 on the train and vessel General Gordon, by Geraldine Holt, as she and Paul returned to Hong Kong.

May 8, 1950
Via Western Springs to Chicago, via Santa Fe to Oklahoma City. We left Western Springs at 8 pm in Holt"s 1950 Ford.. A truck ran into us putting a big dent in the trunk of the car. Jack Carney called and we proceeded to Polk Street station and Mom Holt and I boarded the wrong train. Mom discovered it at 8:45 when our train was do to leave. Paulie was half undressed but Mom got them to hold the train for us. A porter carried Paulie and Mom and I carried our belongings. When we boarded the train it left the station. We slept well through Illinois, Iowa and woke up at Kansas City. Had a happy day. Arrived Oklahoma City at 6 pm.

May 9, 1950
Mom Holt greeted Rose, Bob, Grandpa Bierworth, Susan and the twins. Then Mom got back on the train going to Texas. Paulie and I went home with my folks. Paulie had a big time with Susan and the twins.They have two dogs—"Skipper" and "Rip". Everyone looks good!

May 10, 1950 at Oklahoma City
Visited with my folks. It rained all day. Paulie enjoying the chickens, turkeys and ducks. The twins stayed home all day from kindergarten to play with Paul.

May 11, 1950
More rain! The Santa Fe is on strike, how that will affect our trip to the coast remains to be seen.

May 12, 1950
Paulie played outside today. Tried to help Grandpa fix a chicken coup and got hurt with a saw. Went for a ride with Uncle Bob and had a frozen custard. Paulie got bitten by some ants. Everything day is something new!

May 13, 1950
Paulie had a big day outside. He was naughty at night. He got out of bed 3 times and ran around much to the enjoyment of the twins.

May 14, 1950
Went to Zion Lutheran Church in Oklahoma City. Talked to the Sunday School. Attended church. Paulie and I visited with Dad Bierworth at his house. Paulie gave mommie a red carnation for Mother's Day.

Mother's Day. May 15, 1950
Paulie played outside. He had such a good time and he is getting sun-kissed. Paulie got his head caught in the ironing board.

May 16, 1950
Rose and I went shopping downtown. Paulie had a good day playing with Susan, the Twins, the dogs and grandpa. Sante Fe strike is settled.

May 17, 1950
Had a surprise pre-birthday party for Rose. Said good-by to Dad Bierworth. He took a new job outside of Oklahoma City and left for it.

May 18, 1950
Getting ready to leave tomorrow. What a job trying to pack again. I'm sure Paulie will miss everyone here. Paulie played in a mud puddle—what a mess!

May 19th—Fort Worth, Texas
Paul and I left Oklahoma City. Rose, Bob and the twins took us to the station and saw us off. Ken met us at the station in Fort Worth. Lois and Ken have a beautiful home. Paulie enjoyed playing with Linda. We had a picnic at Lake Worth. It was very hot in Texas. Lois, Ken and Linda saw us off at the train in the evening.

May 20, 1950
Via Santa Fe to California from Texas. Traveled all night. Changed coaches at Clovis, New Mexico. Enjoyed the trip all day. Comfortable and so much to see.

May 21, 1950
On the Santa Fe to San Francisco.

The Journey   Chapter Three

Through New Mexico and Arizona and California. It was a beautiful trip through the mountains all morning. We arrived at Oakland at 5:30 pm . Mr. and Mrs. Karl Steinbeck met us at the train and took us to the LLL supper at the Rollingwood church—it was a District convention. Went home with the Steinbecks for the night.

May 22, 1950—
Oakland, California

Had a lazy day. Unpacked and rested and visited. The Steinbecks are lovely people and certainly are Christians. They are very friendly and warm. I'm sure we shall feel at home here. Mrs. Steinbeck is on the welcome committee of the LWML of this area.

May 23, 1950

Went to San Francisco via the Bay Bridge. Got our Philippine visa and passport pictures. Took care of our foot lockers at Santa Fe Station. Checked on the Mission Board freight. A beautiful day. Took a ride up the hills. What a thrill. Lectured at Zion Church's mens club and had supper there.

May 24, 1950

Took care of our laundry and helped clean today. Mrs. Steinbeck had a reception for me today.They took many pictures of Paulie and me. We had 2 Bon Voyage cakes. I got an orchid.

May 25, 1950

Lectured at the Concordia College today. Had lunch at the famous Cliff House. Beautiful view. The seals were swimming and putting on quite a show. Visited with Rev. Menzel. Checked our boat ticket. In the evening I lectured at the Vocational Womens club. Busy Day!

May 26, 1950

Talked to the children at Zion Lutheran School. Tried to get all of our things in order. Mailed out cards and pictures. "Uncle Karl" took us out to supper at "Shroader's". Drove through Chinatown and we went up Telegraph Hill. Saw the wonderful view! Paulie also enjoyed the sight-seeing and dinner out. Paulie said, "I saw the sights".

May 27, 1950—
Oakland, California

We waited all morning to see Mrs. Leone. Had a nice visit when she finally arrived. In the afternoon we went to the Zoo. Paulie rode on the Merry-Go-Round and train. The seals put on a good show. Went across the Golden Gate Bridge to Muir Woods. Beautiful tall redwoods. Came home on the Ferry Boat. Went out for supper to an Italian place. Packed and ready to leave tomorrow.

May 28, 1950—Pentecost—
Oakland to
Board the General Gordon

Went to St John's Lutheran Church at 22nd Street and South Van Ness in San Francisco. I spoke to the congregation about 5 minutes. They had a prayer for us. Arthur Brohn D.D. was Pastor. Had dinner at the Brohn's home. Max Cheigner took us to the boat. Steinbecks, Mrs. Sylvester and Brohms saw us off. After supper I was sea-sick! What a feeling! Boat left San Francisco at 4 p.m. Had a bon-voyage cablegram from dad.

May 29th On Board the General Gordon
(time back one hour)

I feel terrible but Paulie is fine. I was upset after breakfast. On deck all morning so I feel better. Had a good lunch. Had a nap and was out again until supper. I have my sea legs now. Good appetite and to bed early.

May 30, 1950

Paulie and I explored the ship. Paulie played on deck all morning and got so dirty. Paulie has many playmates. Our ship travels 480 miles a day. Today is Memorial Day!

May 31, 1950
Turn time back 1 hour

Played all morning, blew bubbles and played deck tennis. Paulie found new tunnels. Played on the Promcade Deck. Paul loves to run and looks and shouts in all the holes, doorways and such. Today Plaulie saw some Catholic sisters and asked, "What are they?"

June 1, 1950
Turn time back ½ hour

Paulie was running in the lounge, before breakfast. He bumped into a table. The impact knocked him into the floor and on way down he cut his eyebrow, a wide gash. Our first visit to the doctor. Had a fire and boat drill in the afternoon. Aloha dinner. The dining room was decked out in flags and balloons. We all got paper hats and noise makers. A good dinner, fun and noise!

June 2, 1950
Arrived Honolulu at 8 a.m.

Rev. Hafner met Paulie and I with a flower lai for me and a paper one for Paulie. He took us to Wai Kiki Beach and then to his home, a beautiful place. Mrs. Hafner and Pastor, Paulie and I ate lunch at the Wagon Wheel. Took a ride to "upside down falls" (not much stream) Looked over the island from Pali (cliff) A beautiful view! Saw Diamond Head, Pearl Harbor and Wahiwa. Went thru Foster Gardens. Had supper with the Hafners back in Pearl Harbor. We sailed at 10 p.m.

June 3, 1950
On Board the General Gordon.

Paulie's eyebrow is healing nicely. Played all morning. A nap in the afternoon. Took our evening run on the Promanade deck. Had our shower and to bed.

June 4, 1950
Time back 1 hour

Sunday—Rain at 11 a.m. Played indoors. The boat is sure rolling today. After our nap, played on deck. Rather cool. Had a run on the deck after supper and then to bed.

June 5, 1950
Time back ½ hour

Played on sun deck all morning. Paulie has the bandage off his eyebrow. Healed okay. Days are much the same. Weather is good. Paulie enjoyed his Chinese friend.

June 6, 1950

No June 6th—we lost it crossing the date line.

June 7, 1950—Time back ½ hour Well I have a bumpy rash from sun and salt air combination. I'm a mess on arms, face and legs. Played all morning. Napped. Shower and bed. The days can't go fast enough to bring us to our daddy and dear Joe!

June 8, 1950
Time back ½ hour

Rain in the morning. Heard a Japanese lady speak at devotions. She is president of the YWCA. Had a fire and boat drill in afternoon. Paulie woke up crying hard at 4 a.m. He sobbed, "my socks fell in the water" over and over he said it and he cried so hard I had to get up and show him all his socks. He then quieted down and went to sleep.

June 9, 1950
Time back 1 hour

This is children's day on the boat. Paulie is so excited he couldn't take a nap. At 2:30 pm the children went to a movie. Got a paper hat and mints before the movie. Saw "The Bad Wolf" "Mary had a Little Lamb", "The Headless Horseman" Puss and Boots". Had ice cream and cookies. Got balloons. Each child got a gift on the way out. Paulie got a big rubber ball.

June 10, 1950
Time back ½ hour

We are now on Japanese daylight savings time. Foggy all last night. Foghorns blew every 10 minutes. Had a farewell dinner. Noise makes, paper hats, mint cups. Paulie always enjoys these parties. Tomorrow we bid good bye to many of our "voyage" friends. How I wish we were landing in Hong Kong tomorrow.

June 11, 1950
Yokohama and Tokyo

Arrived Yokohama at 10:30 a.m. Iggy and Sue Kreyling, Norman Lenshow and Heidi Muellar met us at the boat. I received a corsage of red carnations and Paulie a corsage of 2 pink and red carnations. Visited with Rev. George Shibata's. Had lunch with Kreylins. Went shopping and sightseeing. Had a Chinese meal with the Egolf's, Meyers, Kreyling, Norma and Heidi. Paulie loves chopsticks. He kept showing me what to "catch" in his chopsticks for him. Went thru the Egolf;s house. Beautiful place with a view. The Richard Meyers had a open house for us with the Dinkers, Egolfs, Kreylings, Norman and Heidi and the chaplain and his family. Paulie got a "mewins" cat pullboy from the Dankers. Paulie was a good boy and played all evening. We came back to the boat at 11:30 pm. All Paulie's playmates are gone. He wanted to live "in a pan:"—the children told him they were going to live in Japan.

June 12, 1950
On Board the General Gordon

Boat sailed from Yokohama at 6 a.m. We got up at 7:30 a.m. Rain and fog. Nicer in later morning. Saw some of the isles of Japan. We only have 4 adults, Paulie and I in our cabin. Paulie has an infected toe nail! He had to soak his toe so we been reading all his books.

June 13, 1950

Nice morning—played outside. Nap in afternoon. Played on deck in the evening. Showered and repacked to fit in our Japanese gifts. Paulie got a haircut.

June 14, 1950—Okinawa

Arrived at Buckner Bay, Okinawa at 7 a.m. Paulie and I jumped out of bed and dressed in a hurry. Ran out on deck in time to see and hear the Negro U.S. Army band and a local school band. 2 Army L.S.T. Boats came as a welcome. We got off the boat. Paulie rode in a walker. Had a good hike, took pictures and hunted shells. Paulie played in the sand and went swimming with his Chinese friend. Back on the boat at 12 noon. The boat left at 3 p.m. And what a send off! 4 jet planes were "buzzing" us. Paulie has diarrhea.

June 15, 1950
Time back 1 hour

Took Paulie to the doctor for some medicine. He still has diarrhea but seems better. Did not eat anything. Rain in the morning. Paulie played in the big box that a nurse gave him. Napped and more play. In the evening Paulie and I played on the sun deck which was fixed for a dance. Paulie wanted me to dance with him.

June 16, 1950
Time back 1 hour—Manila

Arrived at noon in Manila. Took Paulie to the doctor. No temperature—gave him some other medicine. Dorothy and Herb and James Kretzhean and "Red "Burck met us. Had a little trouble with a box of soap but paid no duty". The heat and dampness of Manila was terrific! Slept under nets. Paulie had an awful night. Met Burbecks and Prange. Drank Pop and water and water and water.

June 17, 1950—Manila

Still hot and stcky! Visited with Buucks, Kretzhans and Pranges all morning. Ate with the Kretzhans. Paulie ate well and played hard all morning with David Buuck. Went back to the boat at 3 p.m.. Boat sailed at 5 p.m.. Had supper and went to bed. HOT! Only two more nights of this!

June 18, 1950
Time a head ½ hour

Hot and sticky! Caught in a shower this morning and we would be on the top deck. The hours are dragging by tomorrow, God willing, we'll be together as a family. I have butterflys in my stomach!

June 19, 1950—Hong Kong!

What a shock! How could this be! When she saw her beloved Joe in such terrible physical condition, she could hardly believe her eyes. It was so difficult for her to accept that she no longer wrote in her diary! She was heart broken!

Rev. Holt, Geraldine and Paul left Hong Kong in the fall of 1950 for the United States. They went immediately to Wheatridge Sanatorium near Denver, Colorado because Rev. Holt had a contagious disease, Tuberculosis.

Return to Hong Kong — 1953

After being completed healed from Tuberculosis, Rev. Holt, his wife and 3 sons returned to serve in Hong Kong. They were filled with joy as this is the ministry where they loved to serve.

Rev. Holt was trained during the past two years to focus on training young men to be Evangelists and local pastors. Basic Bible schools were started. Many language schools were set up. Great teachers were principals of high schools. The school system was a big thing at that time. The Hong Kong government fully supported this work.

Rennie's Mill was expanded to include a Tuberculosis Sanatorium called the Haven of Hope which Deaconess Martha Boss was instrumental in establishing. Geri Holt was involved in the blind work and the Hong Kong government also became involved. They established a School for the Deaf, supported by funds given by friends.

A Seminary was started when evangelism got to a point where deeper study was necessary. Classes included Speaking, History, Lutheran Doctrine and training of pastors for 4 years. The text was in English and translated into Chinese.

In 1959 the Mission Board approved establishment of the Hong Kong Concordia Seminary. Rev. Holt was the first President. He preached every Sunday to the Missionaries and teachers in English. By 1962 the new Seminary was going well.

Farewell Hong Kong — 1962
Geri Holt got the Sprue, a disease which keep the body from assimilating food. Her doctor said she must leave the Hong Kong climate. So in 1962, the family including six sons returned to America.

In 1963 God sent them to San Francisco, where Rev. Holt was called to serve a Missionary to the Chinese. The rest is history!

Visiting Hong Kong — 1968
In 1968 Rev. Holt, Geri Holt and Amy Mui visited Hong Kong, speaking at many churches which Rev. Holt had helped to start. The CNH District also sent representatives of Lutheran Womens Missionary League to visit the churches and the Handicraft center which they helped to support by selling handicrafts made by the immigrants, to churches in the United States.

"God be with you 'till we meet again, by His banner uphold guide you, God be with you 'till we meet again"

Geraldine and Wilbert's Wedding Day

The Journey   Chapter Three

Congregation in China

Missionaries on Boat to China

Denver Sanatorium

Geri Returning to USA on plane

Geri and Wilbert dating

1958 Hong Kong

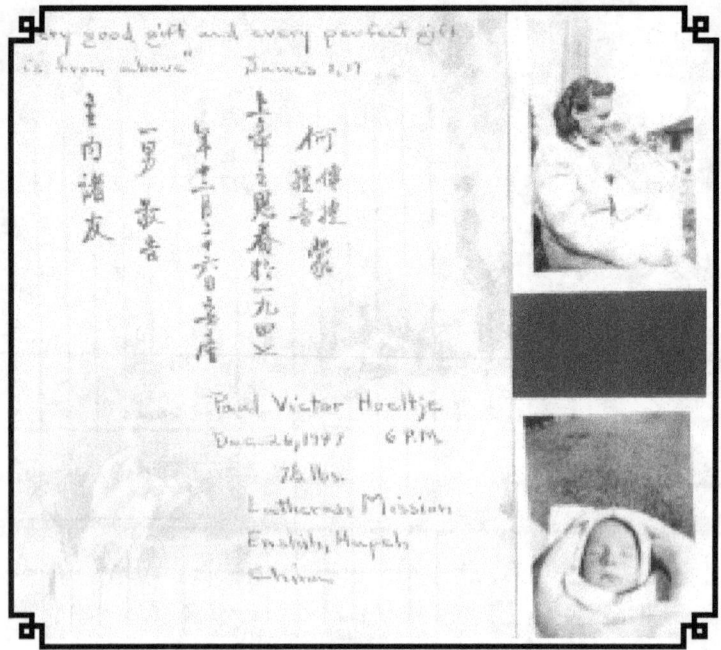
Paul's Birth in China

Geri and Paul

Chinese Doctors

Rickshaw Ride

Missionary and Helpers

Bea Richards in Handicraft Room

Missionaries in Hong Kong

Chinese Children being carried in baskets

Bringing Christ to the Chinese

Hong Kong Staff 1951

Doctor and Patients

China Congregation

Easter Egg Hunt

The Journey   Chapter Three

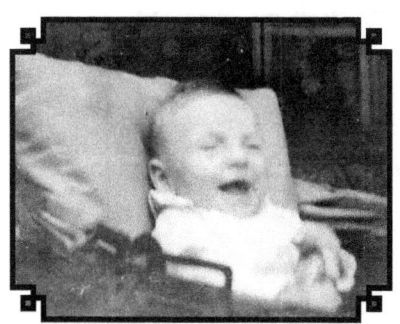

Paul

Geri, Pastor and Paul

Missionaries and Helpers

Congregation

Hong Kong Staff 1950

Andrew Chiu and Family

Rooftop School

Children of the Sanatarium

Pastor Holt and Family

Bringing Christ to the Chinese

The Rooftop School in Hong kong

Pastor Holt and graduates

The Journey   Chapter Three

Holt family 1957 in Hong Kong

Farewell to Hong Kong

65

It was a summer Sunday morning in Kowloon, the three-square-mile peninsula city across the harbor from Hong Kong. It was a very special Sunday because forty refugee children were baptized.

The children's faces were radiant when they returned to their seats from the baptismal font. But one little fellow could sense the joy of the event only by imagination. He was blind.

It wasn't that there was no joy in his full soul. There was much too much to contain. Suddenly, despite the dignity of the worship setting, he stood up and clapped his hands with holy glee — perhaps the purest worship the Lord Christ received in that chapel that morning.

Back in the rearward seats a mother's heart turned a complete flip-flop of compassion for the youngster. She was Mrs. Gerry Holt, wife of Missionary Wilbert Holt.

Now, the thirty-eight-year-old mother doesn't have time for foibles. She is the mother of six boys: Daniel, John, Paul, Joel, James, and David. But the very next week she visited the Social Welfare Office of the British colony.

She learned that there are 1,100 registered blind in Kowloon and no doubt hundreds more not registered. Only two schools for blind children. These are limited to sixty children.

She copied the addresses of 400. Enlisting help from the women of the mission, she and her friends

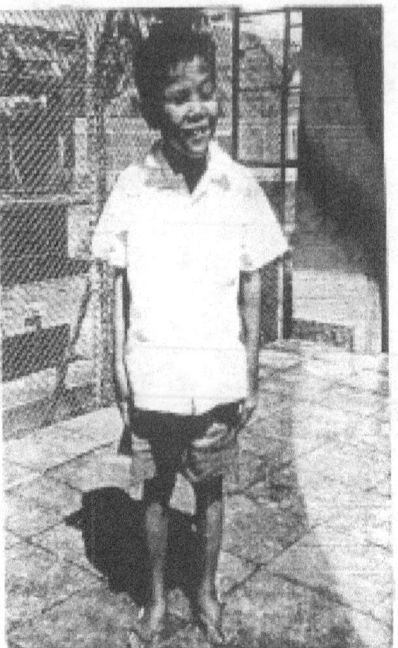

visited hundreds of them in two months of Tuesday-afternoon home calling. Purpose of the visits was to get acquainted, to witness for Christ, to invite the unchurched to come and hear more of the Gospel.

In August she arranged a tea party for the blind children. American sailors in the harbor heard of it, sent money for gifts. A bakery sent cakes; another firm sent soft drinks.

The director of the Sacred Music School of Hong Kong opened a music center for blind children. Private citizens pay the room rent.

At regular music education classes, Mrs. Holt and her helpers now have their opportunity to let the children know that God loves them, that His church is interested in them. Many are now coming to our chapel for church and Sunday school.

It's a fine story of the women in our mission fields. It lets us know that busy men and women can do great things for Christ if they want to, but they've got to want to. We give it the Number 10 position among our mission stories for 1957.

—*Adapted* from *"The Hong Kong Letter"*
Published by Immanuel Lutheran Church, Bridgman, Mich.

Geri's Work With Blind

Mrs. Holt addresses Women's group at Concordia in Cowloon, Hong Kong, in 1960.

Nathan Road Lutheran Church Founded 1956

St Mark's Lutheran Church

True Word Lutheran Church

St Phillips Lutheran Church in Hong Kong

"I will instruct you and teach you the way you should go;
I will counsel you with my eye upon you"

Psalm 32:8 RSV

Lorraine Behling

Chapter Four

The Mission Field

Missionary Lorraine Behling

A message given by Olive Gruen at the Concordia Teacher's College, River Forest, Illinois caught the attention of a student, Lorraine Behling. This missionary pleaded for help for the work in China. "Won't some of you come over and help us? We need teachers! I'm in my 70's! Who will come to take my place?"

When the war ended, the Mission Board recruited Missionaries for China, among them was Lorraine Behling. Getting to Wanshien, was not easy for Lorraine. All boats were packed with refugees, fleeing from the armies. She waited six weeks in Hankow.

After seven days, hardly able to move around since the boat was so packed with people, she finally arrived at Wanshien on November 9, 1948.

Due to the seriousness of the Communist situation, ten days after arrival they were given orders to evacuate. Lorraine recalls - "There was so much to do to get the local Chinese workers prepared to take over the work ". In Chung King she met Rev. Wilbert Holt, and Gertrude Simon, who had flown in from Enshih. The Communists were coming closer and in a short time they took over Chung King. Rev. Holt and Gertrude Simon flew to Hong Kong and wired us to COME OUT! Finally we agreed to leave and waited for the Lutheran plane to come.

It took several hours to get to the airport because of the truck loads of fleeing soldiers.

About midnight we arrived and found the airport deserted except for the little Lutheran Plane, "St Louis," which had made a special trip to rescue Martha and me! It was a turbulent flight and we all got sick! Then we saw the island city of Hong Kong and we knew God had brought us out of China! Our German pilots took us to the Presbyterian mission home. What luxury! Running water and hot baths. Paved streets and sidewalks. Beautiful blooming poinsettias all over. Restaurants with foods of every kind. Bananas. Peanut butter. Doughnuts. How we feasted our eyes and stomachs.

But there were other sights. Thee million Chinese refugees crowded into a city that had numbered 600,000. Refugees were living all over the sidewalks. Hillsides everywhere were covered with tarpaper shacks of squatters. Courtyards of churches and hospital and other buildings were f i l l e d with refuges. All the building had flat rooftops, and these too were filled with refugees. The British government had a problem and it was trying desperately to meet the challenge.

Then there were schools. There were many Anglo-Chinese schools where all the subjects were taught in English to Chinese students. The British government required all schools to teach Scripture as one of their subjects.

Many refugee missionaries were full-time teachers in these school. There were no public schools. All schools charged tuition.

Missionary Holt and Gertrude Simon had been in Hong Kong only 11 days and had already discovered this great mission field. They were busy preaching to refugees on streets, in courtyards and camps and were also doing substitute teaching in schools.

The Lutheran Church—Missouri Synod had never worked in southern China or Hong Kong. It wasn't planned. It wasn't in the budget. We didn't have permission to stay. In fact the Mission Board did not know we had been brought out of China. We had no Bibles or books or Sunday School materials.

The telephone calls began, telegrams and letters, going back and forth. We were given permission to stay—then it was withdrawn! We had been called to China and here were three million Chinese refugees. The Mission Board reconsidered. They sent Mission executive, Dr. O.H. Schmidt to visit Hong Kong to check out the situation. On February 13, 1950 we were given official permission to begin permanent mission work!

I have never seen a team of more dedicated, loving, hard working missionaries than the little group that started the work in Hong Kong.
Our first home in Hong Kong was the Basel Mission, located on a hill in Kowloon. The missionaries spent much time praying, studying the Word and planning.

The government build a new refugee camp called Rennie's Mill out side of Kowloon. 20,000 refugees lived there and many of them were well educated. They were given two meals a day by the government and could not find any work. Finally the government built a chapel right in the middle of the camp and Gertrude Simon moved there. She opened a Bible school and trained students to be evangelists.

Then bad news came! Rev. Holt, whose family had just rejoined him, became ill. He was exhausted from the heavy work load and he had contracted tuberculosis. He and his family had to go back to the United States—and we didn't know for how long!

More bad news! Paul Chang was also diagnosed with tuberculosis. Then we discovered that Gertrude's faithful helper and interpreter, Andrew was ill—and it could be tuberculosis! We gave these men extra rest and good food and prayed. We needed them! Before long, they were tested again and found to be well. Praise God!

The good news was that we found a storefront in Kowloon which we rented for a chapel. It was a miracle! The ground floor became Our Savior Chapel, the floor above was a home for Gertrude and myself.

In October 1950 we held our first service in this building and soon it became the busiest chapel in the world, on the busiest street in Kowloon.

Sunday morning, evening worship, every night was scheduled with baptism, confirmation classes, English Bible classes, children's meeting, women's meeting and clothing distribution. What a happy time we had!

There were 50,000 refugees in a hillside squatters area. A fire broke out and most of them lost everything and were on the streets again. The British government build apartments seven stories high, housing 5,000 refugees in each one. Rooftops were flat and could be rented for schools and churches. We rented three roof tops and conducted Christian schools there. We had three sessions a day with 300 children in each session.

In October 1950, the mission board sent Rev. Herbert Hinz to replace Rev. Holt. Nurse Ruth Proft, the Thode, Karner, Winkler and Kieschnick families joined the missionaries. What busy, blessed years! Working in their homes, the refugees made all kinds of dolls, metal wall silhouettes, brocade jewel boxes, purses, house slipper and painted cards. Martha asked the Lutheran Women's Missionary League to adopt a project for distributing the handicrafts. It was a big business!

Another project which Martha Boss was deeply involved in was the Haven of Hope Tuberculosis Sanatorium. Because so many people were dying of tuberculosis weekly, several Protestant churches worked together to open the sanatorium and large grants from Wheatridge Ministries helped make this possible. Half the patients and many of the nurses and staff were members of the Lutheran church.

Since my area was education and teaching, I was privileged to help open nine primary schools and Concordia High School. During this time in Hong Kong we saw more than 5,000 people baptized.

Rev. Wilbert Holt returned to Hong Kong in 1953 with his family. He was instrumental in founding many churches in Hong Kong. In 1959 he was co-founder and first President of Concordia Theological Seminary in Hong Kong. Rev. Holt and his family left Hong Kong in 1962 when Mrs. Holt contracted the Tropical Sprue and needed medical attention.

What a joy to work with Rev. Holt and all the other missionaries that God sent there.

Plane Makes Night Flight, Evacuates Trio

CHENGTU, CHINA — (Æ) — A Lutheran plane, the St. Paul, slipped into Chengtu in the night to evacuate two American women missionaries—and left for Hong Kong with three.

Miss Lorraine Behling and Miss Martha Boss (home towns unavailable) of the Lutheran mission were startled by a midnight messenger saying their plane was waiting.

A telegram sent them four days earlier was not delivered and the two feared they would be stranded here.

An unscheduled passenger was Miss Mary Shearer, Freeport, Pa., a Methodist missionary.

Miss Shearer originally had planned to remain in Chengtu. Then e heard her mother is ill and d ded to go home.

Gertrude, Lorraine and Pastor Holt

1958 Hong Kong
Pastor Holt, Geri, Paul
Lorriane Behling and Gertrude

The Mission Field   Chapter Four

Hong Kong Staff 1958

Lorraine Behling, Ruth Proft, Martha Boss

"I will sing of thy steadfast love, O Lord, forever; with my mouth I will proclaim thy faithfulness to all generations."

Psalm 89:1 RSV

Jackson Street Church Choir

Chapter Five

Seeking The Way

A 45 year old Mandarin speaking white American, former Chinese missionary was not the most ideal person to begin a Mission in a predominately Cantonese speaking Chinatown.

At that time there were already 20 Chinese churches with Chinese pastors in Chinatown, many of them with 100 years of history in San Francisco. The number one challenge was how to prepare the Anglo Church to understand the Chinese mind, culture, their religious and history backgrounds. What methods should be used and what impediments do we face for them to receive the message of Christ? The Chinese culture is centered on the written word in characters. Some reasons for his success and acceptance by the Chinese people are his love for people and his commitment to saving souls, his compassion and willingness to spend time to help people, and his great faith in God and the power of the Gospel. He also knew how to choose and work with his co-workers. Although no congregation was yet ready to open their churches for a Chinese ministry, their support for a separate Chinese church was superb and gave sufficient compensation.

The Lutheran churches of San Francisco were excited about the prospect of a Lutheran work among the Chinese. After returning to the states, because of poor health of Pastor Holt and his wife, they settled in San Francisco.

Comissioning Of Rev. Wilbert V Holt as Missionary-At-Large

On September 29, 1963, the California Nevada Hawaii District of the Lutheran Church Missouri Synod commissioned Rev. Wilbert Victor Holt as Missionary-at-large, particularly to the Chinese of that area. The commissioning took place at St John Lutheran Church, San Francisco, Circuit counselor Rev. Herbert Schroeder officiated. Holt had been a missionary in China and Hong Kong for 16 years. During these years he founded churches and was one of the founders and first president of Concordia Theological Seminary in Hong Kong. His fluency was in Mandarin and the San Francisco Chinatown was predominately Cantonese and Toishaness speaking.

Founding of The Lutheran Church of The Holy Spirit

The California Nevada Hawaii District Lutheran Women's Missionary League gave $4200 to begin the work in San Francisco among the Chinese. The funds from LWML provided an architect and a contractor to convert a store front at 606 Jackson Street into a very pleasant chapel.

50 women of San Francisco Lutheran churches volunteered to keep the chapel reading room open from 1:00 to 8 p.m. every day, serving as English tutors or reading room atten-

dants. Rev. Holt used large printed characters to tell the story of salvation. He taught simple songs in Chinese like "Jesus Loves Me" and "Jesus was nailed on the Cross for You and Me". There were no written Christian books in Chinese at that time. David Raff and Mr. Gehrke served as carpenters for many years. We acknowledge assistance from Ralph Hough and Dr. Ulich and other district workers who provided the best the District could give in support of our mission.

On March 26, 1964 the first regular Lutheran Chinese-English service was begun in Chinatown The church at 606 Jackson Street, San Francisco was dedicated in a special service on April 5, 1964. Rev. Paul E. Jacobs, District President officiated and Pastor Holt preached. "I praise God for establishing the Church of the Holy Spirit in the heart of Chinatown here, the 'Chinese capital of America' ", said Pastor Holt at the dedication.

The Holy Spirit congregation, in order to begin such an outreach to the Chinese Community, needed to find a liaison or bridge person to the Chinese community. It could be a Chinese Pastor or a Chinese Christian who knew the scriptures well, had the gift of evangelism, a deep concern for souls and be fluent in Chinese and English. History of this church is the history of God providing just that kind of liaison persons.

One of Rev. Holt's first contact was the Dicksen Lau family and their son John. John and his brother and sisters were the first children Rev. Holt baptized in Hong Kong in 1951. The family moved to San Francisco and had joined the Zion Lutheran Church. John, now a 25 year old man, volunteered to be a Sunday morning interpreter from English to Cantonese. Although Rev. Holt had spent seven months learning Cantonese, it was inadequate for preaching, so the first liaison worker was John Lau. Paul Holt, son of Rev. Holt, studying at Oakland Concordia College, served as a Sunday school teacher, along with Geri Holt, pastor's wife. A young man, 17 years old, Lauffer Hong, served as a volunteer janitor. Thelma Wutke, a legal secretary, served as part-time volunteer secretary. Elaine Wong was the first organist. Another family that joined soon after was the Jimmy Chan family. Their son Henry became one of the leaders of our youth group and additional interpreter. A retired Parochial School teacher, Elmer Eggert, became the children's choir director.

In the summer seven College students spent three weeks helping to arrange all day activities for children. They would parade through Chinatown with Chinese children beating on drums and pans, carrying balloons and signs, to invite children to the play days. It was a successful pied piper operation. There were few recreation facilities at that time. So our first work involved children and elderly persons. One of the first elderly converts was Mrs. Kiu Ying Lew, who for many years served as the cook for youth retreats and dinners for Chinatown visitors. Some of the children who took part in the youth activities are still involved in Lutheran churches today.

In January 1965, Mr. Henry Lai, another member of the Lutheran Church in Hong Kong joined. He worked as youth worker and assistant until the middle of 1967. Today he is a Pastor of a Lutheran church in Oakland, California.

In 1967, Miss Amy Hau had been a secretary for the Director of the Lutheran World Relief in Hong Kong. She came to San Francisco on behalf of the Lutheran World Federation on a fund raising tour to raise money for the poor immigrants in Hong Kong. On a visit to meet Rev. Holt, she volunteered to interpret one Sunday. He recognized her ability to do simultaneous translation as an interpreter, her enthusiasm and her commitment to the Christian faith. The CNH District decided to hire her as a secretary and youth worker on a trial

Seeking The Way   Chapter Five

basis. This fulfilled Rev. Holt's search for the ideal liaison worker to enable an Anglo congregation to reach out to the Chinese community.

These were:

1. Fluent in both English and Chinese.

2. Understands both American and Chinese cultures.

3. Interested in winning souls for Christ, preferably having the gift of evangelism.

4. One who is humbly submissive to the Word of God, interested in living for & sharing Christ with others.

Bringing Christ to the Chinese

Pastor Holt and members of Holy Spirit Church in San Francisco's Chinatown

Chinatown

Dedicate Mission In San Francisco

Plans to open a mission in San Francisco's Chinatown, discussed as early as 1896, reached fulfillment on March 29, when a former missionary to China conducted the first services of Lutheran Church of the Holy Spirit in a rented chapel.

"I praise God for establishing Church of the Holy Spirit in the heart of Chinatown here, the 'Chinese capital of America,'" said Pastor Wilbert V. Holt, who served as missionary to China and Hong Kong from 1945 to 1963.

As California and Nevada District missionary at large to some 100,000 people of Chinese descent living in the San Francisco Bay area, Pastor Holt followed up contacts established in his overseas work.

Twenty Chinese were among the 31 people who gathered for the first service. At April 5 dedication rites Rev. Paul E. Jacobs, District President, officiated, and Pastor Holt preached.

More than 65 members of San Francisco churches contributed their labor to help ready the chapel and reading room in the mission's quarters.

Among many gifts from area Lutherans were an organ given by the students of California Concordia College, Oakland, and $4,200 from the mite-box funds of the Lutheran Women's Missionary League of the California and Nevada District.

Activities of the mission include Sunday services in Cantonese and English, Sunday school and Bible classes, and Bible classes and citizenship classes during the week. There are daily vesper services.

The mission's reading room, staffed by 50 volunteers from local churches, is open daily from noon to 8 p.m.

Pastor Holt, a 1945 Springfield seminary graduate, was first assigned to the Missouri Synod's mission in Enshih, Hupeh, West China, which included a church and school, a hospital and nurses training school, and an orphanage.

While on tour of missions in Free China he was cut off from his station by the rapid advance of the communists. Leaving Chungking the day that city fell to the communists, he arrived in Hong Kong in November 1949.

In Hong Kong he joined other refugee missionaries and workers in starting the mission program of the Missouri Synod there at a time when Chinese refugees were pouring in at the rate of from one to five thousand a day.

church will sag with the spring thaws is not known, he added. "If it holds, repairs to the church and parsonage are not expected to exceed $50,000."

Since "some of our people lost very heavily" and because "it may take weeks before the full story of need from outlying areas is clearly known," Director Kuntz expressed the hope that the special offerings "gathered in our churches will be adequate."

(241)

Jackson Street Church Front

Bible Study

Jackson Street Church

One of the first interpreters

Communion at Jackson Street Church

Pastor in office at Jackson Street

Laufer First Janitor

Amy in office at Jackson Street

TO CREATE

1968 1st fellowship group

Seeking The Way   Chapter Five

LUTHERAN CHURCH OF THE HOLY SPIRIT

聖靈堂　　　　　　　　　　　　　　　　　路德會

606 JACKSON, SAN FRANCISCO, CALIF. 94133

WILBERT HOLT, PASTOR

TEL—DO 2-3829
RES—AT 2-2023

January 4, 1967
(Dict. 12/28/66)

Dear Friends:

It seems that the "robin" is showing signs of middle-age - it is losing feathers; it is losing speed; however, it is not lacking in interest, and problems in family, in church, in personal health - but in this Christmas season it is truly wonderful to know that we have a Lord who shared completely our human life, its temptations, its sorrows, its death, and has overcome all of the great enemies of humanity. Truly earth has no sorrow that Heaven cannot heal in Christ.

1966 was a pleasant and profitable year for the Holts, although in November Gerry had extensive repair surgery and is doing fine now. Our eldest son, Paul, 19, is in his second year of college at Oakland. John attends a public high school - a junior - and Joel is a freshman at St. Paulus Lutheran Jr. High, where Daniel is an eighth-grader. James is in sixth grade, and David a fifth-grader at Zion Lutheran School.

Our Chinatown church is now three years old. We have lost our store-front lease, so we must find new quarters before March 3, 1967. The congregation numbers about eighty baptized souls and about forty confirmed souls. We are considering beginning the Lutheran Hour in Chinese in 1967. Chinese immigrants continue to come to San Francisco by the thousands, so already there are perhaps 45,000 in San Francisco.

We thank you for your interest and your prayers. We pray that the Lord will grant each of you a full measure of the Holy Spirit, so that you may have the peace, the faith, the love, the joy, the power to witness to the Message of Reconciliation in the year of grace, 1967.

Sincerely yours,

Bud Holt

Wilbert Holt

WH:tw

上帝差他兒子的靈進入你們的心　GALATIANS 4:6

MRS. LEW, DEACONESS CAROL HALTER, DONALD CHAN — people of all ages are helped through Deaconess Halter's tract ministry.

Retreat with Little Yellow Bus

Seeking The Way   Chapter Five

"For I am not ashamed of the Gospel; it is the Power of God for Salvation to everyone who has faith"

Romans 1:16 RSV

Amy Hau Mui

Chapter Six

The First Co-Worker

Amy Hau Mui

After graduation, she took a job as a secretary at the Lutheran World Federation. Because of her fluency in English, Amy later was chosen by the LWF director for their Sweden Headquarters, to travel aboard on a fundraising trip for three months to raise funds for the poor immigrants in Hong Kong. She was an excellent fund-raiser and the trip was very fruitful, generating US$360,000 to provide education for 6,000 refugees in Hong Kong. Later she made a second fund-raising trip to the United States, this time speaking to more than 200 Lutheran Churches in the State of California. Amy was thankful she learned from her father good communication skills and in many ways, Amy reflects her father: tall, handsome, nicely dressed, and had a good taste for color and design. However, the parent who molded her to love God and to serve God was her mother.

Amy's mother, Mrs. How Yuk Hau was a born-again Christian who struggled with her faith like many new Christians did at the beginning. She did not fully commit to Christ because of her parents' disapproval, and her love to play Mah-Jong (in hope to win some money to help the family financially). Thankfully, God strengthen her faith through a trial. When Amy's mother had an eye problem that might cause her to become blind, she prayed whole-heartedly all night in the hospital bed. Her prayer was answered during re-examination the following day. The doctor told her: "Amazing, you are fully cured and you are free to go home." The miracle inspired her to fully commit her life to Jesus Christ. She became a praying warrior. Amy's mother would visit the hospitals and pray with the patients weekly. She had to travel long distances (old Hong Kong had poor transportation), but she was committed to this ministry for over 20 years. After Mrs. Hau immigrated to the US in 1970, she continued her hospital visitations and prayed for patients in San Francisco Chinese Hospital for over 10 years, until her health no longer allowed her to do so.

Mrs. Hau's prayer life and her love of souls had a strong influence on Amy as how to love God and serve God. Amy's mother was a good teacher, very influential in her ability to teach, she never gave up any opportunity to show her children the importance of loving God and being a good person. Her mission statement to her children was "If you have Christ and a good education, you have everything." She would say it to her children again and again. To her credit, her eight children, all became Christians. and one of her children, Amy, became equally bold to share God's love.

Bringing Christ to the Chinese

Pastor Holt and Amy Mui met in 1966, in the church office at the Lutheran Church of Holy Spirit in San Francisco's Chinatown. Recognizing her fluency in English and Cantonese, Pastor Holt asked Amy to interpret for him at a Sunday service, while Amy was on a fundraising trip to California. Impressed by her commitment to Christian faith, Pastor Holt later invited Amy to work with him at the Lutheran Church of Holy Spirit. To accept Pastor Holt's invitation meant to give up her current job as a fundraiser for the Lutheran World Federation, leave Hong Kong, and start a new life with a great deal of uncertainty.

After long consideration and much prayer, Amy agreed. Amy knew it was God's calling for her to serve Him, fulfilling a promise Amy had made during her youth. When Amy accepted Pastor Holt's invitation to serve God at Lutheran Church of Holy Spirit, she was hired as Pastor Holt's secretary with a trial period of 3 months. With the congregation's focus on outreaching to the Chinese community in San Francisco Chinatown, Amy translated for Pastor Holt during home visitations, interpreted for him during Sunday Services, and served as the church secretary. Interestingly, both Amy and Pastor Holt forgot about the 3 months trial period. What we do know is that they served the congregation together for 35 years, until Pastor Holt's death in 2003. Amy continues to serve the congregation today.

Pastor Holt answered many of the questions Amy had concerning the Christian Faith and slowly helped Amy to build a strong foundation in the Lutheran Doctrine. Amy saw Pastor Holt as a faithful servant of the Gospel, humble shepherd of the congregation, a bold preacher of the Word, and a missionary with great love for the Chinese people and their souls. Pastor Holt was also a very generous giver, and Amy was often a beneficiary of his generosity, especially during Amy's earlier years in the United States. Serving the Lord together for 35 years, many of Pastor Holt's good deeds and characteristics have become part of Amy's own Christian makeup.

One of the interesting characteristic Amy learned from Pastor Holt was how to compromise in marriage. On one occasion, Mrs. Holt unloaded many cans of vegetables onto the kitchen table. Pastor Holt, eager to help his wife, opened all the cans not knowing only one or two cans were needed for that evening. Mrs. Holt, showing her kindness, rearranged dinner plans for the next several days so the opened cans of vegetables would not be wasted. She showed no frustration. Doing so, she eased Pastor Holt's guilt. Witnessing this incident, Amy saw how a Christ-centered couple live out God's Word.

Amy met Jason Mui in Pastor Holt's office in Chinatown. Jason's father was a colleague of Pastor Holt while Pastor was teaching in Hong Kong. Jason was not a Christian at that time, but he boldly invited Amy on dates, and Amy boldly witnessed her faith to Jason on all occasions. Jason was from a large family, 2 brothers and 3 sisters. Jason accepted Christ as his savior, and Amy conceded to Jason's gentleness, nice dressing, and good sense of humor. Jason and Amy married on July 30, 1967.

His mother became a Christian, while living with Jason and Amy, as Amy shared Jesus' love with her.

During more than 43 years of marriage, Amy and Jason had their share of disputes. The blessing was that they were quick to forgive and forget. The trick for Amy and Jason was that they would calm themselves down by going to separate rooms knowing it is not worth it to dispute over minor thing. Amy and Jason grew up in different environments and have different personality. Jason was out spoken and sporty while Amy was quiet and Bible-centric. The difference between the two required major compromises. Knowing how devoted Amy was to Christ and her ministry, Jason gave Amy a lot of freedom in their marriage. He never complained about the hours Amy was away from home on visitations or on the phone with members of the congregation. Amy gave equal freedom for Jason to travel. For the two, God has nurtured their marriage with an amazing trust between themselves.

On May 17, 1992 Jason and May celebrated their 25th Wedding Anniversary and Amy's 25 years of serving the Lord in the Lutheran Church of the Holy Spirit. A celebration was held at Raddison Hau Inn in Sunnyvale.

June 13, 1997, Concordia University in Irvine, California presented Amy with the Christus Amundo award for her encouragement to 10 young people to study for full time church work at the university.

May 2005, the California-Nevada-Hawaii district, with Rev. Ted Iverson as MC, and the Lutheran Church of the Holy Spirit, gave Amy a special celebration for her 38th Anniversary of serving the Lord at Lutheran Church of the Holy Spirit.

The First Co-Worker   Chapter Six

May God continue to bless the Ministry of Amy Mui as she uses her Gift of Evangelism to reach the souls of many people.

All Glory be to our Lord!

Pastor Holt, Tim and Amy

Amy's Mother, Sister, and Pastor Holt

Daniel Woo and Amy Mui

Pastor David and Amy Mui

Pastor Holt, Pastor David and Amy

Bringing Christ to the Chinese

Amy, Pastor and Rosyln

Amy and Jason

June 2004 Amy's Celebration

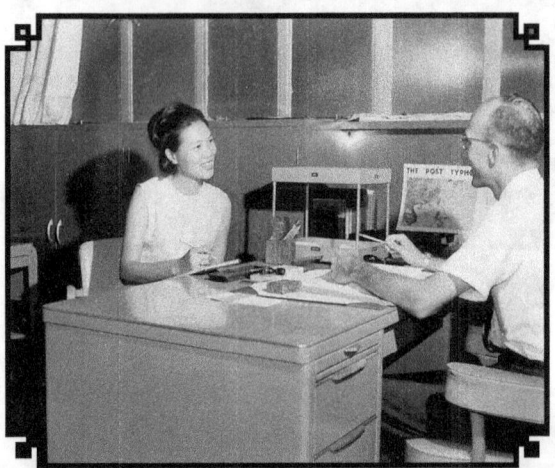
Amy and Lutheran World Federation President in Hong Kong

Amy and her Mother

Amy in Park

Amy Interpreting for Pastor Holt

Chinese Language School Choir

Amy with Youth Retreat

Faithfulness Fellowship

Amy with Church Youth

Amy, Jason and families at Christmas

Amy in Hong Kong

Early years Amy and Jason

Jason and Amy

Amy in office at 1725 Washington St

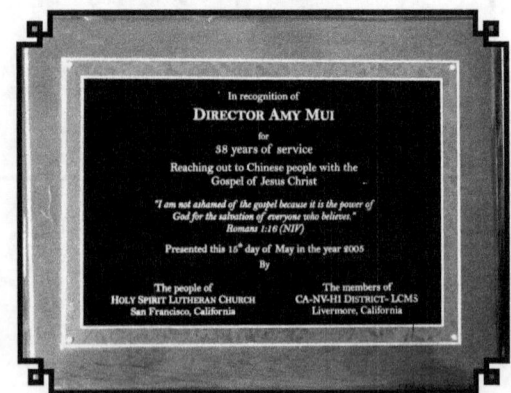
A Plaque given to Amy for 38 years of Faithful service.

Amy's 25th Aniversary

Amy and Jason's wedding

Amy and Jason's Marriage

Amy at Chinese New Year

Christus Amundo Award given Amy by Concordia University

"You shall teach them diligently to your children, and shall talk of them when you sit in your house, and when you walk by the way and when you lie down and when you rise."

Duet 6:7 RSV

606 Jackson Street, San Francisco.

Chapter Seven

Immigrants at 606 Jackson Street

Tom Lee

In 1968, I was a wide-eyed lad recently immigrated to the United States. Knowing very little English, lacking any friends, I had nothing to do during the weekends. At that time, one of my newly met friends from school asked me if I would like to play some ping-pong with him. I said, "Sure" since I had no other commitments. He brought me to this place on Jackson Street in Chinatown. As I walked into the place, I didn't see any ping pong table. What I saw was a room with a cross on the wall and several people sitting around a table. I was a little astonished but my friend assured me that we would play later. He introduced me to this friendly lady named Amy and the people around the table. Amy welcomed me warmly to this "Bible Club" that met every Saturday afternoon. We sang songs from this red songbook and then we studied the Bible. Her voice and the way she spoke captivated me. After the Bible study, I had another surprise. From a room in the back, a thin, tall Caucasian man emerged. He was speaking Cantonese! It was like, "Wow!" He shook my hands and introduced himself as Pastor Holt. He was very friendly. Although I did not get to play any ping pong that day, my church life with the Lutheran Church of the Holy Spirit had begun. It was some kind of a day for this young fellow!

During the couple years that I spent at the Jackson Street location, I had many great memories. This is the place where I got to know Jesus Christ and received Him as my Savior. It was there I was baptized. Although it was not a very big place, it was a place where many people could meet God and receive His love. The sanctuary seated about 60 people (maybe less) during a Sunday worship. Behind the sanctuary there was a tiny room as an office for both Pastor Holt and Amy. Leading out of the office is the door to the back alley where you can smell garbage and sewer from the neighboring restaurants. From the side of the main entrance, there was a stairway that led to the basement with very dim lights. This was where we had the two Sunday school classes, a Chinese one by Amy and an English one by Mrs. Holt. The older folks had their Sunday school in the sanctuary with Pastor Holt! The church was centrally located in the heart of Chinatown. We passed out Gospel tracts on weekends to passer-bys. As the membership grew, we had to find a bigger place to accommodate all the worshipers. In 1969 we moved to a new site at 1725 Washington Street.

~~~~~~~~~~~~~~~~~~~~~

Looking Back
Barbara Lee Louie

In 1968, my sisters went to a church on Jackson Street. One day Pastor Holt and Amy came to visit our home. We were surprised he spoke Chinese although it was hard to understand. He was very warm, friendly, listened with a caring heart and answered our questions. Amy had a warm smile and shared the Gospel. They invited me to come on Sunday with my mom to the bilingual service. I was very excited and couldn't wait till Sunday. On the way, I asked my sister many questions about church; she tried to answer them and told me "just to go there". We sang a lot of songs before going to Sunday School. Our class was taught by Fay Wong and met in Pastor Holt's office. During those days I had six other teachers, including Paul Holt, Mrs. Holt and Henry Lai. Mrs. Holt was very quiet and stuck to her Bible lesson on Sundays. Switching teachers constantly was very difficult. After the church moved to 1725 Washington Street, Deaconess Carol Halter came.

We were told she would be our teacher and we wondered how long it would be before someone took her place. She taught us for 11 years. I really learned a lot from her applications from the Bible. She telephoned weekly to answer our questions. She also led our youth fellowship, directed our choir, took time each summer to talk with us individually, to pray and recreate with us. We had vacation Bible school during the summers. It was the best time of my life.

~~~~~~~~~~~~~~~~~~~

A New Immigrant 40 Years Ago
Debbie Lim Louie

I immigrated to San Francisco with my family on January 13, 1968. I was 18 years old. Since I was the oldest of four children and my mother did not speak English, I had a heavy responsibility on my shoulders. I was excited, sad, and scared. I cried for six months. I shouldn't have cried because God was always by my side.

I will always remember the day I took the bus to look for a school. I got lost and I rode around and around on the bus. Finally, I got off and I ended up in front of Zion Lutheran Church in the Richmond District. Since I attended a Lutheran church in Hong Kong, I figured someone at the Lutheran church would be able to help me. I also had a letter from my pastor in Hong Kong recommending that my family find Pastor Holt in San Francisco's Chinatown. When I introduced myself to the pastor at Zion, I showed him my letter. The pastor immediately called Pastor Holt, who quickly arrived at Zion with Amy Mui. Both Pastor Holt and Amy were very friendly and helpful. I was especially impressed with Amy, who was very charming and gracious.

Pastor Holt and Amy helped my family with everything we, as new immigrants, needed. From assisting my siblings to enroll in schools, to teaching us about life in the U.S., they were a tremendous help. Pastor Holt even gave me my English name. I am very thankful for Pastor Holt and Amy. Soon after, I got a job as a salesgirl in a gift shop in Chinatown. My hourly wage was 75 cent an hour. I saved all of my earnings for my school tuition.

My whole family attended Lutheran Church of the Holy Spirit on Jackson Street. It was very convenient because we lived in Chinatown. At the time, about 30 to 40 people were in the congregation. I remember Mrs. Ying Tit Hui, Ruth Hui and Pauline Hui, who are Pastor David Chan's grandma and aunts. Everyone was very friendly and helped each other. The church was one big family. I played the piano during fellowship and also at special church events. I also was a Sunday School teacher for the children. God has greatly blessed me. I have been a member of Lutheran Church of the Holy Spirit for over 40 years. I thank God for bringing my family to this church.

A Very Special Pastor
Po Gee Hui Chan

My mother, Hui Ying Tit, was baptized by Pastor Holt in 1958 in Hong Kong at Savior Lutheran Mission. After being baptized, Pastor Holt came to our home and helped my mother destroy all the ancestral plaques of our relatives. This was a big event and my mother truly wanted the family to worship only the one true God. I was baptized in 1964. I had to learn a lot of scripture before I could be baptized. One year later I was confirmed. David was 3 years old and Ricky was only 1 year old. They were baptized at Easter time in Hong Kong. Jim was born in Hong Kong later.

In 1965 my mother and two sisters came to San Francisco. One day my dad was walking with her on Jackson Street, across from 606 Jackson. My father pointed out the Lutheran Church of the Holy Spirit sign and just then Pastor Holt came out of the front door of the church and my mother waved to him. He recognized her and was so glad to see her. From then on she attended the church at 606 Jackson Street. My sister Pauline also attended the church and interpreted for Pastor Holt sometimes.
When the church moved to 1725 Washington Street, my mother and sisters went to there to Church and Sunday School.

When we came to San Francisco in 1969, my mother took us to the Washington Street church and introduced us to Pastor Holt and Amy Mui. I remember Peter and Debbie were my Sunday School teachers. I remember Pastor Holt's radiant smile and how he always shook hands so friendly every time we met. In 1971, I got a job but I told the boss I could not work on Sunday because we went to church on Sundays.

David actually learned Chinese at the Chinese Language school where Amy Mui was the principal. After graduation, he got a job at Bank of America. When the church opened the extension church on Noriega Street, his friend Charles Lee brought David to fellowship there. I also encouraged him to go there. Later Amy and Pastor Holt were suggesting he consider going into the ministry. In 1991 David and Lucy married and in 1992 he decided to enter the Seminary at St Louis. Lucy had a good job with the Government and she was able to transfer to St Louis. The Lord provided for them. He graduated in 1996. He was assigned as Pastor of our church and was ordained later that year.

We had a warm relationship with Pastor Holt and Mrs. Holt over the years. My husband, Jimmy often gave them rides to the hospital or doctor appointments. I remember one time Jimmy took Pastor Holt to have a pacemaker put in. I especially remember Mrs. Holt's delicious German Potato Salad which she made often for all special events. She was always smiling!

I was president of Yun Deen LWML from 1981 until early 1990's. During those years the women in our Yun Deen group visited Laguna Honda Chinese patients, once a month for many years. There we talked with the patients in Cantonese, brought them tea and dim sum. Pastor Wang or someone from our church would bring a Gospel message in Cantonese. Sometimes we sang Chinese gospel songs.

Now my eyesight is failing, I can not read the LWML directory. I have memorized all the telephone numbers of our ladies and I spend my days calling them on the phone to encourage them and reminding them of church events. I also have written in Chinese, by use of a small magnifying glass, many psalms and memorized them so I can recite them at picnics or other church events. It makes the time go faster.

"How can a young man keep his way pure? By guarding it according to thy word. With my whole heart I seek thee; let me not wander from thy commandments! I have laid up thy word in my heart, that I might not sin against thee. Blessed be thou, O Lord; teach me thy statutes! With my lips I declare all the ordinances of thy mouth, In the way of thy testimonies I delight as much as in all riches. I will meditate on thy precepts, and fix my eyes on thy ways, I will delight in thy statutes; I will not forget thy word." Psalm 119:9–16

Jackson Street Sunday School

Immigrants at 606 Jackson Street   Chapter Seven

Pastor and Amy at Jackson Street

Jackson Street Congregation

1968 Amy and Fellowship at Jackson Street

"God is able to provide you with every blessing in abundance, so that you may always have enough of everything and may provide in abundance for every good work"

2 Cor 9:8 RSV

Pastor Wilbert Holt

Amy Hau Mui

Chapter Eight

Sharing The Gospel

Pastor Holt offered many suggestions to an Anglo congregation reaching out to ethnic people such as the Chinese:
* Study and get an appreciation of the history and culture of the Chinese people.
* Study and understand the history of prejudice against Chinese in America.
* Get to understand why many Chinese have a natural feeling of prejudice toward the white race.
* Realize the diversity that exists among Chinese in language, in dialect, in places of origin, and various other influences.
* Be willing to allow every Chinese person to tell you his/her spiritual, cultural, familial, educational, and economic pilgrimage.
* Beware of the "ugly American" paternalistic, condescending contemptuous attitude toward anything that is not "American".
* Remember to have an attitude of "learners together" of the Word of God in Christ.
* You may weep over but never ridicule the superstitions or religions of the Chinese.
* Make sure when you plan an additional ethnic mission that you are prepared to have some space set aside for the new mission "Two objects cannot occupy the same place at the same time".
* Remember the Lutheran Church—Missouri Synod has great financial resources.
* Pastor Holt wrote "Commentary for Genesis and Chinese Characters". It is on file in the church archives.

The Ministries of Amy Hau Mui

"Train up a child in the way he should go, and when he is old he will not depart from it." Proverbs 22:6

Youth Ministry

Amy began her youth ministry by teaching Sunday School. Pastor Holt gave Amy four young students to teach. Soon, it became 8, then 16. With these youths, Amy started a "Bible Club", a first for this congregation. The Club later became two fellowships because of the age difference. A third fellowship was started for the parents (mostly mothers) of the youth. As the youth of the two fellowships aged, they became college fellowships and later couples fellowships. These were the early fellowships of the congregation.

Soon, Amy took the group of young adults on their first retreat (which also was the first for Amy). Amy's goal was to increase interaction between the fellowship by dividing them into small groups where each group had tasks of presenting topics, cooking, and games. Through the inspiration of the Holy Spirit, Amy felt that the daily life of the young adults lacked a moment where they could be alone with God and confess their sins to God. Thus, she created a candlelight service at each retreat, where the young adults had a life changing experience with God. Since then, Amy continued to organize retreats for youths with the focus on application of messages for daily living, deeper brotherhood/sisterhood bonding, and dedication to God during the candle light service.

Amy has a special gift of easily remembering names and related details whenever she speaks to a person about Christ. At the end of the day she would write down people's names and their specific needs—and pray for them many times. Her work of evangelism was very effective. She has three goals for her ministry: First, to enable others to have a firm relationship with Jesus; Second, to equip the youth through Bible studies; Third, to encourage young men to enter the ministry. Today this congregation has sent out 12 young men to become pastors of the Lutheran Church.

One of the early challenges for Amy in her youth ministry was how to invite new friends to fellowship. She quickly discovered that young adults have amazing ability to invite new friends. Amy also discovered that these young adults were eager to listen to the Gospel and eager to follow Biblical guidance. Their spiritual growth astounded Amy. One example of astonishing spiritual growth in the youth group was a young adult's dramatic change to become a newborn child of God.

A troubled young man at the age of 20 came to church in pursuit of a young lady who was in Amy's fellowship. The young lady sought Amy's help on how to handle the young man. Amy asked the young man to meet with her. On the first meeting, the young man spoke first in a cynical tone: "So, tell me about Jesus." Amy replied: "You have wasted 20 years of your life. Are you happy at this moment? You need God to teach you what is said in Psalm 90:12—Teach us to number our days aright, that we may gain a heart of wisdom. " With that verse and from that meeting, God turned the young man's life around. He met with Amy 7 more times, often expressing how lonely he was and the guilt he felt from the smoking, drinking, credit card frauds, and other wrongdoings. Afterward, he joined one of the church's young adult fellowships. For more than 15 years, Amy continued to follow up on the young man's well being, ranging from teaching him Chinese/English at the early age, to marital advice and parenting at the present time. Today this young man has become a radiant Christian, teaching youth and leading fellowships. His spiritual revival gave true meaning to the Bible verse: "Therefore, if anyone is in Christ, he is a new creation; the old has gone, the new has come!" 2 Corinthian 5:17

Chinese School

Not long after Lutheran Church of Holy Spirit moved from Chinatown to Washington Street, Pastor Holt and Amy started a Chinese school at the Washington church facility. Amy served as the school principal. The purpose of the school was to teach the next generation of Chinese descent the Chinese language, culture, and custom. More importantly, Chinese school was a channel where Amy and her staff could share the Gospel with students and their parents. Amy had some unique requirements for the enrolled students and their parents. All the students must attend the weekly gospel seminar while their parents were required to attend the quarterly gospel seminar during the school year.

The parents also were required to work closely with the school in order to ensure proper nurturing for their children. Thus, Amy was able to preach the Gospel effectively to the students and their parents. In her goal for administering to children, she uses everyday practical events and visual objects relating to God, and based on biblical principles. Conveying the message with enticing words and appropriate diction, can speak volumes in reaching young hearts whose attention span is sometimes short. When ministering to adults and elderly, she uses simple and understandable illustrations with empathetic persuasion. She guides them to God as their Heavenly Father, Provider and Creator of the Universe. She instructs them to write down Biblical verses and read them out loud to develop good memory and fluent articulation. The life of a believer is transformed by the Holy Spirit. She readily says she has personally nothing to boast, except to give all the glory to the Lord. The Holy Spirit is victorious in winning souls for Christ.

During one school year, the mother of a Chinese school student asked for Amy's phone after a parent seminar. She called Amy from the street phone (this was in pre-cell phone era) that evening, asking Amy to help her husband. The husband had been very hostile to the Gospel and refused to attend the parent seminar for Chinese school. Amy agreed to help and took the initiative to meet the husband. Since the husband worked from 8 O'clock in the morning until late in the evening, Amy set up a one-on-one session with the husband at 7 O'clock in the morning, where she was able to share God's Word for 3 months. The couple was baptized that Christmas and moved to Canada shortly after. 20 years later, the couple still maintain a good relationship with Amy. They would call Amy up on the phone for parenting advice and continue to share their serving experience with Amy. Their experience gave testament to the Bible verse: "Believe in the Lord Jesus, and you will be saved—you and your household." Acts 16:31

The Chinese school ministry was commissioned on three separate occasions in three separate locations. Altogether, Amy ran the Chinese school for 26 years and over two thousand students have attended. The staff of the Chinese school were devoted Christians, filled with the compassion of the Lord and they dedicated their wages to God. At the closing of the schools, all of the teachers' salaries, totaling $220,000, was donated to the Church Building Expansion Fund. The ministry itself was extremely fruitful. Many of the students and their parents accepted Christ as their savior. Some became members of the congregation.

Trials

Amy's ministries at Lutheran Church of the Holy Spirit were not without difficulties. She was constantly troubled by the gradual spiritual dwindling of the Christians she nurtured. She often found the young adults to have a strong spiritual growth period of 5 years. Afterward, their love for God and eagerness to serve God began to fade. It was also the time when their relationship with Amy also began to dwindle as well. Bearing witness to such dilemma, Amy prayed continually for these individuals and asked God to grant them the spiritual awakening once more.

In her long tenure at Lutheran Church of the Holy Spirit, Amy's biggest challenge was her health. When Amy got ill, she often got very ill and stayed ill for a long time. On three separate occasions, Amy had to close down her ministry for a whole year due to health problem. Each time, she faced anxiety attacks and a great deal of physical pain. Though she was deeply attached to the congregation and its ministry, God asked her to stop and rest. She learned to focus just on prayer and trust God. Through these experiences, the Lord granted her a compassionate understanding of how to support the members who struggled with illness or spiritual turbulence.

One of such occasions came from stranger. A young mother who heard Amy's sharing on the radio program of the Chinese Lutheran Hour, reached out to Amy for help. She was burdened with family issues, mainly issues with her husband. The young mother stated that she was a Christian but her husband was not. The two had a troubled marriage where extramarital affair was part of the issue. The two were on the verge of divorce, and the young mother often cried out: I just want to die. Amy agreed to provide counseling to the couple. Knowing only God could repair the broken marriage, Amy provided Bible studies with the couples, along with counseling. It took more than 6 months of counseling and Bible studies for the couple to begin repairing their marriage. Today, the couples loudly proclaim the name of Lord, Jesus Christ, and offered their home as place for Bible studies for new seekers. "You turned my wailing into dancing; you removed my sackcloth and clothed me with joy." Psalm 30:11

43 Years Serving the Lord !

For 43 years, Amy has faithfully served the congregation. Her ministry ranged from secretarial work to interpreter, from choir to evangelism committee, and from youth fellowship to senior fellowship. She never ceased to witness for God. She is eager to teach the Word of God, ready to provide advice that is Christ-centered, keen to lecture when one sins against God, and passionate to pray for one troubled spiritually. She introduced many members of the congregation to the Lord, and helped them mature with God's word. For 43 years, Amy's ministry has being fruitful, and it is a testament of God's grace that is showered upon her. Her ministry will continue to be fruitful, knowing God will continue to grant her wisdom and strength to share God's Word with lost souls.

Dear Heavenly Father, I praise and thank You for guiding our Lutheran Church of the Holy Spirit over the past almost 50 years. Each time I think about our church, my heart is filled with gratitude and thanksgiving to you.

Missionaries in Hong Kong listening to the Chinese Lutheran Hour broadcast for news during the time they were interned by the Japanese" Oh, Heavenly Father! Workers may pass, surroundings and situations may change, but your work will not cease. It will continue to move forward, for You are the Lord of our church, Lord of the harvest, and Lord of the threshing field. Thank you for giving us co-workers and believers who are faithful and who love the Lord with all their hearts.

You have been the head of our church from the very beginning. Ever since the day you called Rev. Wilbert Holt to establish our church, our brothers and sisters have been committed to share the gospel, and today your power strengthens us as we continue to proclaim your gospel. May our hearts be filled with your word as our foundation, and a sacrificial love that is rich in giving. You are the same yesterday, today and forever. You, who began a good work in the hearts of the brothers and sisters in our church, will surely complete this work, until the day of Jesus Christ. Guide us so we may continue to conduct ourselves in a manner worthy of the Gospel of Christ, united in one mind, standing firm, and working hard together to proclaim your gospel and not compromising with the ways of the world.

I pray the Holy Spirit will fill our hearts with unity, sincere love and passion, making us pure and trustworthy persons, seeking to give encouragement, comfort and fellowship to one another. Help us use our days on this earth, bearing good fruits for you. Always seeking to please only you!

May our attitude be the same as that of Christ Jesus, humble in learning, respectful and loving, good examples as children of God in this sinful generation. May we shine like stars in the universe as we proclaim your words of life. Help us lift high the Cross of Jesus Christ. May His name be glorified and His kingdom return soon.

In Jesus' name I pray. Amen. Amy

Sharing The Gospel   Chapter Eight

"Rejoice always, pray constantly, give thanks in all circumstances, for this is the will of God in Christ Jesus for you"

I Thess. 5: 16–18

1725 Washington and the Green Bus

Chapter Nine

Moving Forward

After 4 years, the rent for the Chinatown chapel became unreasonable, and the church was in danger of loosing its lease. We thank the Lord for the timely and generous contribution of $100,000 from the International Lutheran Women's Missionary League's 25th Anniversary in convention at Washington, D.C. Pastor Holt's wife, Geraldine traveled to DC to receive this mite offering from the LWML's Silver Anniversary. It was used to purchase and renovate the new church location.

After much prayer and many frustrations, an old but well-built church was found, which had been used as a theatre for many years. A fire had burnt out a section of the balcony and thus the building was condemned. However, the building was basically sound and contained about 9,000 sq. feet of usable space. This building and land was purchased for $118,000—the land itself being worth $90,000.00. The Mission Board of the Calif-Nevada District decided to completely renovate the building. The result was that the building's interior was completely rebuilt; the end product was most functional and beautiful.

It was a church with a seating capacity of 250, a large parish hall, a handicraft room, a Chinese kitchen, a teen-center, meeting rooms and church offices. The theatrical facilities were also retained—the chancel area, about 37 feet in depth, could also be used as a stage for religious drama and musical events.

The banners in the chancel were made by the women of the church under the direction of the architect. The central banner of the flame symbolized the Spirit of God who kindles faith and love in our hearts so that like the apostles on the Day of Pentecost we might be aflame with love, zeal and boldness to confess the Crucified and Risen Savior to all men.

The late Pastor John Rische reminded us many times of the prayer preparation involved in establishing our Lutheran mission in Chinatown. One of the great praying people in our congregation was Mrs. How Yuk Hau, mother of Amy Mui, who for more than 35 years made our ministry the very heart of her prayer life.

Today this congregation thanks the Lord for and shall never forget the human resources who gave, served and loved this mission into existence, including the members of the San Francisco Lutheran churches, our Missouri Lutheran Synod and C-N-H District, the L.W.M.L. and Church Extension Fund. The final and greatest resource was and is the prayers of the many people. Our Lord says "Pray the Lord of the harvest that he may send forth laborers into His harvest".

This is the Green bus which LWML District mites helped us to purchase for $5000.00. It helped to transport members to and from their homes in the Richmond and Sunset Districts to Church worship services and other activities. We thank God for LWML's assistance

"Now to Him who by the power at work within us is able to do far more abundantly than all that we ask or think, to Him be glory in the church and in Christ Jesus to all generations, for ever and ever. Amen".

Eph 3:20 RSV

1725 Washington Street, San Francisco

Chapter Ten

Dedication of 1725 Washington Street

After many months of planning, praying and renovation, the Lutheran Church of the Holy Spirit at 1725 Washington street, was dedicated on November 30, 1969. A specialdedication service was held with many friends from District, other Lutheran Churches and representatives from the Lutheran Women's Missionary League in attendance. It was a wonderful time to praise the Lord for what He had done or His church.

Worship services were held in Cantonese and English. The Lord's Prayer, the Apostles Creed and Hymns were sung or spoken simultaneously in both languages. The sermon was interpreted, sentence by sentence. Yes, we thank God that we are one body in Christ, each member doing the part assigned to him and all to the glory of our Lord and Savior, Jesus Christ.

We give thanks to God for the obedience of the Lutheran Church, Missouri Synod, California Nevada Hawaii District, to the Lord's command to make disciples of all nations and thus for the establishing of the ministry of God's Word and Sacraments among us. We give thanks for the support of the district congregations and mission board in generously subsidizing this congregation until it became self-supporting. And to the Church Extension Fund who gave us the low interest loan of 1 ½ % to cover the renovating expenses of the Washington Street building.

Pastor Holt spoke about our hope for the future when he said, "Today as we praise God for His direction in the past, we trust Him to empower us in the future so that whatever we do, as individuals and a congregation, we shall glorify God. As we are faithful in the use of God's Word and Sacraments, we rejoice that His Holy Spirit will ever enable us to share the message of reconciliation with others." "The Lord will give strength unto His people; the Lord will bless His people with peace." Psalm 29:11.

Interior of 1725 Washington Street at Dedication

Opening Ceramony at 1725 Washington Street

Dedication of 1725 Washington Street   Chapter Ten

Procession at Dedication

Circuit Pastor and Pastor Holt
at Dedication

Pastor Holt at
Washington Street Dedication

Choir at Washington Street Dedication

Amy at Dedication

Dedication of 1725 Washington Street   Chapter Ten

Guests at Dedication

"That which we have seen and heard we proclaim also to you, so that you may have fellowship with us; and our fellowship is with the Father and with his Son Jesus Christ".

I John 1:3 RSV

Ribbon Dancers

Chapter Eleven

The First Ten Years 1969–1979

Junior Youth Fellowship

This group meets Saturdays from 10 am to Noon. They learn God's Word, not just man's word. They share His precious Word, sing His praises, and serve Him by cleaning around the church. This is the place where they feel very happy and close to our wonderful Lord Jesus. Everyone is full of love and concern for one another. They work and play and worship together. If a person doesn't know God, they welcome him to come and find out about his need for God and how wonderful it is to have the gift of everlasting life. If they knew God already they were invited to come so that their faith can be strengthened by the Word of God and by fellowship of His children.

Chinese & English Speaking Youth Fellowship

The goal of this fellowship is to strengthen each other through God's Word and to proclaim that Word to our world about us. Meetings begin at two o'clock every Saturday afternoon and are usually led by one of the members of the church staff. The Bible study group was divided into two groups depending on whether you prefer to speak English or Chinese. Sometimes there are special guest speakers from other churches. Some were Pastor Jung from Taiwan, John Payne from Child Evangelism, Pastor Wahl or his son teaching "Transactional Analysis" and members of the Lutheran Social Service helping us with the Lutheran Youth Survey. One of the regular activities was to share the Word of God at the Laguna Honda Hospital and to help wheel patients to the worship service there. During that worship we would sing together as a choir. Another activity was singing and passing out tracts in the park or from door to door. Sometimes we would go to different churches to bring testimonies in word and song to them. Several times a year there would be a special musical or drama program to invite our non-Christian relatives and friends.

Young Adult Fellowship

Formed in March of 1974, this fellowship is typical of the way God has so generously showered blessings upon the Lutheran Church of the Holy Spirit and its members during the past decade. Its members strive for a closer walk with Christ through insightful and inspiring Bible studies held bimonthly on the 1st and 3rd Tuesday night of each month. There were about 15 members including an army veteran, schoolteacher, nurse, cab driver, telephone man, secretary, clerks and students. Diversified backgrounds and experiences aided the fellowship in assuming their tasks of hosting outside church functions, ushering and visiting the sick and elderly Chinese at Laguna Honda Hospital. It was a truly redemptive and fruitful fellowship which became more constructive and productive for the church and community.

L.W.M.L. Women's Society

Although the ladies of this congregation have been active since the beginning of the mission, it was not until 1970 when they officially organized as members of the Lutheran Women's Missionary league and received a charter from the California-Nevada-Hawaii District LWML. Bible study was held every Sunday morning during the Sunday school hour. It was through the study of God's word that they drew close to the Lord and in fellowship with one another. Some of their activities were providing candles and flowers for the altar; visiting Chinese patients at Laguna Honda Hospital, making altar paraments, providing a center aisle rug for our sanctuary and cooking food for church dinners. Through collection of mites and prayers they strive to do a woman's part in glorifying Jesus Christ.

L.L.L. Men's Fellowship

The goal of this fellowship was to glorify God by helping the men of the congregation to assume their responsibilities and with the privilege of studying the scriptures; leading their family devotions; training their children in the Word of God; being a Christian example to their families, to their colleagues at work and school and to the congregation. Intensive Bible study relating to concerns of adults such as marriage, family living, social concerns and Gospel evangelism were held. A special concern was support for the Chinese Lutheran Hour Radio Broadcast and Patterns for Living TV Broadcast. They sponsored the annual church picnic and other congregational outings.

One of the highlights of every fellowship was the annual Bible retreat. Every year five fellowship groups have a three or four day retreat. Participants were challenged to rededicate their lives to Christ. These usually took place at churches out of the San Francisco area. Much time was spent in the study of His Word with special speakers and in singing in the morning and evenings. On the last evening there was usually a candlelight service, which gave, an opportunity to dedicate or re-dedicate lives to Christ. We also had recreation such as swimming, hiking, playing softball, volleyball and other sports. It was even fun to prepare meals, to wash the dishes and clean up the camp. One of our favorite and most frequently visited retreat centers was the Messiah Lutheran Church in Santa Cruz. Groups have also gone to Yosemite, Clear Lake, St Andrew's Lutheran Church and Lake Tahoe. God truly blessed the young people each year through these retreats.

The First Ten Years   Chapter Eleven

Pastor and Mrs. Holt and young mothers

Youth of Church 1969

1970 Retreat

Pastor Holt Exercising

Pastor Holt Teaching

Holt Family 1970

The First Ten Years   Chapter Eleven

Singers at 1725 Washington Street

Pastor Paul. Grandmother Hoeltje
and younger sister

1978 Hope Boys Group

Confirmation Thanksgiving 1978

Women's Retreat Walnut Creek

The First Ten Years   Chapter Eleven

Pastor Holt

Dr. of Divinity, Wilbert V Holt

LUTHERAN CHURCH of THE HOLY SPIRIT
1725 WASHINGTON STREET
SAN FRANCISCO, CALIFORNIA 94109

WILBERT V. HOLT, Pastor
CHURCH: 771-6658
PARSONAGE: 752-2444

JULY 17, 1972

YOUR PRESENCE IS REQUESTED AT A SURPRISE PROGRAM AND CHINESE DINNER, SUNDAY JULY 30TH AT 5 P.M. AT THE HOLY SPIRIT LUTHERAN CHURCH, 1725 WASHINGTON STREET, SAN FRANCISCO, WHEN THE CONGREGATION WILL HONOR ITS PASTOR, REV. WILBERT V. HOLT, RECENT RECIPIENT OF AN HONORARY DOCTOR OF DIVINITY DEGREE FROM CONCORDIA SEMINARY AT SPRINGFIELD.

AS THIS IS A SURPRISE DINNER, PLEASE RETURN THE ENCLOSED CARD BY JULY 25TH AND NO PHONE CALLS TO THE CHURCH, PLEASE.

"For we are his workmanship, created in Christ Jesus for good works, which God prepared beforehand, that we should walk in them"

Eph 2:10 RSV

Pastor Holt

Chapter Twelve

Lives Touched By Pastor Holt

Bringing Christ to the Ma Family
Jerry Ma

It was 1969! My sister Joanne was attending the Chinese youth fellowship of this church. Having heard the Gospel for about a year, she wanted to be baptized. For some reasons, my mother objected to the baptism of my sister. Pastor Holt and Director Amy visited our home to explain the meaning of baptism to my mother. I was at home during their visit and heard their sharing of the Gospel. Before they left, they invited me to come to the fellowship. The following Saturday, I went with my sister to the Chinese youth fellowship and have been part of the church ever since. My sister was baptized on Christmas day of 1970. I was baptized on Christmas day the following year. That was the beginning of an amazing story of "Bringing Christ to our Chinese Family"—The Ma Family. Besides my sister and I, there were nine other members of the Ma family baptized in our church: Jessie Mah (my cousin), Kwan Shou Wong Ma (my mother), Frank Mah (my cousin), Kwan Ying Mah (my aunt), Tony Ma (my cousin), Jonathan Ma (my son), Wah Ma (my father), Theodore Ma (my nephew) and Rebecca Ma (my niece). God has been gracious to my family, to the Ma family with His love and salvation. The promise of God is "Believe in the Lord Jesus, and you will be saved—you and your household" Acts 16:31. He has fulfilled His promised in the Ma Family and many other Chinese families.

Remembering Washington Street
Debbie Lim Louie

After two years in junior college, I transferred to UC Davis. Although I was a good student in Hong Kong and junior college, UC Davis was very challenging, especially during the first few months. I struggled and I was lonely. I will always remember when Deaconess Carol Halter visited me at Davis. She encouraged and motivated me. I am very grateful for her help. I met my husband, Bat, at City College of San Francisco. Both of us transferred to UC Davis. After college graduation, we got married. We were one of the first couples who were married at the Washington Street church. Pastor Holt officiated at our wedding.

We were very active in various church ministries. I continued to teach Sunday School. Sometimes I played the piano and the organ. A few years ago, Pastor David Chan and Susan Woo reminded me that I was their Sunday School teacher at that time.

Deaconess Carol Halter coordinated the Laguna Honda ministry. Every Saturday, we visited and wheeled the patients to the Laguna Honda church service. The patients eagerly waited for us in their best outfits. We wore bright colored clothes because it attracted and cheered up the patients. The patients knew we were visitors by the bright clothes we wore, unlike the nurses who wore white.

During one special event, Bat's mother made rice porridge for the patients. They were all very excited to try the rice porridge. Carol also had an evangelism ministry at the Chinese Playground in Chinatown. Many kids accepted Christ through her ministry at the playground. In 1981, Carol was commissioned a fulltime Missionary to Hong Kong. During the past two years, Bat and I were able to join Carol on two short-term mission trips. It was a blessing to serve God with her.

Growing up in the Church
Barron Fong

I was first made aware of Pastor Holt and the church as a young teen growing up in the Chinatown/North Beach area in the late 60's. The church located at Jackson St. opened its doors on Saturdays for local youths to gather for time of recreation in the basement for ping pong and other activities. I was not yet a believer back then, but just went there to have fun times with my friends.

Whenever I saw Pastor Holt, he would invite me to attend Sunday services with his nice gentle voice. It wasn't until the church moved to Washington St. in 1969 that I began to attend church regularly with my good friend, Frankie Choy. I remember attending Sunday School classes, with just a few other people, sitting in his small upstairs office. During those days, when we were still too young to drive a car, we would gather at the old location on Jackson St. and catch a ride in the yellow van driven by Deaconess Carol Halter to Washington St. Over time from hearing God's Word and through the ministry of Pastor Holt, I was baptized and confirmed as a member in 1970.

As a youth, I recall the experiences going away from home for summer retreats to Santa Cruz and one time to Southern California. These summer retreats were special times for us to get closer to God and to get to know others much better. These were times for work, play and spiritual renewal.

It's now 40 years that I've been a part of the Holy Spirit Lutheran Church. Much has changed in terms of physical locations and the people, but yet God's Word of salvation remains the same for all to receive. I've taken on different roles over the years. I was one of the first church Treasurers, since I studied accounting in college. More recently, I have taken on the role as an Elder and assisting in various ministries among the English speaking members of the congregation. It is by God's grace and the work of the Holy Spirit that the various ministries within the church have grown.

**Early years at 1725 Washington Street
Peter Ng**

Through Frankie and Sue Choy, our family started coming to our church in 1993. At that time, even though things seemed to be fine on the surface and our family was doing okay as others saw us, but deep inside, I knew something was missing. Agnes and I both had pretty good jobs and our kids were getting good grades at school. We owned a house and drove a Lexus, yet we were not happy. I was confused, lost, and desperately looking for answers.

It was at our church at Washington Street that the love, grace, and mercy of God came upon me and my family. The Holy Spirit convicted me and I realized how selfish and sinful person I was. He revealed his unconditional love to me and in so many occasions in my life he rescued me from danger and saved my life when I was a sinner. It is so true that "God shows his love for us in that while we were still sinners, Christ died for us".

I praise God that he gave me a second chance. In that same year, I committed myself to follow Jesus all the days of my life, and received baptism. Since that time, I have witnessed God's faithfulness and tasted his wonderful grace. Although my family went through a number of difficult times since that year, but each time God was by our side, holding our hands and guiding us through safely. Praise God for his goodness! Praise God for his amazing grace!

**Our Goal
Cindy Lim Jeong**

The Chinese Youth Fellowship began at the end of August 1969. Our motto was taken from Philippians 4:13 'I can do everything through Him who gives me strength.' (NIV) Every Saturday afternoon, over a dozen of us gathered together at two in the afternoon to study the Bible. There were all kinds of recreation activities such as picnics, debates, concerts, ping pong contests, Bible trivia, games, …etc. After each meeting, we learned a little bit more about the Bible. We understood a little bit more of Christ's love and became closer to Him and came to know that Christ loved us. Because of His death and resurrection, we are called children of God, our sins are forgiven and we were given a new life from then now on. This fellowship was built on Christ the Rock and therefore our faith will not be shaken, no matter what problems we may face. Our group of young people quickly blossomed in pure companionship, and to this day, years later, we still maintain a deep bond of endearment and caring for each other in Christ.

Two years later, our fellowship's motto was changed to: 'Growing Holistically: Loving God and our fellow men! Walking Hand In Hand, Sharing Our Blessings From the Lord!' Through the Father's protection, Jesus' guidance, and the Holy Spirit's transformation, we learned that 'faith by itself, if it is not accompanied by action, is dead'. Jesus said, 'whatever you did for one of the least of these brothers of mine, you did for me.' We visited senior citizen homes and hospitals, bringing Christ' love and salvation to the patients. Seeing the tears of joy and gratitude in their eyes, often gave us an urgency of giving more care to those in pain and those forgotten by people.

Our church did not have a custodian so we divided into groups after each fellowship meeting, to vacuum, empty garbage cans, clean the glass doors, desks and chairs...etc. The tasks were done quickly in the midst of laughter and sharing. These simple acts of service allowed us the opportunity to show our love and gratitude to God through actions. At the same time, the fellowship members shared many happy moments together.

Today, many of us have become teachers, secretaries, doctors, merchants, policemen or engineers and because the roots of our faith are deeply grounded in the ROCK, we will still be able to revere and honor God and bring people to the Lord within our work and our lives. We are willing to offer ourselves completely to God and since 1972 to the present, our fellowship motto has been 'Giving Our Heart to the Lord'.

Thanks be to God for the establishment of this Fellowship where we can hear the True Word and understand God's salvation. We are able to have activities that are beneficial to our body and soul and at the same time, we are able to be separated from this evil world which is filled with sin and temptations. In summary, the purpose of this Fellowship is to lead young people into God's salvation and to love the Lord our God with all our heart and with all our soul and with all our strength and with all our mind; and, love our neighbor as ourselves.

My memory of Pastor Holt!
Yuen Hui Lee

Like many families in our congregation, Pastor Holt was very close to our family. When I first started attending our church, one Bible verse that Pastor always instilled upon my heart was Acts 16:31 "Believe in the Lord Jesus, and you will be saved—you and your household". After I became a Christian, Pastor Holt always encouraged me to pray for my family and lead them to Christ. My oldest sister, Lisa was the first member of the Hui family baptized by Pastor Holt. I was baptized the follow year. Then few years later, my Mom, my paternal grandmother at the age 94, my youngest sister, Anna, my younger sister Simmy, my Dad, my maternal grandmother, my older brother Wilson. Later our children Nathaniel, Kathy, my four nieces and nephew (Nicholas, Candace, Victoria and Danielle) were brought to faith and baptized.

When I first came to church on Washington Street, I attended the Youth Fellowship on Saturday afternoons. Many times, on Saturday evenings, our churches had dinners to raise money for Chinese Lutheran Church

Hour Program. Along with some members of the Youth group, I stayed around to help serve dinner and clean up after the dinner. At that time, most members of our church lived near Chinatown or church, we were one of the few families that lived in Sunset District so usually Pastor Holt would drive me home. I remember it was during these many car rides that I had the opportunities to talk to Pastor about many different issues.

Pastor Holt always had time to talk with us. Many times, after our Fellowship group ends, we would help to clean the church. When it was my turn to clean the Church office areas, Pastor Holt would always stop what he was doing and asked me to sit down to talk with him. He always called my parents or came to our home to talk with my parents. Even though at that time my parents were not Christians yet through the love and prayer of Pastor Holt and Director Amy, they became more interested in the gospel and later became Christians. I thank God for placing Pastor Holt among us. He was there when I needed advise as a teenager, young adult, wife or mother. We will always miss you Pastor Holt.

Because of Pastor Holt!
Anna Hui Hirano

Because of Pastor Holt, I was introduced to God. Because of Pastor Holt's love toward me, I learned and understood how much God loves me. Because of Pastor Holt, I became a Christian. Because of Pastor Holt, I'm still one today! Pastor Holt always had time for me, he made me feel as if I was his priority. When I was a teenager we had one-on-one Bible study sessions, for our pre-marriage counseling sessions he worked around my schedule. I was able to call him anytime and he would lead me to the right answer through his love, kindness and understanding. He was there through each important event of my life.

To this day when I come across challenges, I still think about what he has taught me. Pastor Holt was, and still is a God sent to my whole family!

Pastor Holt, an Amazing Person
Simmy Hui Lee

One summer day, my friends and I were playing in the school yard. Carol Halter walked by the school yard and invited us to church. The church had just moved from Chinatown to Washington Street. That was the first time I met Pastor Holt. Both Carol and Pastor Holt left a lasting first impression.

Pastor Holt was an amazing person. He was the most sincere, gentle, kind, and caring, loving, generous and humble man. I can remember the time when Pastor Holt was mugged by a homeless man. Instead of being angry and upset, Pastor apologized to the man because he didn't have a lot of money in his pocket for the man to steal. Pastor was a friend to everyone. His selfless dedication to church is what

God would want us all to be. His passion was to spread the gospel. I can still remember his smile when he talked to us; especially, when he talked about God. His face would light up, and there would be no stopping him.

Pastor Holt was a big part of our lives. He baptized us, performed our marriage ceremonies and baptized our kids. God truly blessed our church when he sent us Pastor Holt.

My Friend Pastor Holt!
Ernie Louie

Pastor Holt was the greatest influence on me outside of my father. He was like a father to me. He, along with Deaconess Carol Halter helped to disciple me. I could call him at any time and talk with him about any subject. I can not recall one time when he was annoyed by anyone. He always took time to listen to people, and to help them. He was like a real Jesus, right here. He was a light to the community.

~~~~~~~~~~~~~~~~~~

The Walk that Changed My Life
Dr. Robert Kong

I met Pastor Holt under the direst circumstances. I was a Christian who had fallen away in my faith, and my marriage was falling apart. I called my brother (who had gone through previous multiple divorces) for the name of a good divorce lawyer. He said he would call me back. A few minutes later, I received a phone call from Pastor Holt. All he said was, "Let's take a walk." I hesitated a moment, but then answered, "OK". It was after midnight as I drove over to his house in the inner Richmond.

He met me at his doorway wearing a well-worn pea coat, and we headed off on our walk. During the walk, I related my marriage problems and emptied my deepest feelings. After many minutes, he finally said, "I guess you're all played out". I agreed with him. "You know what your problem is?", he asked. "No, please tell me", I thought and answered. He told me that I was looking to my marriage, my family, my job, my house, everything to fill my cup. But only God can fill our cup—the rest is overflow. Immediately, the figurative light bulb went on in my mind, my heart, and my soul. I immediately prayed to God for forgiveness and recommitted to Him.

Thereafter, my entire attitude and behavior changed. I returned to my local church; I began attending a Bible study; My life began to change. I never reconciled with my wife, but I was reunited with my children, and we all attended church together.

Remembering a Special Husband
Susan Yee

"Thank you, my dear." Those words of gratitude were often spoken by Pastor Holt to his beloved wife, Geri. He and Mrs. Holt had a sweet and loving relationship. Wherever God called Pastor to serve, she was right by his side serving along with him. They were supportive of each other all the years they were married.

Mrs. Holt was a wonderful cook and always had a hot dinner ready for Pastor after work. Sometimes he would surprise her by bringing a guest home for dinner. Graciously and quickly she would set up another table setting and shared their meal. Pastor really enjoyed her desserts. I remember her delicious homemade cookies.

Pastor was a gentleman and treated Mrs. Holt like a lady. He opened doors, helped her with her coat, and assisted her in and out of his little car. When their vacuum cleaner got too heavy for Mrs. Holt to maneuver, Pastor would come to work a little late every time it was "vacuum day."

Pastor Holt had many joys in his ministry and church life, but nothing made him happier than the joys that he shared with Mrs. Holt and the large family that God blessed them with. Susan Yee, church secretary 1989–1994.

My family came as immigrants in 1965 to San Francisco's Chinatown. I met Pastor Holt at his Lutheran Church of the Holy Spirit on Jackson Street. Through his warm personality and love for bringing the gospel to the people of Chinatown, my entire family of ten accepted the Lord and were baptized shortly after. This blessing expanded to our second generation where my four children came to know the Lord and were also baptized.

My most vivid memories of Pastor Holt were his genuine greetings of "Hello, friend" and warm smile. Whenever I heard him greet me as "friend," I always felt the love of God flowing through him just like the bright light shining from a light house in the night. I could write a book talking about our beloved Pastor, but to put it shortly, I want to thank him for:
All the Summer Vacation Bible Schools where we heard many great Bible stores and ate cookies and drank Kool-Aid.

All the Summer Camps at South Lake Tahoe and Santa Cruz where we learned the love of God. All the long sermons where we learned to examine our relationships with God. Most of all, thank you, Pastor, for bringing my family the Gospel and leading us to Christ.

What Pastor Holt Did For my Family
Otto Fung

I want to share with you what Pastor Wilbert Holt has done for me and my family.

Coming to the Lutheran
Church of the Holy Spirit
Jason Yan

I came to Lutheran Church of The Holy Spirit in November of 1984. It started when I went to Hong Kong earlier that year in February. I had a chance to go back to my old school and paid visit to my old Bible teacher. Maria Lang, a German lady who served the Lord there.

When we met, she was very concerned about my faith in Jesus. When she learned that I wasn't going to church, she gave me Pastor Holt's phone number and his address. Since she had visited our church a few years before that, she was able to give me info about Pastor Holt.

After I came back to San Francisco, I put away Pastor's number for seven months. When I dug it up one day in November, I decided to listen to my teacher and gave him a call. One week later, Pastor came to visit me with Patty Lee, who was the secretary at that time. Two weeks after their visitation, Pastor Holt and Mrs. Holt came to drive me to church for the first time.

Pastor Holt and Mrs. Holt were always a great pair. They were gentle and kind. Pastor Holt used much of his personal time for church and invited people to his house to share the gospel with them. Mrs. Holt tried her best to work with him by preparing food for the guests. The most memorable time for me with Pastor Holt was about one month before he went to heaven. Since I knew that he won't be around for a long time, I worked with Victor Wright to bring him dinner. During our last dinner together, Pastor Hot was not able to speak and express himself clearly. One thing he never forgot was to have a short Bible study with us. He took out a Daily Bread booklet, turned to a page, and asked Victor to read it out loud. After that, he tried to explained it to us. Even though he couldn't speak clearly, we tried our best to listen.

Yes, Pastor Holt is no longer with us physically, However, there is much that we can still learn from him.

He Was My Friend
Sam Chang

Pastor Holt was my friend. The way he lived his life made a very dramatic impression on a young man who immigrated to the U.S. without a father figure. He was a gentle person when he spoke to you but he had a will of steel in doing God's work.

I remember feeling uncomfortable seeing the homeless people on Polk Street, but Pastor Holt never judged people by their appearance and literally gave away his own shoes if someone needed them.

He told me when I was in Junior High to remember this period of time because it would the happiest and care free time of my life and when I look back, he was so right. I miss you Pastor Holt. I can still hear your voice when you call me "friend".

A Christmas Miracle
May Luu

For many years Pastor and Mrs. Holt sent Christmas letters to their family, relatives and friends. Because I helped type them, I got to read them and enjoyed them very much. Their letters were inspirational—always full of praises and thanksgivings to God. I want to share with you the one I wrote in December of 1996, a truly miraculous Christmas.

Christmas is a miracle—a gift of love, a promise of hope, an assurance of faith ... from God to man.

I experienced a miracle this Christmas. It happened on Saturday, December 14th, on a trip that Pastor Holt and I took to Ukiah, CA, to visit my nephew, Elmer. We left for Ukiah at 9 a.m. that day. It was a beautiful day—sunny, cold and crisp after several days of rain. It was a long two and half hour drive. But the scenery along the way was peaceful and picturesque. The visit with Elmer was great. Pastor Holt had a long talk with him about our Lord Jesus Christ, and we had a Bible study together on the Gospel of John.

Following this, we paid a visit to Pastor Schulz at Faith Lutheran Church in Ukiah. Afterwards, we went to see Elmer's friend, Joy and her mother, Brenda, at the local hospital. Pastor Holt prayed for Brenda and talked to Joy about God. I really felt God's love through Pastor Holt's ministry to these people. We left Ukiah around 5 p.m. It was already dark. I was driving, and Pastor Holt was sitting in the passenger seat next to me. After traveling on a long, dark, winding road, we finally reached Highway 101 and headed south to go home. Suddenly I felt an impact followed by the sight of a black jeep spinning out of control in front of us. I was sure we were going to crash into it. But, miraculously, we didn't! I was almost hysterical with fear.

Miraculously, nobody was hurt. This made a strong impression on the police and everyone involved.

It truly was a miracle!!! It was really something to thank God for!!! At the scene of the accident we were able to share with the people in other cars, Pastor Holt's Christmas tract entitled "You are Miracle—Christmas is a Miracle." My prayer is that you will trust God to be working everything for good in your life as you trust and love Him. Receive God's love that caused Him to give us His Son as our Savior, and live each day with joy as God gives us His spirit's guidance in the New Year.

~~~~~~~~~~~~~~~~~~~~

The Greatest of These is Love
Zoel Zeddies

In 1997 I lived much of the summer with Pastor Holt & his wife Geri. They invited me to stay with them for the summer while I was doing business in San Francisco. It was the first time I had met Wilbert, my mother's cousin.

Not many I know would be so hospitable that they'd open up their home to a distant, unknown relative for 2 months, but this kindness & hospitality I discovered, characterized my "uncle" whom I learned to love and respect. I saw this spirit of love extended to many members of the church, street people, and neighbors.

Pastors may be loving "on the job" but at home may be another matter. Pastor Holt, however, was the genuine article.

Too often I have seen how strong religious faith leads to fanaticism, heavy-handedness, and judgmentalism. This was not the case with Pastor Holt. His faith in Jesus Christ led to an unwavering love and concern for all—for the religious and the non-religious; the righteous, the self-righteous, and the unrighteous. Never once did he speak an unkind word about anyone. There was always a cheerful face on and a heart of love in this man of God. He was great lover of God and man.

It was a privilege for me to know this remarkable man of love.

Memories of Pastor Holt
Karl W. Randolph

I first came to Holy Spirit while on a visit to San Francisco, 1978. At that time people told me that I should visit this church because it is a great, mission minded church. After my visit, I went back to Iowa. During that visit, I did not meet Pastor Holt, rather my main contact was Warren Jow.

The following year I came back to San Francisco for what turned out to be a stay of five years. Warren Jow again insisted that I stay, as a member this time, and so I did. I joined the English Fellowship at that time led by Deaconess Carol Halter.

After five years, I moved to Texas, expecting to take care of my grandfather. We stayed there five years, where two of my sons were born. Then we returned to San Francisco. When we returned to San Francisco, this time Pastor Holt sought me out just for conversations. Discussions covered a wide gamut of subjects, politics, social affairs, theology, literature, etc. As Pastor Holt came to know me, he hoped that I would be one of the members of the congregation who would eventually become a pastor.

After his retirement, Pastor Holt started a Friday evening Bible study. He hoped it would develop into something more than just a meeting between some friends with a Bible study. He had me prepare some of the Bible studies. Sadly, as his physical condition deteriorated, he had to give them up.

One thing that he said was those who attended the Bible studies were needy people, all with problems. We are to accept them as they are, and work to improve them. The only problem is that at that time, I too was so needy that I had a hard time helping others.

Later, after illness made it that Pastor Holt was no longer able to continue his Bible studies, I continued to visit him on Friday afternoons. Pastor Holt was always a firm believer in the effectiveness of written materials, and so we discussed making flyers. But he was too weak to continue. The last Friday I was there was when he died, and years later, I still get emotional about that experience.

The one thing that impressed me most about Pastor Holt's life, that still speaks to me, is that he was a man of prayer. Every meeting had prayer connected with it. Every problem was brought before God. I wish I could say I have adopted that lesson, but I still have not.

"Equip the saints for the work of ministry, for building up the body of Christ, until we all attain to the unity of faith and of the knowledge of the Son of God"

Eph 4: 12–13 RSV

Chinese Children's Choir 1973

Chapter Thirteen

New Ministries

One day Pastor Holt received in the mail from Hong Kong, a half-hour drama produced by the Lutheran Church in Hong Kong. It was directed primarily to a non-Christian audience, although it was a Christian drama.

Pastor Holt wanted a more direct Gospel message to be added to the program. He was excited about this new means of "Bringing Christ to the Local Chinese Community". He enlisted Amy's help in adding a special Gospel message following the drama. They also added helpful news and information of interest to the Chinese Community.

The broadcasting studio was only a short walk from the church. Pastor Holt and Amy visited the recording station and arranged for time to broadcast their program. Broadcasting time was very expensive and there was no church budget for this expense. Pastor Holt would not allow a fund raiser in the church. So ladies of the LWML in the Bay Area were invited to come as a group for a delicious Chinese dinner at the church and learn about this new radio broadcast reaching out to Bay Area Chinese. Sometimes as many as 200 people came in one evening. Soon people from all over the bay area came by busloads to enjoy meals cooked by women of the church and served by the young people. From the money received for the dinners, the church was able to pay for the radio broadcast time. Amy's voice became very familiar to the Chinese community and people came to the church after hearing the broadcast. Thus the Chinese Lutheran Hour was born! "The Sound of Life."

On April 1, 1969 the Lutheran Laymen's League assumed sponsorship of the Chinese Lutheran Hour on station KFAX AM 1100 KC and it continued for 109 broadcasts, until November 30, 1974. It is with great appreciation we acknowledge the financial investment by the Lutheran Laymen's League and thank women of the LWML, which made this Gospel broadcast to the Chinese people possible.

Chinese Language School

In November 1969, when the church moved from Chinatown to 1725 Washington street, many of the families living in the neighborhood were recent immigrants from Hong Kong or China. God gave Rev. Wilbert Holt and Parish Worker Amy Mui, a new vision to start a ministry among these new immigrants. They used the church facilities to start a Chinese Language school. The purpose was to nurture the next generation of Chinese descent, to teach the Chinese language, culture, custom practices and most importantly, to bring the children and their parents the knowledge of the Bible which is able to make them wise for salvation through faith in Jesus Christ. Amy Mui was the principal of the school.

The Lord had given Amy a deep concern for souls, the gift of evangelism, the natural ability to teach, the gift of organization and the gift of interpretation, all which she used in leading this school. It was her belief that in ministering to children, the everyday practical events and visual objects relating to God, and based on biblical principles can be very effective. Conveying the message with enticing words and appropriate dictions, can speak volumes to reach their hearts, as children's attention span is very short.

The Church established the first Chinese Language school, 1971–1975, beginning with 56 students. Many students came to know Jesus as their Savior and are still attending our Church today.

The second school was in the Sunset District at Christ Lutheran Church, 1975–1980, starting with 80 students. During that time, Amy became ill and with Pastor Holt's approval, the entire school and its student body was transferred to Christ Lutheran Church. They had just begun their Chinese ministry in the Sunset District.

The third school was in the Sunset West Portal Lutheran School, Moraga Campus, 1985–2001. Initially 110 students were enrolled.

A Chinese school was an obvious need in the Chinese community. Most churches used every possible means to bring the children, youth and adults to church. Yet, at the Chinese Language school, the parents eagerly brought their children to the language school in the church. Now, there was duel responsibilities. One was to relate the Chinese culture to the next generation; the second was to carry out the Great Commission, bringing Christ to the students and their families. The most crucial factor in running the school was to have good teachers. All 30 teachers were college graduate church members from our congregation.

They responded to Christ's love. Jesus said, "Do you truly love me? Feed my lambs" John 21:15. All of the teachers dedicated themselves to be used by God, and compassionately taught the students. Most of the teachers volunteered their services and offered their wages to God. The school's good reputation spread throughout the Sunset district and people knew "God was at work among us". The School motto was "Train a child in the way he should go, and when he is old he will turn from it" Proverbs 22:6.

Every teacher was trained by Principal Amy Mui with a heart for evangelism and committed to at least one year in this ministry. The school hours were every Saturday morning from 9:30—12:30 noon. The classes were kindergarten to sixth grade. Each report card period, parents attended a mandatory meeting with a 45 minutes Gospel message and parent/child relationship workshop, all led by Principal Amy Mui. Our current Truth Fellowship, Living Spirit Fellowship, and Living Word Fellowship were all established for the parents and students. God added souls to our Church regularly.

The combined total years of the Holy Spirit Chinese Language School history was 26 years, over two thousand students attended, over forty college graduates, Christian teachers faithfully served our Lord. The teachers' salaries totaling $220,000, was entirely contributed to our Noriega Church Building Fund. These have been 26 years of blessings and a testimony that our glorious Lord is the one who generously blesses His people.

HUL-Help-U-Learn
After School Tutorial

DCE Allan Tong

Fresh out of internship, God called Director of Christian Education (DCE) Allan Tong back to The Lutheran Church of the Holy Spirit, the very church he grew up in, and the very same church where intended to serve God, for what would be the next decade or so. You could almost say that God intentionally put him at this church to send him away to college for the specific purpose of coming back to start something new. And this "something new" that God put on his heart to begin, was miles and miles beyond what he ever imagined it to become.

New Ministries

Chapter Thirteen

This is more than just a historical document of some church in San Francisco. It's a story of how faith spurred obedience, and how God blessed a ministry built upon this type of faith. This is the story of "Help-U-Learn After School Tutorial" under the direction of DCE Allan Tong.

A little over a decade or so ago, the congregation decided to move the church site from Washington Street near Chinatown to the Sunset District on Noriega Street. This move was within the same city of San Francisco, but then, if you have ever physically been to both Chinatown and Sunset, you'd know that the two different places are very...well, different.

And now that the church has followed Jesus to the heart of Sunset, what's the next step?

"For I know the plans I have for you," declares the Lord, "plans to prosper you and not to harm you, plans to give you hope and a future."(Jeremiah 29:11, NIV) Just what kind of plan is it that God speaks of?

How obvious was it back then when DCE Allan Tong was given the official responsibility of heading and building up the youth ministry for the church at the new building? An assessment of the new location and its surrounding areas revealed a high makeup of schools and homes within the area, with a high Chinese American population. God inspired in DCE Allan the idea of "Help-U-Learn After School Tutorial" (HUL). There were so many students around, and with their homes so close, there had to be a few that needed some help in their schoolwork.

Thus, HUL was born in the year of 1998. Of course, it wasn't that simple. HUL was first an idea that became a vision, and this vision required some planning. It was hard to get help in the beginning. There was some canvassing that needed to be done, flyers needed to be handed out from house to house to let the community know that HUL was on the way. Yet again, God provided a few dedicated people. To name a few, there was Ms. Lorraine Ma, Mr. Jason Yan, Ms. Helen Lee, Mr. Dennis Lin, Director Amy Mui, Pastor David Chan, and many more. There were these people doing as they're told, helping out in faith, and receiving a blessing that came back ten times more.

HUL started out small. As students started to enroll, this tutoring program called for more than just tutoring and finishing homework. To meet the needs of the community and its growing students, the purpose of HUL ministry was further developed with the heart of wanting to provide a safe environment for students to come after school to a place where not only could they get help with their homework, but a place where they belong, a place where they can build true friendship in knowing Jesus.

It didn't seem likely that students in our society today would find the pleasure of belonging and building up friendship in an environment that primarily focuses on learning and improving your homework. Well, that's why as the director, Mr. Allan, along with Ms. Lorraine, the assistant director, added some special features to HUL throughout the years. Not only does Help-U-Learn help students learn and excel in their homework, but now, with the help of some incredible volunteers, Help-U-Discover (HUD) and Devotion became an extended part of the after school life at HUL. HUD took place on certain days throughout the week, for students who finished their homework early and was on top of their assigned HUL worksheet packets. Sometimes HUD involved creating a delicious snack, or other times there were games and short TV episodes. Because of all these new additions, an award system was developed. It was altered each year, but the idea behind it was the same. You earn points through completing your worksheets, answering handouts of the HUD videos, or just participating.

And through all these bits and pieces that ornamented HUL's program, with the help of committed volunteers, HUL became a place where children belonged, a place where true friendship flourished. This was really what made HUL so unique from any other tutoring program.

Mr. Allen didn't really expect anyone to come, much less know what to expect. It was kind of a hit-or miss type of thing. There was something, he did hold on to. It was the hope of a faithful God, a good God who always loves us and provides for our best interest. It was the hope that if you "Delight yourself in the Lord, (and) He will give you the desires of your heart." (Psalm 37:4). This hope kept Mr. Allan going and with the help of Ms. Lorraine and a few others,

HUL officially began with the first 12 students and their families who came with a need that HUL was able to provide for. Within a few years, parents, teachers and everyone who came across HUL started to see the benefit that it was bringing to the children and families of the community. By word of mouth, news spread quickly and many more families came.

Parents began to develop a deeper trust in Mr. Allan as they saw he genuinely cared for them. Their hearts were opened to learn more about this God that Mr. Allan keeps bringing up. Mr. Allan actually cares, whether you're a cute 5 year-old or a "mature" teen about ready to start high school. He cares to the annoying extent that not only would he speak with your parents about your homework, but your behaviors, who you are, your life, and your potential in life. He not only stopped there but he would then talk to you about it, try his best to understand where you're coming from and somehow tie in a loving God with all of this. It sucked sometimes though, because punishment was involved and maybe, if you were disobedient enough, he'd ask you to stay and help clean up at the end of the day, or make you copy your handbook rules five times. Then he'd offer to drive you home, like a friend, and then give you a yummy snack.

Confusing sometimes, was he a friend or a foe? He somehow invaded your privacy and come into your home for a visit. You actually had to clean your room, for once. Not intimidating, but the idea of it certainly was. But you could tell through all this, Mr. Allan really did care. A lot!

Another vital part of HUL ministry was the parents. Alongside ministering to youth, Mr. Allan, Ms Lorraine, and other leaders within the church also had a passion and heart to reach parents as well.

With this concept in mind, the HUL Parent Ministry took root. Not as easy as it sounds though. The ministry took many years of good foundation building and a great deal of nurturing prayers. It started with mandatory parent meetings. But not too many parents showed up. So, what's another way—the leaders must have thought long and prayed hard—what is another way around this? Let's ring their doorbells— Ding Dong! Family visitations! These families were now generously offering food to these church-working guests, a cultural sign that signified acceptance. The relationship between the Church and the people got stronger. All these visitation volunteers reflected a different light of who the Church was into the lives of these parents. This change led to the birth of a small Bible study group for HUL parents who showed interest in coming. Mothers would invite other mothers, sometimes a father or two, it soon became Joy & Praise Fellowship which met once a month with a Christian group of adults known as Agape Unity Fellowship. Now the entire family was growing together.

Help-U-Learn has reached over 200 families in the past twelve years since it opened its door to the Sunset community. Within the HUL parent ministry, there were over 40 adults who were baptized. Looking back, we see that all Mr. Allen did was delight in the people that God's heart chased after, the people that God so willingly sacrificed His Son for. God gave him what he desired, to not only imprint a physical influence on people, but an eternal one as well. Through his obedience to God's calling in his life, we are reminded that God is the Supreme Planner of our lives.

To Mr. Allan, for the many lives you've changed, taught and inspired, thanks for being faithful to God's calling to start a HUL ministry that serves as a continuing irrigation system of Living Water to so many lives in the desert of a broken world! And last, but not least, thanks to the prettiest and most supportive woman behind the successful Mr. Allan Tong, his wife, Jennifer Tong!

Chinese Language School

Bringing Christ to the Chinese

Lutheran Hour Convention

'SHE'S A DOLL' --- President Thomas D. McDougall accepts a special Lutheran Hour Chinese doll from 6-year-old Suanne Yorn a real "doll." Suanne made a big hit when she opened The Lutheran Hour report to the convention with a mighty clang on a Chinese gong.

New Ministries   Chapter Thirteen

DCE Allen talking at the HUL Graduation

HUL; Help U Learn

HUL Graduation

"For God so loved the world that He gave his only Son, that whoever believes in Him should not perish but have eternal life"

John 3:16 RSV

Rev. Ching Ching Wang

Deaconess Carol Lee Halter

Chapter Fourteen

New Co-Workers
Deaconess Carol Lee Halter Joins The Staff

In November, 1969, a young deaconess, who had served in Hong Kong at Rennie's Mill Village with Deaconess Martha Boss for four years, joined the staff at Holy Spirit Church. She was energetic and a multi-talented worker. She spoke Cantonese and enjoyed teaching the Word to young people. She establish the first English speaking youth group, directed their choir, visited Laguna Honda Hospital Chinese patients with the young people, and took the young people to witness in the parks. She served at Holy Spirit for eleven years before being commissioned a Missionary to Hong Kong in 1981, where she is still serving today. She was unique in that she accepted only a very small allowance during the years she served here. Her board and room was provided by members of the congregation, Eddie and Jean Lee.

Carol Remembers the Early Years

Whenever I think of Pastor Holt, I think of his "serendipity" personality. He was willing to try almost anything that might be of benefit for the proclamation of the Gospel. Just about whatever way anyone might propose to proclaim the Gospel, he was 100% behind it. We covered the whole area of the church with leaflets in English and Chinese inviting people to our worship services. Eddie and Jean Lee heard about the church and came after they received one of these leaflets. For days we set up telephones in the downstairs of the church and telephoned all the Chinese people in the whole area of the church proclaiming the Gospel to them and inviting them to church. From Monday to Friday there was a Chinese school with Amy as the principal. This was an excellent outreach for the students as well as the parents. Each Thursday afternoon I took some of the young people to witness to the children in the local Chinese park. Once a month on Saturday we went to Laguna Honda to bring the English-speaking people to the worship service held by Pastor Riche. For the Chinese people we had a special get-together with Chinese snacks and a proclamation of the Gospel.

Any time there were any events within an hour or so distance from the church, Pastor Holt would be happy to get a group together to attend. Such programs included The Institute for Basic Youth Conflicts, Child Evangelism Fellowship Training, Billy Graham Crusades, etc. On Saturdays everyone pitched in and helped clean the church so that we never had to hire any janitors. Under his leadership, the church was always lively and serving—an excellent example of what a church should be.

Another thing which I appreciated so much about Pastor Holt was his desire always to share the Word of God. No matter what was going on, he wanted to find out what the Word of God said about that problem or matter. And of course when I think of him and his family I always am moved by the generosity of them all. When I first came to the church, his family let me stay with them and share all their meals with them. This was quite a sacrifice on their part since Pastor and Mrs. Holt had 5 sons still at home. I am so thankful to God for the eleven years I was able to serve with Pastor Holt and Amy at the Lutheran Church of the Holy Spirit. May God proclaim His Gospel to even more and more Chinese people as this lovely church continues to be a shining light in San Francisco.

Rev. Ching Ching Wang
Stand Up, Stand Up, For Jesus

In January of 1971, a very cheerful elderly Chinese man, who reminded one of a monk in appearance, came to join the staff at Holy Spirit. He was a very quiet man, who loved nature. He grew up in a Buddhist home, but came to know Jesus as his Savior when he heard a message from a Norwegian Missionary, Dr. K.L. Reichelt. Pastor Wang was the former head of the Christian Mission to the Buddhists in Shatin, Hong Kong for 37 years. His pastoral cross was a Cross on the Lotus, taken from Job 14:4 and I John 1:7.

At his church in Tao Fong Shan, Shatin, Hong Kong, he artistically designed the church and other buildings, high on top of the mountains in Shatin, New Territories, long before real estate developers found the area. He used Chinese art and Lutheran theology to design this exquisite church. There was a narrow gate to the garden area—depicting the words in Matt.7:13, " Narrow is the gate and the way is hard, that leads to life, and those who find it are few." A Thanksgiving Pavilion is in the sacred garden. A School of Religion and small figures on the roof of the temple symbolizes pilgrims who came here to study and then gone out in all directions to bring the Gospel of Jesus to others.

A huge cross, standing on top of the mountain at Tao Fong Shan, can still be seen today from far off China, as it points the way to Christianity for many people. Many monks from the Buddhist temple at the foot of the mountain found there way up the mountain to Toa Fong Shan and became Christians. Many are serving as Christian pastors today in Canada, the United States and other countries.

In order to support these new Christians, Pastor Wang established a porcelain shop. They painted many pictures on porcelain plates, vases and bowls from Bible stories, "Woman at the Well", "Jesus and Little Children", "Jesus washing the disciples feet", a total of 12 pictures were painted and put into book form for a reference. This book is in the archives of Lutheran Church of the Holy Spirit. When he retired, he came to visit his daughter in Minnesota, but feeling he had much talent left and wanting to use it for the Lord's work among Chinese, he came to San Francisco. He was fluent in Mandarin, spoke some Cantonese and English.

He was a talented artist and writer. During the time spent at Holy Spirit church Pastor Wang painted 8 murals on the church walls. Some are shown in this book, and pictures are kept in the Church archives since the murals were destroyed when the Washington street church was sold and torn down.

Pastor Wang also accompanied the LWML ladies to Laguna Honda Hospital where he held a monthly Chinese worship service for the Chinese patients and brought a message of hope to these patients, using a Cantonese interpreter from the church. In December, 1981 there were 4 Chinese patients baptized and 13 patients took Holy Communion. He prepared many Chinese evangelistic brochures for the church. The ministry at Laguna Honda Hospital resulted in a Chinese congregation of 20 baptized people.

He was helpful in senior activities in the

City as well as the church. On December 24, 1984 Pastor Wang celebrated his 75th birthday with a dinner given by the church and attended by many members of his family from far away. The church gave him a special celebration on December 21st, 1986 for his 50th year in the Ministry. Pastor Wang passed away on Dec 15th, 1996. A Memorial Service was held in the church on December 29, 1996 giving thanks to God for this dedicated servant of the Word.

My Father—Ching Ching Wang
Maria Wang Rantapaa

My father Pastor C.C. Wang was born in a small village of Pai-tou, Anhui Province, China, December 14, 1908. Everybody in the village was named Wang. His father was a Buddhist who also took care of the village temple. He had two younger brothers. His sister was a Buddhist nun who died by self-immolation.

He wrote in his diary steadily since 1927. In 1927, he received his medical (nurses'?) training in an army hospital in a city near Shanghai. He wrote about treating the wounded soldiers, what terrible sufferings and pain he saw in them. At that time, Japan had already invaded China!

May 28th, 1927 he wrote, "I got up extra early, enjoyed the exhilarating fresh air. I am thinking about my parents and my brothers. I attended church once. It was a happy experience! We sang hymns and studied the Bible. I plan to continue studying this religion."

January 18th, 1928 he wrote "Bought a BIG Book "Meaning of Life" for $1. He wrote extensive notes about contents of this book! Finally he finished studying the book on January 25th. There were lengthy notes on other books or subjects such as the revolutions in major countries of the world.

October 11, 1928 is the first time he mentioned Li-feng Luk. (My mother's maiden name)

They were married Oct 10, 1930 near the city of Wuhu where he was stationed. My father was the first Chinese pastor ordained in the Scandinavian Christian Mission to the Buddhists..

Tao Fong Shan was a rural area about 15 miles inland towards China from Hong Kong island. There he built the church and Christian Mission to the Buddhists campus with classrooms and dormitory and dining rooms etc. So I was brought up in a very unique environment. Most of the children I grew up with were the Scandinavian missionaries' children. I am still in touch with Dr. Reichelt's grand children who are living in Norway today.

On June 10, 1938 our entire family went to Peking for a couple years while my father was taking some classes at the theological seminary. On the way back to Hong Kong on January 23, 1940, my father stopped by his old home and invited his parents to come and join us to live in Hong Kong. I remember my grandparents diligently studied the Bible and later became Christians.

December 1941 was the beginning of WWII. The Japanese bombed Hong Kong.

The next four years were very difficult because of hunger and poverty. We raised a few chickens, rabbits, and a pig but this was not enough. At one time, in desperation, my father cooked a rat but told us first it was rabbit! Later he confessed it was rat. None of us children had any formal schooling. We spent much of our day roaming the hills nearby looking for berries or anything edible. My parents tried to teach us some basics of reading and writing. I remember that my father often told about interesting historic events and stories of famous people during mealtimes. Many times we were stricken with severe illnesses. It was truly Gods' blessing that we were spared from death!

My father was a man of deep faith. He always quoted Bible verses to us. When he encountered serious situations, he would often go to the Lotus Crypt and pray. The Lotus Crypt was a small, all enclosed by rocks, place of meditation and prayer, built under the Tao Fong Shan Temple. It has a colorful window of the cross and the lotus. It was a favorite place of prayer for many people.

My father's faith was manifested in his daily life. He loved the Lord. He loved to paint, make art pieces and art sculptures. I remember many times when I had serious illness or injury; he would always put his hand on my forehead and pray for me. It really gave me much comfort.

On December 1st, 1948 all people from Luther Seminary in Peking escaped from Communist China. About 60 people moved to Hong Kong. Tao Fong Shan offered them facilities for their seminary campus. Since the Japanese war and the Communist civil war drastically changed the original mission to the Buddhists, most of the Scandinavian missionaries returned to their home countries by 1969. Tao Fong Shan became a small community of members who supported themselves mostly by means of a porcelain shop where they made Chinese style art depicting incidents from the Gospels. These were sold to tourists to Tao Fong Shan and handicraft stores in Hong Kong.

My mother visited my family in Minnesota in 1968. We also invited my father to join us. He came to St. Paul March 19, 1970. Life in Minnesota was not very suitable for my father because the family members were all very busy working. I had classes of piano students and my husband, Larry taught in a high school. At that time the Chinese community in Minneapolis-St. Paul was small and scattered so it was difficult to find a compatible group or church to associate with. Missionaries and family friends from Tao Fong Shan. Former missionary Cora Martinson, suggested he could do more church work in San Francisco. So he moved to California in 1972.

I feel my father was happy with his decision to go to San Francisco even though it meant he was apart from his own family. We were very thankful that Pastor Holt and family received my father as their own family.

1988 Dec. 14th was my Dad's 80th birthday. Our whole family, Larry & myself, Erik and Aaron, as well as my brother Sam and his wife Linda all attended the celebration at San Francisco. In fact, many of his old friends came too. Mr. Ko from Canada, and my uncle Dr. Joshua Wang, Pastor Jing from Modesto and Pastor Kao from the Bay Area. From my father's diary, this celebration was organized by his very special friend from church Mrs. Jean Lee. A special slide show was prepared demonstrating my father's work in San Francisco. Pastor Holt gave a talk about my father's art work at the church. It was a very memorable event indeed.! After a long illness, my father passed away in San Francisco on December 15, 1996.

One of Pastor Wang's Favorite Bible Verses—Psalms 121: 1–2 "I lift up my eyes to the hills, from whence does my help come? My help comes from the Lord, who made heaven and earth."

Pastor Wang Was My Friend
Peter K.S. Lee

I met Pastor Wang between 1971 and 1972 at the Holy Spirit Church in San Francisco. My first impression was that he was a calm and modest gentleman. As I got to know him better, I found he was very intelligent, well versed in Chinese philosophy, and extremely talented, especially in Chinese painting and pottery. Despite my limited awareness and talent in these subjects, he never lost confidence in me but continued to nourish me with his wisdom and knowledge.

I enjoyed spending endless hours discussing and learning about these subjects from him. It was through these discussions, I discovered that he had an awesome capacity for connecting the excellent ideas of various ancient Chinese philosophies and Buddhism with the injection of the salvation of Christianity. As always, he reminded me all the time that all these great philosophies could not lead us to eternal life unless we believed in Jesus Christ as our Savior. To him, this was the clever approach to reach the masses of Chinese and lead them to salvation in HIM.

I also missed the many happy hours I spent with Pastor Wang. Every time I was in the Bay Area, we made sure to visit him. He always brought joy and blessings to our gatherings. Sometimes he would be like a little child updating us about his projects with the Senior Center or other places. In his final couple of years, it was quite agonizing for me to say good bye after we visited him. I could almost touch the sadness in his eyes. He seemed to have sensed that it could be the last time we would see one another. I will always remember his parting words…"love your wife". Pastor Wang taught me a simple way to be a good husband. What a noble assignment Pastor Wang has given me! To me, Pastor Wang will forever be an amazingly uncomplicated and unassuming servant of God and most of all, a good friend and teacher to me and my family. Veronica and I miss him very much.Ca

Carol at Rennie's Mill Hong Kong

Martha Boss and Carol at
Rennie's Mill Hong Kong

Carol and Martha

Carol's Park Ministry

Commissioned 8/01/1981
Shown with "Dad" Eddie Lee

Geri Holt and Carol

Rev Wang and Carol

New Co-Workers   Chapter Fourteen

Meet a Lutheran sister

Chow Shuk-Ching
Chinese Christian in Hong Kong

by Carol Lee Halter

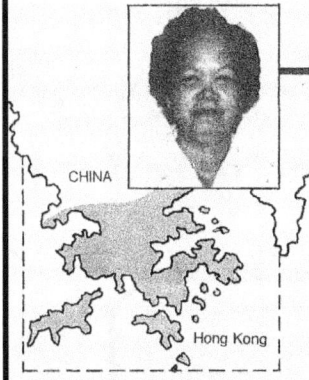

Chinese women often do not use their husband's last name. Their last name is said first and then their first name. Our sister from Hong Kong is Mrs. Chan. Her family name is Chow, and her first name is Shuk-Ching. We lovingly refer to her as "Sister Chow" and that is what she likes to have people call her too.

When Chow Shuk-Ching was 17 years old she resolved to eat no meat, for then the gods would be pleased and would protect her. When she wanted to know her future she went to the Chinese temple and shook a can of sticks up and down until one fell out. She then took it to a man who told her the future written for that stick. Sometimes her future looked bright and sometimes it looked dreadful. When she wanted a favor of the gods she burned incense and offered food to them.

Does this sound like the same person who last year, at the age of 50, had a special worship service to thank the Triune God for making her well after she had been sick? Does this sound like the same lady who, despite having only one lung, climbs seven flights of stairs to visit her friends and tell them about Jesus? Does this sound like the Chow Shuk-Ching who tells her teen-age children to pray to the true God every time they have a problem? How could such a dramatic change have taken place?

In China, Chow Shuk-Ching at 18 was married to a young man her parents had selected for her. As was custom, she had nothing to say about whom she would like to marry. A year later she gave birth to a son. In her culture this was considered much better than to have a daughter and was a great joy. But alas, in five months he died of a respiratory problem. Three years later she left China and came to Hong Kong where she had a second child, a girl. But again her joy was short-lived, for a year later her daughter died of an intestinal sickness.

Life was very difficult for Chow Shuk-Ching in Hong Kong. Sometimes she tried to help her husband make a living by squatting down on the street and selling underwear or facecloths spread out on a sheet on the ground. She did embroidery work twelve hours a day for 15–30¢.

All this time she refrained from eating any meat in the hope that the gods would favor her. She continued to use some of her hard-earned money to offer them incense. How could it be that one so conscientious could get the dreaded disease tuberculosis? She did not yet realize that her false gods *"have mouths, but do not speak; eyes, but do not see. They have ears, but they do not hear . . . ."* (Psalm 115:5–6)

In a t.b. sanatorium Chow Shuk-Ching had to have complete bed rest for seven months. Then she had to wait another year and a half—not just for her body to be stronger, but for room in a hospital so that she could have one of her diseased lungs removed. After this there was more time needed for recovery. To be three and a half years in the hospital surely was not easy.

But the Lord was looking down upon Shuk-Ching in love. It was a Christian sanatorium called the Haven of Hope to which she was sent. And it was there that she heard about a God who had loved her all of her life. She came to faith in the One who died for her sins. She learned that He doesn't want burnt sacrifices but rather our lives as a living sacrifice to Him.

When she was a little girl, Shuk-Ching's schooling had been very sporadic. Her mother needed her to help sell noodles to earn money for the family. Besides, it wasn't the custom for girls to get much education—only boys. Now she longed to read the Bible for herself. Every morning and evening when the head nurse came into the ward Chow Shuk-Ching listened to the Word of God very carefully and tried to follow in a Chinese Bible. When she didn't know some of the complicated characters she asked patients or nurses or anyone she could find to tell her what they said. And when she finally got out of the hospital she could read the Bible for herself.

The Bible says, *"If any one is in Christ, he is a new creation; the old has passed away, behold all has become new."* (2 Cor. 5:17) Now in her 30's, Chow Shuk-Ching's life had begun anew. There was no need to go to the hot, smoke-filled temple to burn incense to appease the gods anymore, because now she had the God above all gods as her good Friend. She was content and happy.

But the Bible also says, *"He who did not spare His own Son, but gave Him up for us all, will He not also give us all things with Him?"* (Romans 8:32) And give He did! A year and a half out of the hospital Chow Shuk-Ching gave birth to a precious little girl whom she named Grace. Three years later she had a son. His name? Adam. More than that! One year later she was able to lead her 65-year-old idol worshipping, superstitious mother to the Lord. After two years the Holy Spirit melted her husband's heart so that he too came to Christ.

And others too! For "Sister Chow" did not forget the Haven of Hope t.b. sanatorium where she came to know the Lord. Even though it is a long trip, she still goes back there to tell other patients about the holy, all-merciful, one true God. She tells everyone she sees, "God loves you. God cares for you. You don't need to do anything to win His favor. He will lead you through all the rough places in your life and bless you on the way. And at the end of this life, through Jesus Christ, He will take you to heaven."

God tells us in Isaiah 55:11 *"My word that goes forth from my mouth shall not return to me empty, but shall accomplish that which I purpose and prosper in the thing for which I sent it."* God has fulfilled His promise in the life of Chow Shuk-Ching and in the lives of many others with whom she shares the word of God. To God be all the glory!

Carol Lee Halter is in charge of the deaconess training program at Concordia Seminary in Hong Kong. Besides her teaching duties she holds weekend seminars on evangelism, Sunday school teaching and youth leadership in the various Hong Kong Lutheran churches.

Lutheran Woman's Quarterly — Spring 1984

Amy, Pastor and Carol

Bringing Christ to the Chinese

LCMS WORLD MISSION

Hong Kong street sleepers come to faith

LCMS Missionary Deaconess Carol Halter trains Hong Kong Christians to reach out to "street sleepers," people who regularly spend nights on the streets, often in carefully marked-out personal spots. Halter estimates that there are over 2000 street sleepers in Hong Kong. About half are registered with the government and receive welfare stipends. Many are involved in alcohol or drug abuse, while others have been abandoned by their families. Almost all are men.

Halter's trainees include youth, seminary students, members of the Lutheran Church—Hong Kong Synod and a few street sleepers themselves. Each Monday night, about 25 people form teams and go out to visit and witness to 80 to 100 street sleepers. Their "regulars" stay at their sleeping places to meet them. More than 20 other street sleepers wait together in a local park. If there is time, the Christians visit new street sleepers.

Periodically, a bus from the Church of All Nations brings the street sleepers to the church's facilities for a chance to receive a good meal and enjoy some entertainment provided especially for them. They also attend a worship service and Bible class.

Halter says that about 70 to 80 percent of the street sleepers with whom her trainees work have already come to faith in Christ. Some even share the Gospel with other street sleepers! One of Halter's evangelism trainees amazes her. Normally people can't understand him when he talks because of his mental and physical condition, but he communicates clearly when he witnesses to fellow street sleepers.

Lutheran Deaconess Association

VALPARAISO, INDIANA 46383   SUMMER 1977

Chinatown, San Francisco

Dear Louise,

You asked for a personal statement regarding my ministry, and I guess the best way is just to write a personal letter to you.

Our congregation is composed mainly of teen-agers and those in their early twenties, so the weekends are the busiest. We have two youth groups on Friday nights, one Saturday morning, two on Saturday afternoon, and one on Sunday afternoon.

On a typical Saturday I drive our church bus to meet the young people in Chinatown at 8 a.m. From there we go to the

Deaconess Carol Halter tutors a Chinese student

Laguna Honda Hospital. After practicing singing, we divide into two groups. One group gathers the non-Chinese patients from all over the hospital for a worship service led by the local chaplain.

The rest of the young people gather the Chinese patients to listen to the "Lutheran Hour" in Chinese tapes.

In the afternoon two youth groups meet for Bible study, singing, and cleaning around the church. (We have no paid janitor and about 50 youth volunteer their services as their way of serving the Lord.)

On Saturday nights we have groups who come from other churches to share a Chinese meal at our church. Often 50 to 100 people come from sister Lutheran churches to hear about the mission work here. We give the proceeds to world hunger.

Each day from 4:30 to 6:00 p.m. we have Chinese school at our church. Here the children, coming from their regular English-speaking day school, learn how to read and write the Chinese language. Most of them learn to speak Chinese at home, but they have no one to teach them to read and write.

Through this Chinese school we can teach the children the way of salvation through Christ and also gain an entrance to their homes to reach their parents.

In our ministry here we try to prepare young people to be strong in the Lord so they can, in turn, bring more people to know the Lord Jesus. As a result of all this work, each Christmas about 25 to 30 are baptized.

When we speak to others about Christ's love, of course, we're also ready to show this love. We might get involved in translating for someone when they go to the doctor or in helping them move with our church van.

Sometimes people long for a little Chinese food in the hospital. At other times they need someone who can speak English to talk to the nurse or doctor.

My time at Valpo was a time of learning to serve — a time of learning to love. After being a deaconess for 12 years, I still

Deaconess Carol Halter meets with group of Chinese young people at Church of the Holy Spirit in San Francisco.

delight in telling people about "the good old days" when I was back at Valpo.

May the Lord bless you in your important work of training young women to love one another and to dedicate their lives in service to our Lord and Master.

All glory to Him for His wonderful love and forgiveness in Christ Jesus.

May He continue to enlighten us as to how to do this best and empower us to do so in His strength.

With love in Christ,

Deaconess Carol Lee Halter
Lutheran Church of the Holy Spirit
San Francisco, California

New Co-Workers   Chapter Fourteen

Geri, Pastor Holt, Pastor Wang and Carol

LWML Ladies at Laguna Honda

C.C. Wang

Pastor Wang and Family

The Master at work

Pastor Wang, Family and Friends

New Co-Workers   Chapter Fourteen

Good Reason to move to San Francisco

Celebrating Pastor Wang's Birthday

Friends in Park

Pastor Wang's Gethsemane

The Prodigal Son Banquet

Disciples Asleep

New Co-Workers   Chapter Fourteen

Toa Fong Shao now in Church Archives

Pastor Wang's Altar at Church in Tao Fong Shan

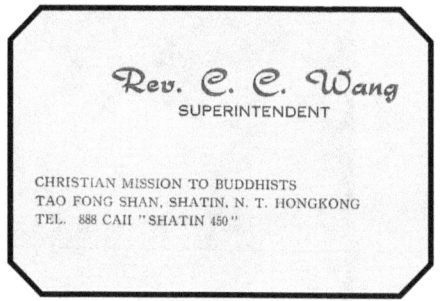

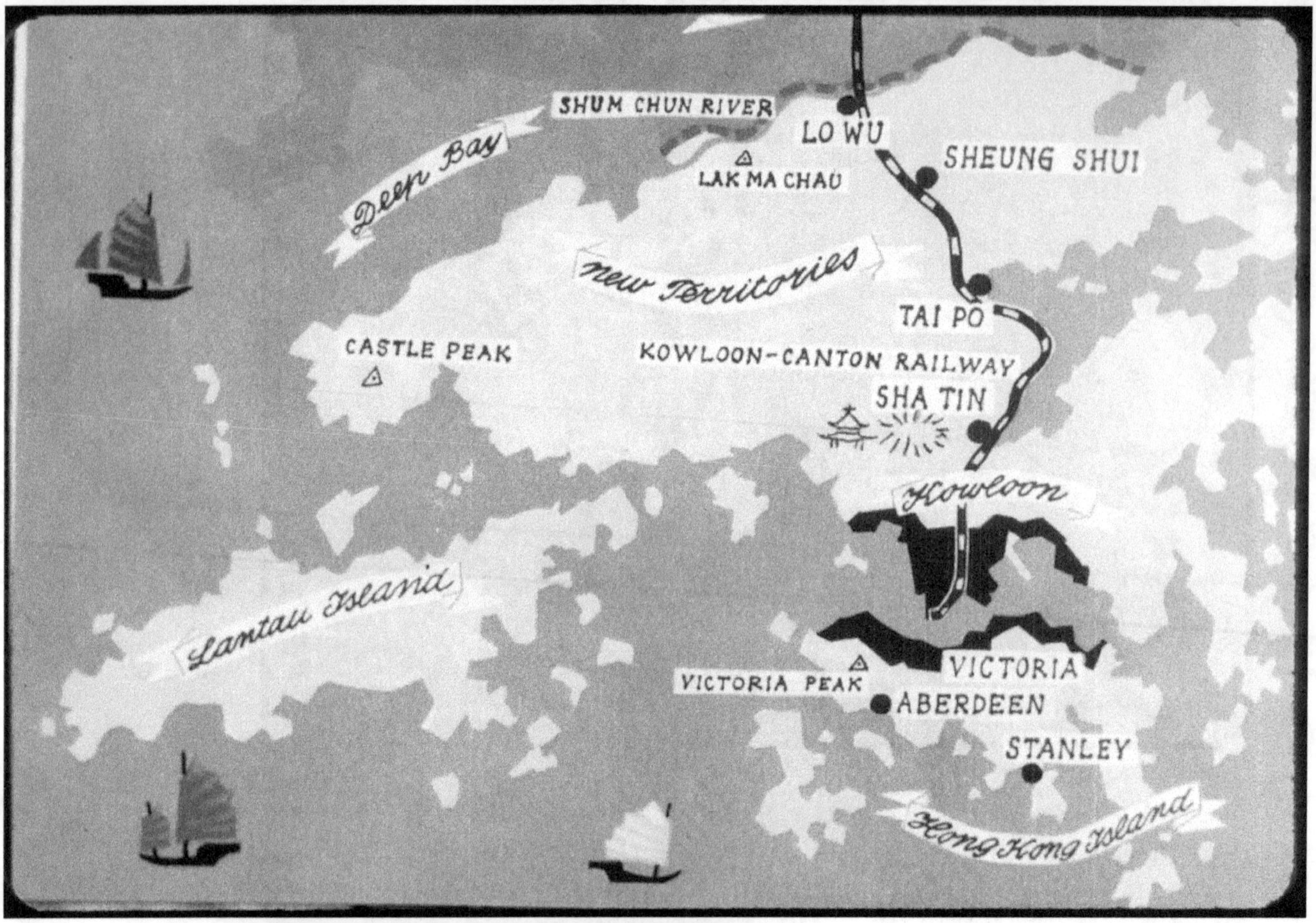

Tao Fong Shan

New Co-Workers   Chapter Fourteen

Congregation before Chapel

It Is Finished

Easter Garden

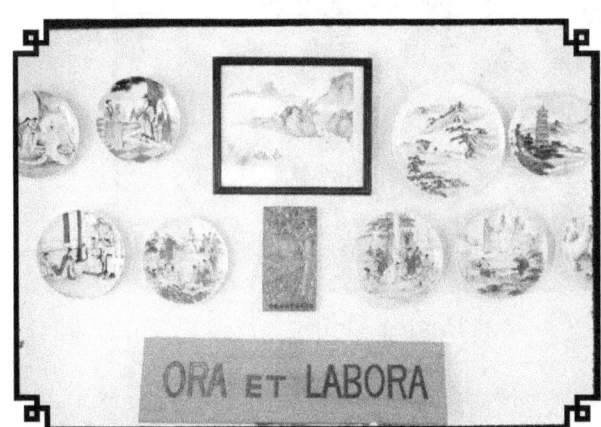

Bringing Christ to the Chinese

Congregation by Cross

In Library

Out Door Service

Lotus Crypt at Toa Fong Shan

Pastor Wang

New Co-Workers   Chapter Fourteen

Porcelain Shop At TaoFong Shan

Ah-Mah Rocks

School of Religion

Stained Glass Window

Signs in The Church

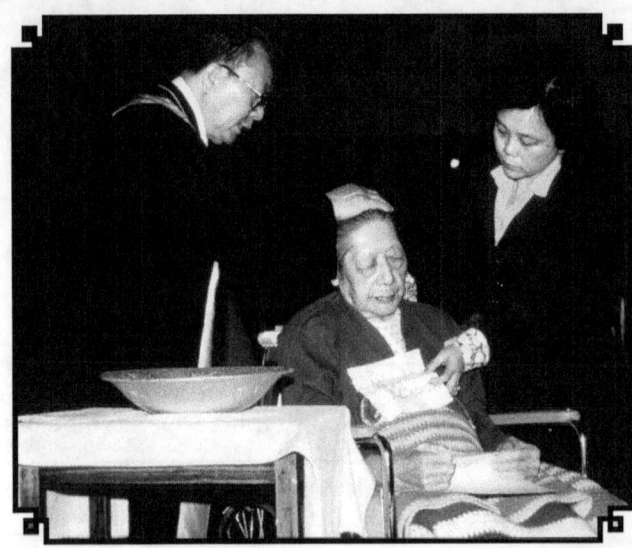
Baptism at Laguna Honda

Baptism

At Laguna Honda

Book written by Rev. C.C. Wang

New Co-Workers   Chapter Fourteen

The Presentation of Pastor Wang's Painting

Pastor Wang with Procelain Vase

Pastor Wang preaching at Laguna Honda Hospital

"And all these blessings shall come upon you and overtake you, if you obey the voice of the Lord your God"

Deut. 28:2 RSV

40th Anniversary of Pastor and Mrs. Holt's Ministry

Chapter Fifteen

Twenty Years of God's Blessings

At the gala banquet celebration, Pastor Holt shared the following thoughts and vision: During the past 20 years, 540 persons received God's salvation through baptism. The average Sunday worship attendance was 250 people. The Chinese are the most numerous race in the world. Our congregation has trained many to bring the Gospel to Chinese people. The church needs to expand her work. Every Christian should learn to see his part in the mission of the church.

Our congregation has the following plans for new work:

1. **Work in The Sunset District**. West Portal has generously given us permission to use their Moraga campus on 37th Avenue and Moraga, without charge, to extend Chinese work in the Sunset District. Many Chinese live in that area. We started a Chinese language school there in July 1984. Now we have 10 teachers teaching 60 students. The goal is to bring the Gospel to them and to their parents.

2. **English Language School**. Many Chinese immigrate to the United States everyday. One of their immediate needs is to learn English. Therefore, we have started a free English language school. The goal is also to bring the Gospel to them. We have 10 teachers teaching over 40 students.

3. **Mission—Promotion Center**. We hope our congregation will become a Chinese mission-promoting center. Since we have so many well-trained Christians ready to do His work, we can help other congregations to start their Chinese ministry. If the congregation stops reaching out with the Gospel, she has lost her reason for existence!

You might ask, "What can I do?" Every Christian can participate in one or more of the following: Pray for the outreach to the Chinese people. Support the outreach with your offerings. Actively participate in the work. Support the outreach by encouraging those who are participating. Consider becoming a church worker yourself, even though you may be an employed person. Just think if every Christian tells ten persons about Jesus, every person in the whole world would hear the Gospel. The Gospel of Christ is the only way of salvation in the whole universe! Reach out to the lost now!

Special Characteristics of this Congregation

Pastor Wilbert Holt wrote the following on the Twentieth Anniversary of the church, about the special characteristics of the Lutheran Church of the Holy Spirit and what it means to be a Lutheran.

Holy Spirit congregation is predominantly a *youthful* congregation, made up of members most of who were converted to the Lord in their teens or early twenties. The median age is 24. Because almost all members are converts, there is a strong desire to share their faith with others. The Holy Spirit has given the staff and the members of the congregation a spirit of **unity**.

Although some members came from South East Asia and some were born in the United States, their members have a strong feeling that the church is one and that the ministry of the Gospel is their joint responsibility. The Holy Spirit has worked in the **Fellowship Groups and Couple Groups** to help over 200 members to grow in their relationship with the Lord and with other Christians, and together to reach out to others with the Gospel. Many people have been converted through fellowship activities.

The Holy Spirit has given the staff and many members recognition of the importance of **Personal Evangelism and Personal Discipleship**. Often when people come to worship or attend fellowship meetings, their personal questions may not be answered, and their personal needs may not be met. Therefore it is important to spend time to help individuals to know Christ personally and to grow in Him.

The Holy Spirit has given the members a spirit **Willing to Serve**. When each person learns to serve, he learns to appreciate the church more.

The Holy Spirit has given to many members the **Willingness to Give**. Many of the members use one tenth of their income as a starting point in their offering to the Lord.

The Holy Spirit has given many members a strong desire to read, to study, and to follow the BIBLE. The Word of God gives motivation and power for faith Christian living.

The Holy Spirit has given this congregation a core of people who support the church by praying faithfully. "The prayer of a righteous man has great power in its effect." (James. 5:16) This congregation believes that we have the responsibility to be **Totally Loyal** to the Lord Jesus Christ and everything He taught us.

"You shall not add to the word which I command you, nor take from it". (Dt. 4:2) St Paul told Timothy to "charge certain persons not to teach any different doctrine". (1 Tim. 1:3) 1977 The Chinese Mission, Lutheran Church of the Holy Spirit, became self-supporting. All Glory to God!

Twenty Years of God's Blessings   Chapter Fifteen

"Let my prayer be counted as incense before thee; and the lifting up of my hands as an evening sacrifice"

Ps. 141:2 RSV

DCE Patty Lee

Chapter Sixteen

The Church Grew 1980-1990

In February 1981 Patty Lee joined the church staff as a called worker. She was a very creative, cooperative person to whom the Spirit of God had given a very caring spirit, the ability to help others in a most practical way. She was a graduate of the Director of Christian Education program of Concordia College, Portland, Oregon. She worked very effectively among the youth groups and the English tutoring class. She taught in the Chinese language school at Holy Spirit congregation and also formed about 20 Vietnam Chinese into a fellowship at Pilgrim Lutheran Church in Oakland, California. She left Holy Spirit congregation to pursue work toward a teaching credential.

There Were Many Firsts In The Next 10 Years

In 1980 A 'first', the calling of Concordia student Timothy Yip to be the first vicar.
In 1981 we said goodbye to Deaconess Carol Lee Halter as she was commissioned a Missionary to Hong Kong. Her departure left a great void in the English Ministry.

Easter—12 persons were baptized.

Thanksgiving—four persons baptized and 30 persons confirmed.

At Laguna Honda hospital, Pastor Wang baptized 4 persons and 13 persons received Holy Communion.
A son of our church, Patrick Jow, a graduate of Irvine College, interned at Holy Spirit Lutheran and Pilgrim Lutheran Church, Oakland for 1 ½ years.

Life at Holy Spirit in 1982 was busy with visits to Laguna Honda Hospital once a month by the ladies and young people.

100 young people had a retreat at Santa Cruz church.

The Voters Assembly discussed calling a pastor, later they issued a call to Timothy Yip who had served as a vicar to our congregation. November 14th he accepted the call. Christmas time—eight persons baptized and eight persons confirmed.
In 1983 Pastor Holt greeted all and encouraged everyone to read the Bible through in 1983. Bible reading schedules were passed out.

January 16th, 1983 Seminarian Timothy Yip was ordained and installed at our church as Assistant Pastor and Mission Enabler.

May 22, 1983, Pentecost Sunday—six persons baptized.

July 1983 the congregation gave $95,000 to Synod's Forward in Remembrance, over $70 Million was collected nationwide.

September 11th, our first Chinese Language school opened with 27 pupils. Amy Mui was the principle of the school.

November, Love Loaves were passed out to collect for World Hunger.
December–Pastor C C Wang's 75th birthday

was celebrated.

Christmas Day—17 baptisms and 20 confirmations. Again, we thanked the Spirit for working among us.

Each year gets busier and more exciting.
April, 1984 West Portal Lutheran Church approved use of Moraga Campus for our Chinese Language School. This was an added blessing because many young families now live in the Sunset area..

In September Faith and Unity Fellowships held retreats in San Rafael and Santa Cruz, using local churches as their retreats.

A legal question arose at the September Voter's Assembly, "Do we want to be a Non Profit Corporation?" The vote was yes! Pastor Holt always required a unanimous vote for issues to be passed.

October 24th, 1984—Incorporation Articles of the Lutheran Church of the Holy Spirit were filed on with the State of California, signed by Edward K. Yee, President and Patty Lee, Recording Secretary.

November,1984—a special Thanksgiving program commemorating the 20th Anniversary of the founding of our church!
Christmas worship—nine persons baptized. Praise the Lord for a busy year of growth and progress!

1985

May 19, 1985 the congregation gave Pastor Holt a surprise dinner and appreciation for his 40th year in the ministry. It was held at the Dunfrey Hotel in San Mateo. The CNH District presented him with a special certificate honoring the occasion.

July 18, 1985 the State of California, March Fong Eu, Secretary of State, issued Articles of Incorporation # 361442, dated July 12, 1985 to the Lutheran Church of the Holy Spirit.

September, 1985 there was sadness among us as we learned our faithful bus driver, Cliff Wright, passed away. Our big blue bus was garaged in San Rafael, across the Golden Gate bridge and Mr. Wright would go early on Sunday mornings to pick up the bus, drive it on a route in the Sunset and Richmond districts to pick up congregation members for Sunday school and services at Washington street church. He would then take them home and return the bus to the garage in San Rafael.

September—Mid Autumn Festival with Evangelistic outreach was held. We thanked God for the 50 non-Christians who attended the service. Thanksgiving time the congregation gave $10,079 to World Hunger.

December the LWML women's group gave a large altar screen to the congregation.

It was thought fellowship groups had outgrown their names. The Young Disciples had become high school and even college age students. The Senior and Junior Youth members were no longer senior and junior high students, but had become college student or graduates. The names of the fruit of the Holy Spirit were chosen to be the names of the fellowship groups: Unity, Faith, Agape, Joy, Praise and Hope. We pray the fruits of the Holy Spirit will abound in the life of every member.

1986 is here!

Pastor Holt again encouraged members to be faithful in studying the Bible daily during the New Year. March 1986 there was a special offering for the Mid West Flood Victims. Our member, Mrs. How Yuk Hau, gave $10,000 to this fund. Our members knew how to give generously because God had graciously blessed them!

Easter Sunday—five persons baptized.
April we had some structural problems with the church building and during repairs we worshiped on April 11 & April 18 at the Zion Lutheran Church on 9th Avenue in the Richmond district.

June 1986, a celebration was held when Rev.

The Church Grew 1980-1990   Chapter Sixteen

Patrick Jow, a son of this congregation, was ordained in our church. He was installed in a Lutheran Church in Alhambra, California on August 31, 1986.

In December 1986 the congregation celebrated Pastor C.C. Wang's 50th year in the ministry.

1987—A New Year

Pastor Holt encouraged the congregation to resolve to have quality time for meditation and prayer.

February plans for construction at 3830 Noriega street were revealed.

March 22, 1987 a sign was put up at 3830 Noriega identifying the building as Lutheran Church of the Holy Spirit.

May 26, 1987 the city approved plans for remodeling 3830 Noriega and it became officially our church extension. Building pledges have reached $100,000. This is the 1st phase of pledges.

June 7th Pentecost Sunday—9 persons baptized.

June 1987 as the church grew, there was a need for an English speaking ladies group. Love in Action was formed as an LWML society with election of officers. Geri Holt and Jean Lee were appointed by Pastor Holt as advisers to this group. July, 1987 a member, Eddie J Lee, gave $3001 to World Hunger.

September 1987, in a Voter's Assembly, the congregation voted to call Vicar Terrence Chan as assistant pastor. He accepted the call and was ordained and installed on October 25, 1987. Rev. Chan is a "son" of this congregation.

Praise be to the Lord, November pledges for building at 3830 Noriega Street reached $228,000. December 20th a ground breaking ceremony was held at the 3830 Noriega building.

The congregation gave $9000 to World Hunger. Christmas Worship—14 baptisms and 11 persons confirmed.

1988 was another busy year with the ministry becoming an outreach to the Sunset area of San Francisco.

February Pastor and Mrs. Holt took a trip to the Holy Land given by the congregation.

April 10, 1988 the Extension Church at 3830 Noriega Street was dedicated.

Lutheran Lay Ministry began meeting at the Extension church on April 13, 1988, Rev. Fred Stennfeld and other pastors were instructors and 44 persons attended.

April 28, 1988 Love in Action received its charter from LWML District Office.

With plans to return to a teaching career in Hong Kong, Pastor Timothy Yip preached his farewell sermon on May 15, 1988.

May 15, 1988—Five ladies were confirmed.

On May 29th, 1988 the first Chinese Worship service was held at the 3830 Noriega Extension church. 33 persons attended, over half were newcomers.

September 10, 1988 the Chinese Language School began with 146 students and 17 teachers.

A Moon Festival celebration was held on Sep 24, 1988 at the Sunset Extension.

September 21, 1988—A fall session of Lutheran Lay Ministry began with 45 persons enrolled.

In October the congregation gave $5000 to the Bangladesh Flood Victims Fund.

On November 6, 1988 the congregation celebrated Pastor Holt's 70th birthday

Thanksgiving time—$5000 was given to print Bibles in China and $1750 to the SF Food Pantry.

Thanksgiving Worship—ten persons were baptized and nine persons confirmed.

December 11th the Congregation gave Pastor

Wang a party for his 80th birthday and many of his family members and friends came to celebrate.

Christmas 1988—three confirmations and one baptism.

Time Marches On! It's —1989!

Our Holy Spirit church is 25 years old!

Faith fellowship was busy distributing sandwiches to the homeless and the congregation gave $500 to the city for care of the homeless.

March 25, 1989 a great celebration was held to celebrate our 25th anniversary with a banquet at Ferry Plaza Restaurant on the wharf.

April 2nd Mayor Art Agnos brought greetings and thanks for our help for the homeless.

April 16th, Lutheran Lay Ministry began the 4th session at Sunset extension church. Congregational retreat was held in Vallejo with 155 persons attending.

More blessings were received when International LWML designated $50,000 to the building fund at 3830 Noriega street extension church.

August 5, 1989—Wedding bells for Rev. Terrence Chan and Heather Wu at Hope Lutheran Church, Daly City.

October 1, 1989 Susan Chiang was employed as part time office secretary. The congregation gave $3000 to victims of the Hurricane Hugo.

This congregation has a great heart for giving ! Thanksgiving—$4000 was sent to Watsonville Earthquake fund and $2111 to San Francisco Homeless Shelter—all from a White Elephant sale.

Christmas Day Worship—ten persons were baptized and seven persons confirmed.

A New Year—1990!

January 18th, DCE Patty Lee began as a Called Worker.

May 11, 1990—The Lutheran Church of the Holy Spirit filed as a Domestic Non-Profit Corporation signed by Tom C. Lee, President and was granted Certificate #C1186715 as a Non Profit Corporation.

In June 1990 a Congregational Picnic was held at Serra Park in San Bruno.

Vacation Bible School was held at Sunset extension with 50 children attending.

June 24th, Rev. Walt Tietjen preached on "The Characteristics of a Mission Church".

July 1, 1990—four persons baptized and one person confirmed.

$3000 was given to the Iran Earthquake Fund. July 29th Rev. Stephen Tsui, Chairman China Lutheran Hour, Hong Kong, spoke about cassette ministry.

August 5, 1990 Rev. Orval Oswalt, President of CNH District brought the message.

November 25, 1990, Thanksgiving offering of $2764 sent to the Concordia Theological Seminary Food Bank.

Christmas Day—15 persons baptized and seven persons confirmed.

The Church Grew 1980-1990   Chapter Sixteen

Fellowship

English Fellowship

Young Men 1980's

Bringing Christ to the Chinese

Celebrating Graduation

Graduation

Graduates with Diplomas

The Church Grew 1980-1990   Chapter Sixteen

Laguna Honda 1984

Baptism of Janet Lim

Women in Kitchen

Bringing Christ to the Chinese

Mrs. Lau and Mrs, Holt

Pastors amd Families

The Church Grew 1980-1990   Chapter Sixteen

Mrs. Geri Holt

1983 Faith Fellowship

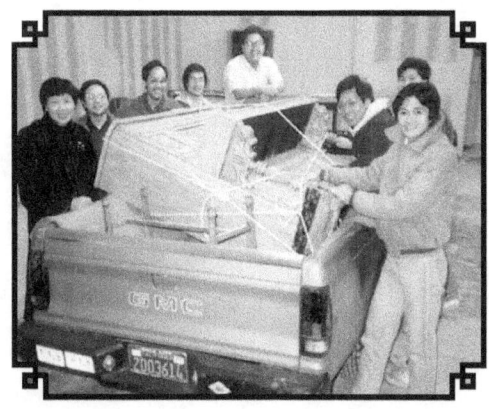

Moving to Sunset Extension

Pastor Yip at Protest

Protest 1981

The Church Grew 1980-1990   Chapter Sixteen

"Be watchful, stand firm in your faith, be courageous, be strong. Let all that you do be done in love."

I cor. 16:13–14 RSV

Pastor Timothy Yip

Chapter Seventeen

The First Pastor Called

Rev. Timothy Yip

In August 1982, the congregation unanimously called Rev. Timothy Yip as Assistant Pastor and Mission Enabler. During the interim between his call and installation at Holy Spirit church, he completed his studies at Concordia Seminary, Ft. Wayne, Indiana for the Master of Sacred Theology Degree. He was installed on January 16, 1983 at the Lutheran Church of the Holy Spirit.

Pastor Yip had many God given talents and spiritual gifts—a keen and well-trained mind, experience as a teacher in both Hong Kong and America, good training at very fine theological schools, strong faith in the power of the Gospel of Christ, deep concern for the evangelism of the world, great gifts in teaching, writing and speaking. On May 21, 1988 he left Holy Spirit to accept a call to teach in Hong Kong.

Pastor Yip wrote a book—"The Way of Salvation"—to make it easier to tell the Way to Salvation when talking with unbelievers. It is stored in the church archives.

God Is Love! God is Righteous and Just. Man Turns from His Creator. Man Loses Himself in Sin. The Result of Sin and Death. Who is Jesus Christ? How can God Possibly Forgive Us? God's Answer. Christ Rose from the Dead. Christ Ascended into Heaven. Christ will Come Back! The Way of Salvation! 2 Destinations—Heaven or Hell? Pray to the Lord! Assurance of Salvation!

Graduate Tim and Amy

Pastor Holt, Patty Lee, Amy and Pastor Yip

The First Called Pastor   Chapter Seventeen

Rita and Pastor Yip

Pastor Yip serving 1990

Pastor Yip and Youth

Young Pastor Yip

Bringing Christ to the Chinese

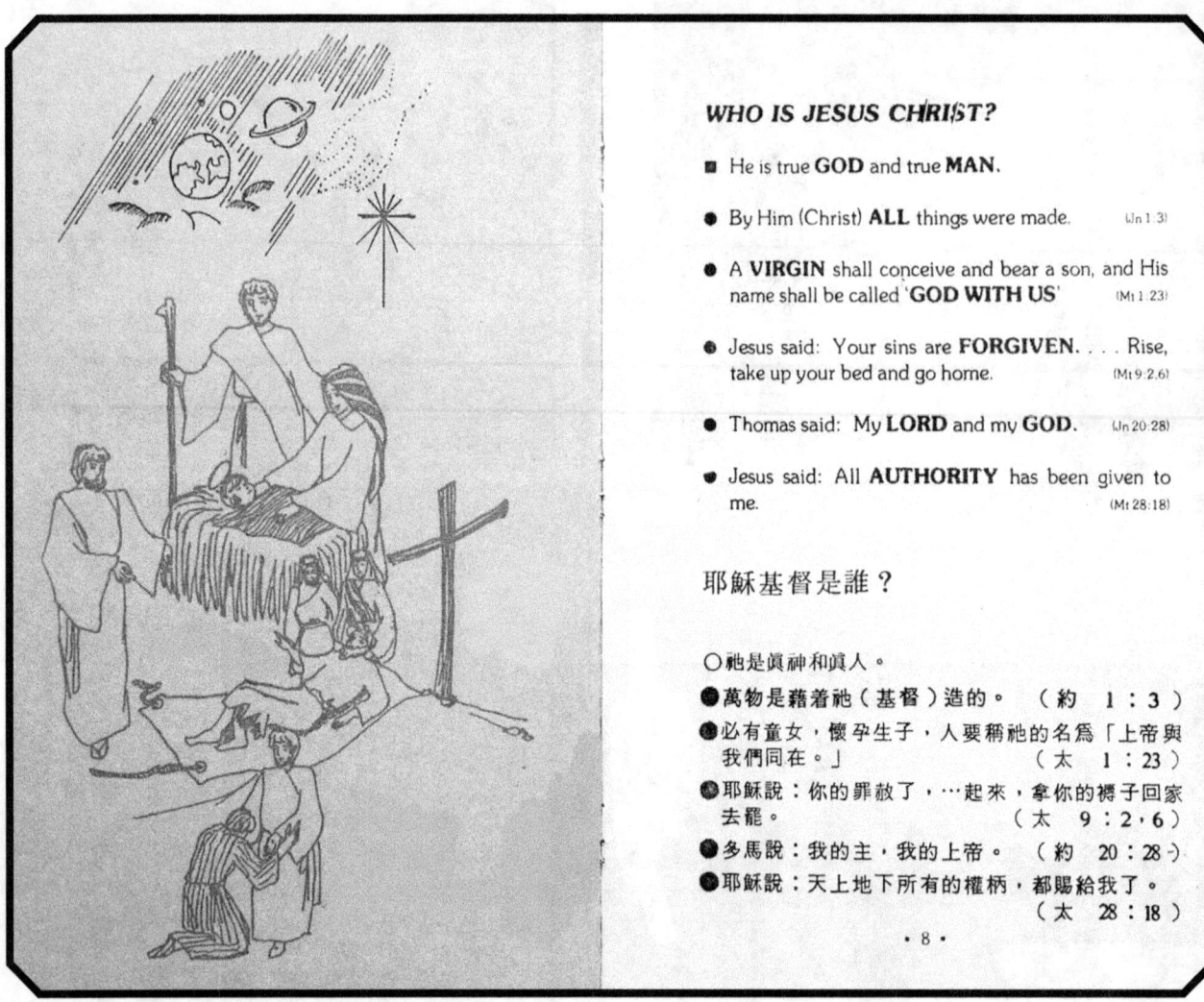

Page 8 From Pastor Yip's Book

The First Called Pastor   Chapter Seventeen

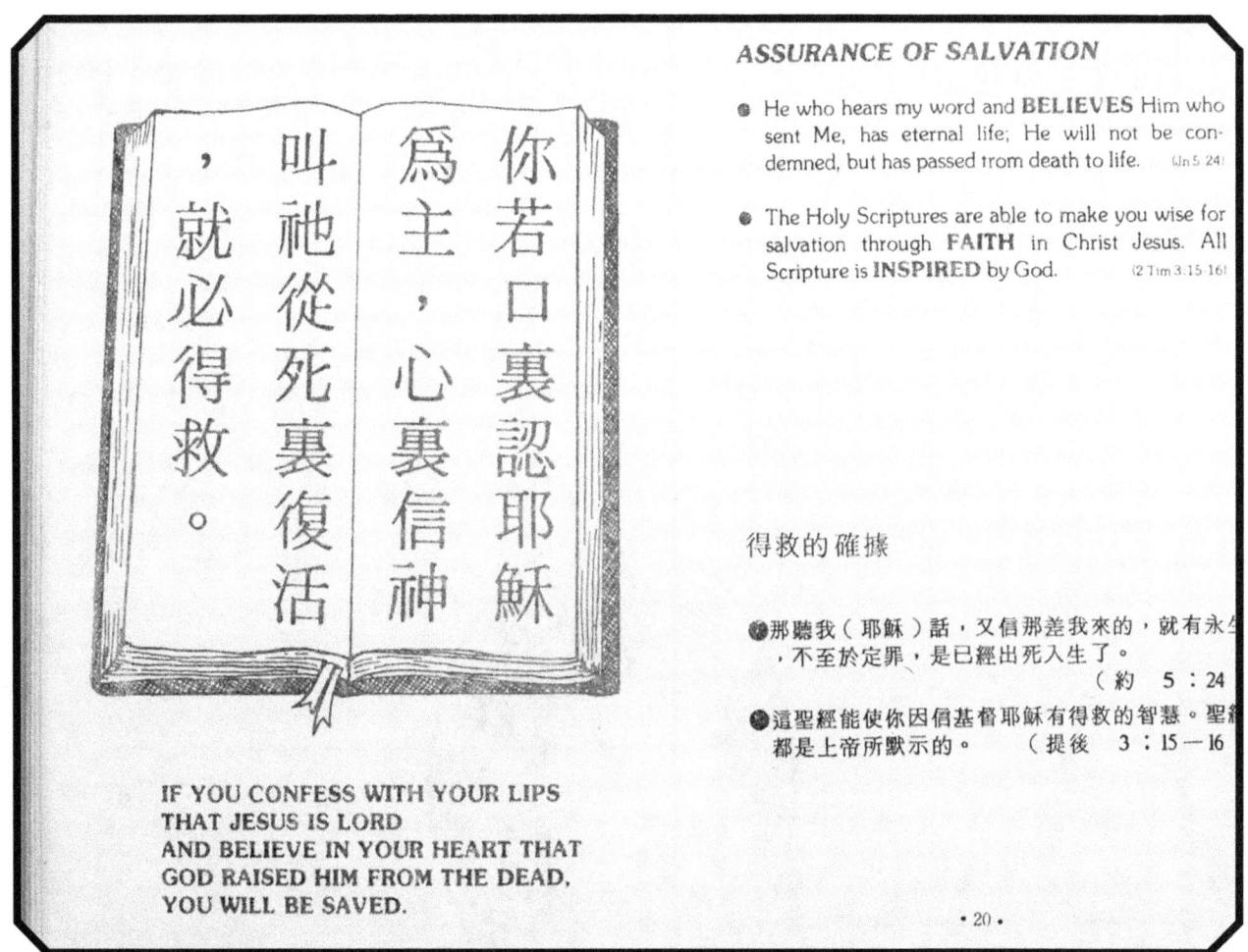

Page 20 From Pastor Yip's Book

"I beg you to lead a life worthy of the calling to which you have been called, with all lowliness and meekness, with patience, forbearing one another in love, eager to maintain the unity of the Spirit in the bond of peace."

Eph. 4:1–3 RSV

Rev. Terrence C. Chan

Chapter Eighteen

Calling The Second Pastor
Rev. Terrence C. Chan

Rev. Chan was born in Hong Kong in August 1958 and moved to San Francisco with his parents when he was a young child. On June 6, 1976, at age 17, he was baptized into the faith. After high school graduation he attended Concordia University in Portland, Oregon from which he received his B.A. Degree in Christian Education in 1981. He received his Master of Divinity Degree from Concordia Theological Seminary, Fort Wayne, Indiana in 1986.

August 1986 Seminarian Terrence Chan was installed as Vicar at the True Light Lutheran Church in New York City.

In 1987, Lutheran Church of the Holy Spirit called Rev. Terrence Chan as Chinese Assistant Pastor. He was installed on October 25, 1987.

Pastor Chan had many God given gifts. He was well-trained in Christian schools and was a good speaker and writer. A good administrator, he brought many new ideas to promote good stewardship He planned leadership retreats and various committee guidelines for fellowships, including a 10 week training course for church elders. He was instrumental in using Extension church at 3830 Noriega Street, for numerous meetings. On May 10, 1988 the building at 3830 Noriega was dedicated and the first English/Chinese worship service was held May 24, 1988.

Rev. Chan was appointed Chinese Ministry Field Counselor on September 3, 1992 by Synod where he served as field counselor for ten years and then 2001–2004 as a member of Synod's Board for Mission Services. In 1992 he founded the LCMS national Chinese Ministry Conference (CLiMB) and served as chairman for four years. June 26, 1994 he accepted a call as Mission Developer to begin work in the Sunset District for the English District of the Lutheran Church.

July 24, 1994 Lutheran Church of the Holy Spirit held a celebration giving thanks for the 7 years Rev. Chan worked among us. September 18, 1994 an inaugural service was held at West Portal Lutheran Church (English District) for Rev. Terrence Chan and his new mission venture.

January 29, 1995 the Lutheran Church of the Holy Spirit, in a special service, officially acknowledged the New Life Chinese Church Task Force. Pastor Chan preached and Frankie Choy spoke about the vision of the New Life Chinese Church.

In April 1995, New Life Chinese church requested Lutheran Church of the Holy Spirit to provide collateral of $140,000 for the new church; however in a congregational voters' meeting on May 14, 1995, the Holy Spirit congregation declined to provide the collateral but said it would support the new church in other ways.

Today, Rev. Terrence Chan is serving as Senior Pastor at Bethel Grace Lutheran Ministries in San Francisco, CA.

Fellowships 1992

Summer Retreat

Calling the Second Pastor   Chapter Eighteen

Pastor Chan and Simi Lee

Pastor Terry Chan

Rev Chan at 25th Aniversary

Rev. Chan's Birthday

Calling the Second Pastor   Chapter Eighteen

189

Bringing Christ to the Chinese

Congregation Retreat

Youth Retreat

Men's Retreat

Calling the Second Pastor   Chapter Eighteen

25th Aniversary

Farewell ToVicar Ryan

Pastor Holt, Pastor Reed and Wife

Dedication of Classrooms

Deanna Jang Baptism May 1993

Bringing Christ to the Chinese

Geri and Pastor Holt; Jean and Eddie Lee

Mission Spring Retreat 1992

Calling the Second Pastor   Chapter Eighteen

193

"Hallelujah! I want to express publicly before His people my heartfelt thanks to God for his mighty miracles. All who are thankful should ponder them with me. For his miracles demonstrate his honor, majesty and eternal goodness."

Ps. 111:1–3 LB

Pastor Wilbert V. Holt

Chapter Nineteen

Words of Advice
What it Means to be a Lutheran
Pastor Holt

To be Lutheran means to be faithful to the teachings of the Scripture. We recognize that the principles and teachings by which Martin Luther attempted to refer the church were biblical and therefore correct.

We Believe that

The Bible is inspired by God and does not contain errors. It instructs us in the way of salvation and Christian Living.

Jesus Christ is true God and true man. He died for our sins so that all who repent and trust in Him will be saved.

The creation of faith is purely the work of the Holy Spirit. Man can not decide to believe in Jesus by his own power or free will. "No one can say 'Jesus is Lord' except by the Holy Spirit". (1 Cor. 12:3). Some Christians say that there was a moment that they "wanted" to become a Christian and then they made a decision to become a Christian. Actually when a person "wanted" to become a Christian, the Holy Spirit had already worked in his heart through God's word to give him a willing heart, and he was at the point a Christian already.

Baptism is not just a ritual. It is a visible form of the Gospel. (The Gospel of Salvation comes to us through God's word, baptism, and the Lord's Supper).

Baptism forgives our sins and gives us salvation as we trust in Jesus who died for us. "Rise and be baptized, and wash away your sins"(Acts 22:16). Baptism is "the washing of regeneration and renewal of the Holy Spirit"(Tit 3:5). Baptism "now saves you... through the resurrection of Jesus Christ(1Peter3:21).

Infants are also to be baptized because: a) Our Lord's baptism is powerful, as was explained in the previous paragraph. b) the promise of baptism is for infants too, "Be baptized... for the promise is to you and to your children" (Acts 2:38–39). The Lord can work in the hearts of infants and give them faith, salvation and spiritual life. "Out of the mouth of babes and sucklings, Thou hast brought perfect praise" (Mt. 21:16). "Thou has hidden these things from the wise and understanding and revealed them to babes" (Mt 11:25). For example, even when John the Baptist was in his mother's womb, the Lord worked in him so he was "filled with the Holy Spirit" (Luke 1:15).

The Lord's supper is the true body and blood of Christ. It forgives the sins of all repentant believers. "The cup of blessing which we bless, is it not a participation in the blood of Christ?" (1Cor 10:26) "For this is my blood of

Bringing Christ to the Chinese

the covenant, which is poured out for many for the forgiveness of sins" (Mt 26:28).

If a Christian continues to sin without repentance, he can lose his salvation. The scripture warns us not to sin. The teaching "once saved, always saved" is not scriptural. "Now the Spiritual expressly says that in later times some will depart from the faith by giving heed to deceitful spirits and doctrines of demons"(1 Tim 4:1). "Take care, lest there be in any of you an evil, unbelieving heart, leading you to fall away from the living God......" (Hebrews 3:12).

Although some Christians do not feel that it is necessary to follow every teaching of the Scripture, it is obvious that God expects faithful following and faithful interpretation of His Scripture.

Consider The Following Passages

2 Timothy 1:13, 14, says: "Follow the pattern of the sound word" and "guard the truth." We should realize that "no prophecy of scripture is a matter of one's own interpretation" (2 Pet 1:20), but we should interpret the scripture with the scripture itself.

"We praise God that we may boldly stand with Christians of all times and clearly confess all that Christ in His Word has commanded us. We are humbly grateful to be Lutheran Christians."

Blessings

Forbidden

Ship

Spirit

Words of Advice

An Eager Heart for Evangelism
Dir. Amy Mui

Evangelism is a spiritual war in which one can not rely on flesh and blood to gain victory. You must remember Jehovah your God is the ONE fighting for you. You must rely on the Word of the Bible and the strength from the Holy Spirit when you enter the battlefield.

The seventy people whom Jesus sent returned joyfully to report: 'Lord, even the demons submit to us in your name.' (Luke 10:17) You can only imagine their excitement. However, Jesus did not join them in the celebration. Rather, he immediately helped them focus on several important reasons for serving:

Evangelism is declaring war against Satan. The outcome has been fixed. Satan will be defeated. We have set foot on a journey that will lead to victory. We must set our eyes on the outcome in the future, not the gains or losses of the moment.

God has given us the Great Commission to bring the Gospel to all people. He also grants us His promises and strength. Hudson Taylor once said, 'Depend on it, God's work done in God's way will never lack God's supply.'

A key to Evangelism is in seizing the moment. Recording a person's name in heaven, in the Book of Life is exactly God's intention for His Salvation Plan.

We must not become discouraged but set our eye on long-term perspectives. Everything we are doing now is setting the stage for the final victory. What did He mean when our Lord Jesus said, 'Come follow me.'? What Jesus was trying to say is, 'My goal for life and all that I seek shall become all that you seek.' Jesus' goal for life was: 'For the Son of Man came to seek and to save what was lost.' (Luke 19:10) and 'I have come that they may have life, and have it to the full.' (John 10:10) Jesus came into the world to complete His Father's Salvation Plan. For the sake for our redemption, He paid the ultimate price, pouring out His life on the Cross. He commanded us to spread the Gospel all over the earth.

Evangelism is a formidable task, yet we do not become afraid. All that we need to do is to trust and obey the Lord. We should not rely on our own strength but on God our Father. When believers of the church have the same mind in advancing the Gospel, then the One Who began the good work in us will carry it on to completion until the day of Christ Jesus. Our God's mercy and grace shall be with us forever.

Let us rise up to accept the challenge, seizing every opportunity of sharing the Gospel. It doesn't matter if they are a multimillionaire and a homeless drunk, their souls are of exact importance and value in God's sight. The Lord's love compels me, allowing me to serve with joy in the church for over 40 years. The Holy Spirit urges me on. I don't dare to turn away from the Great Commission, given to me by my Lord, to bring the Gospel to all people. Strength belongs to God! Only He is worthy of praise and glory. Anyone that obeys Him will be satisfied. All those who follow Him will shout with joy. Our Lord God's wondrous work is magnified through the history of the Lutheran Church of the Holy Spirit.

May many people pray for this book so that it will become a great witness for the Lord and empower believers to offer themselves to be used by the Lord, without reservation, for the sake of the Gospel. Our Lord really loves sinners. Many people who are hopeless as withered grass spring forth like beautiful flowers once they believe in the Lord! When their lives are connected with the Lord, they are changed completely! Since we are surrounded by such a great cloud of witnesses, let us put down our 'SELF' but give our heart to the Lord and seize the moment in bringing the Gospel to the Chinese.

Jesus is coming soon! The Earth shall see His glory! May God's people be fully prepared, because God's kingdom will be here soon. HE is Lord and King forever and ever!

Bringing Christ to the Chinese

"So the word of the Lord grew and prevailed mightily"

Acts 19: 20 RSV

路德會聖靈堂

The Lutheran Church of the Holy Spirit

Chapter Twenty

Ten years of God's Blessings 1991-2001

The Annual LWML District convention was held at Cathedral Hotel in San Francisco. Jean Lee of Holy Spirit's Love in Action was chairman of the convention.

February 2, 1991. Wedding bells for David Chan and Lucy Wong, married at our church

May was a busy month, $4000 sent to Lutheran World Relief to help Kurds in Northern Iraq.

Pentecost service—one person was baptized, nine persons confirmed and two persons transferred to our Church.

June 22, 1991, Special Mission Adventure for Youth was held for six Saturdays.

July 28th, 1991—four persons were baptized.

August 18, 1991, celebration of Red egg and Ginger party for Pastor Terrence and Mrs. Chan's daughter, Elizabeth.

September $4000 was given to the China Flood Fund.

December 18th, Pastor Holt had major surgery and the congregation created a special, round the clock, prayer chain for his recovery. He was able to return to part time work in March 1992.

Christmas Day worship—19 persons baptized and five persons confirmed to the Glory of God!

It's now 1992!
May 10th—Pastor Holt received a special award—"Gift of Life" for social work in the city.

He was very active in social affairs, always helping those in need.

May 17, 1992, Amy Mui celebrated her 25th Wedding anniversary and her 25th year of church service with a program and dinner at Raddison Hau Inn.

May 24, 1992, Pastor Chan was elected Chairman of Chinese Ministry Conference, and the Synod Board of Missions appointed him Field Counselor for Chinese Missions.

1993
Pastor Holt was active in opposing the Freedom of Choice Act and encouraged the celebrating of Sanctity of Life. He received a special award from Sanctity of Life.

January 31, 1993, Pastor Terrance Chan received a call from the Board of Missions to serve as Mission Developer in Greater Los Angeles Area. He later declined the call.

May 28, 1993 the Congregation celebrated its 30th Anniversary with a gala party at Empress of China.

In July more than 255 persons attended the Congregational picnic.

July 25th, Pastor Holt held a Valediction Service and Farewell with God's speed to Candidate Marty Reed, a son of this congregation, as he left to be ordained and installed in another Lutheran church.

August 21, 1993 two "sons" of the congregation were installed as vicars in local churches: David T. Chan as Vicar at Mt Olive Lutheran Church, Milpitas; Bill S. Chu as Vicar at Shepherd of the Valley in San Jose

August 22, 1993—$6000 was given to Midwest Flood Victims fund.

Christmas Worship Service—20 persons baptized and 25 persons confirmed.

1994
The congregation gave thanks for the members studying for full time church service: Daniel Woo, Ministry; Allan Tong and Julie Jue as DCE's; Cathy Fong, Jenny Szeto and Lisa Gin as teachers. David T. Chan and Bill S. Chu were serving as Vicars.

October 26, 1994 the Title of the 1725 Washington church building was transferred from Calif-Nav-Hawaii District to the Lutheran Church of the Holy Spirit. A milestone in our history !

November 24th offering was designated for the New Organ Fund 3 persons were baptized on this day.

Thanksgiving Food Fest proceeds were sent to the Rwanda Relief Fund.

Christmas, we celebrated "Sharing Peace & Joy of Christmas" with a congregational dinner at 1725 Washington street. Christmas day—17 persons were baptized.

1995—How time flies!

Pastor and Mrs. Holt celebrated their 50th wedding anniversary and Pastor's 50th year in the ministry with a banquet dinner given by the church at the Empress of China. Pastor and Mrs. Holt gave a $2430 love gift to the Church's Scholarship Fund.

A special gift of $28,000.00 was given by the Holy Spirit congregation to New Life Chinese Lutheran church on April 2, 1995; also the use of 20 telephone outlets for New Life's October 7th convassing program.

In April, Pastor Holt became very ill. Mrs. Holt also had surgery. There was great concern for their health and a 24-hour prayer chain was maintained. During the next months, there were 23 visiting pastors and vicars who came to preach during Pastor Holt's absence.

June 16–18, 1995 a congregational retreat was held at Alliance Redwood Camp with 160 members attending.

July 27th, a church leadership retreat was held at Mt. Olive Lutheran Church in Milpitas.

September 17th, contractors began work to add 4 classrooms to the building at 1725 Washington street, which was paid for by the $50,000 from mite offerings given by the International LWML and originally slated for remodeling the building at Noriega street

The Chinese Language school began a new fall school year.

November 26, 1995—The first Church Constitution and By Laws was presented to the congregation.

December 10, 1995—Reverend Fred Stennfeld, Circuit Counselor, met with the call committee. A call for a Chinese/English bilingual pastor was issued.

December 25, 1995—11 persons who received baptism and 4 persons were confirmed.

1996

In January, California-Nevada-Hawaii District sent a list of names of pastors to be considered by the call committee.

February 11th, 1996—62 members of Holy Spirit congregation were released and transferred to the New Life Chinese Lutheran Church, English District, where Rev. Terrence Chan was the pastor.

February 15, 1996, Voters Assembly unanimously voted to request the Concordia Seminary to assign Seminarian David Chan to be our new pastor. On May 5th Concordia Theological Seminary Board of Assignments assigned Rev. David Chan to be pastor of Holy Spirit Lutheran Church.

June 16, 1996 Pastor Holt dedicated 4 new classrooms and a new organ at 1725 Washington Street church.

June 23rd, Retirement and Appreciation Banquet was held for Pastor Holt at Empress of China. Pastors from CNH District and Circuit representatives attended to share their appreciation for the many years of ministry of Pastor Holt.

June 30th, 1996 The Ordination of David T. Chan and his installation as Pastor of Lutheran Church of the Holy Spirit was celebrated. Celebrants were Service of the Word, Dr. Ihno Janssen; Rite of Ordination, Rev. Theodore Mueller and Rite of Installation was Rev. Fred Stennfeld. Lectors were: Service of the Word, Rev. Wilbert V. Holt and Rite of Ordination Rev. Michael Gibson. Dr. Glenn Nielsen, Assistant Professor of Practical Theology and Director of Vicarage, Concordia Seminary, St Louis, MO gave the sermon.

August 18, 1996—Rev. Bill S. Chu, another son of this congregation was ordained and installed on at Our Savior's Lutheran Church in Pinole, CA.

November 28th—Thanksgiving Food Fest was held with proceeds of $3000 given to the SF Food Bank.

December 15, 1996—Pastor C. C. Wang passed away. A Memorial service was held at the church on December 29th, 1996.

Christmas Day—six persons baptized and 2 persons confirmed.

1997

February 16th, 1997—the family of Rev. C. C. Wang gave $2800 to the Memorial Fund in memory of their father.

May 4th—members of our congregation were called to serve in other churches: Lenny Szeto to Vicar at Hope Lutheran Church, Daly City; Allan Tong as DCE at New Life Chinese Lutheran Church; Jenny Szeto as Music teacher at West Portal Lutheran Church..

June 1st, a member, Eddie J Lee, gave $7625 from his 81st birthday celebration to the church's scholarship fund.

June 28th—An annual Congregational Picnic was held at Coyote Point Park, San Mateo.

June 13th—Dr Martin Shramm, Professor at Concordia University, Irvine, CA presented Pastor Holt and Amy Mui the "Christus Mondo" award for their work among Chinese.

July 28, 1997 Pastor David Chan had emergency surgery to repair an Aorta blood vessel. He took medical leave through October and the congregation activated a 24-hour prayer chain for his recovery.

September 14th, Pastor David required additional surgery. Many guest pastors filled the pulpit, including Pastor Holt, during the months Pastor Chan was recovering.

October 5th—$6000 was given to the Sunset building fund in memory of Mrs. How Yuk Hau mother of Amy Hau Mui.

November 27th Thanksgiving Food Fest proceeds of $2161.15 sent to the SF Food Bank.

December 14th a Christmas Celebration was held at Irish Culture Center in the Sunset area.

1998
February 22, 1998 Pastor David Chan brought the message but he was unable to preach more than once a month because of damage to his vocal chords during surgery.

May 3, 1998 the Voters Assembly voted to call DCE Allan Tong as Director of Christian Evangelism for the English Ministry. On June 14, 1998 he accepted the call and was commissioned and installed at Holy Spirit congregation on July 5, 1998.

July 26, 1998 Daniel Woo, son of the congregation, was ordained and installed at Hope Lutheran Church, Daly City.

November 5th Pastor Holt celebrated his 80th birthday.

November 8, 1998—revised Church Constitution and By Laws was completed and members of the congregation signed the new document.

November 15, 1998—proceeds from the Thanksgiving festival were sent to LWR Honduras Relief.

At Thanksgiving, Pastor David Chan baptized one person and confirmed 10 persons.

Christmas Day worship—baptism of seven persons and one person confirmed.

1999
A new ministry—Help U Learn was established by DCE Allan Tong and a new spring semester of this after school tutorial was begun—Jan 5th to June 4, 1999.

January 31, 1999—In Voters Assembly, the congregation voted by 84 Yes, and 32 No votes to seek an additional location in the Sunset area and relocate the church there.

March 29, 1999 Lenten services were held at 3830 Noriega Street—the Extension church. Easter services were held at 1725 Washington Street and Chinese services at Sunset Extension church.

A Children's' Day Camp was held at the Sunset extension church—June 24–July 30th.

July 11, 1999 Rev. Lenny Szeto, son of the congregation, was ordained. He accepted a call to a Lutheran Church in Shawnee, Oklahoma.

August 8, 1999—Congregational retreat was held at Mt Gilead Bible Conference Center.

Fall session of Help-U-Learn after school tutorial began, lead by DCE Allan Tong and Lorraine Ma.

In September we said goodbye to Patty Lee with an Appreciation Party as she left to pursue a career in teaching.

Thanksgiving time—$2000 was given to S F Food Bank.

December 25th, 1999 Christmas Day— 11 persons baptized, 9 persons confirmed.

2000
Time rushes by—This is the last year of the 20th Century.

Ten years of God's Blessings   Chapter Twenty

Pastors Holt and Chan both encouraged members to read the Bible daily & pray.

March 26, 2000—We were filled with sadness, when our beloved Geraldine Holt, wife of Pastor Holt, passed away. What a shock! We have lost a great friend! She is now with the "Dear Jesus" she loved so much! April 1st a celebration of her life was held at West Portal Lutheran Church. A Scholarship fund was set up in her name at Lutheran Church of the Holy Spirit for young men entering the ministry.

April 1—we praised God with a celebration for the First Anniversary of Cantonese worship at the Holy Spirit's Sunset extension.

April 23rd—Easter three young men were confirmed.

Pastor David began six months training for church Elders.

Seminarian Warren Jow, a son of the congregation, was assigned to Trinity Lutheran Church in Howard's Grove, WI as Vicar.

June 18—a Sending Off ceremony was held for Raymond Lau, for a short term mission trip to Macau.

November 5, 2000—Another "first" for the congregation, Pastor David appointed the first elders: Tom Lee, Daniel Lam, Peter Ng and Ernest Louie. November 12th they were confirmed in a Voters Assembly and installed on 12/31/2000.

November 23, 2000—Thanksgiving services, four persons were baptized.

December 17, 2000, two persons were transferred to the membership of Holy Spirit congregation.

Warren Jow

Youth Retreat

1992 Retreat

Bringing Christ to the Chinese

Choy Guen and Son

Ray and Anita Lau

Quok and Jane Lee

Patty Lee 1993

Amy and Elaine 1993

Cindy and Mabel Co-Workers

Pastor Jow and Mom

Janet Lim's Wedding

Ten years of God's Blessings   Chapter Twenty

Barbara Lee's Wedding

Ma Family

Cindy, Mom, and Debbie

Patties on the fire

Wing Szeto, Chef

Memorization Champs

Herman Kwan Family with Pastor

Mr. Wong 1993

"There is one body and one Spirit, just as you were called to the one hope that belongs to your call, one Lord, one faith, one baptism, one God and Father of us all, who is above all and through all and in all,"

Eph. 4:4–6 RSV

Pastor David Chan

D.C.E. Allan Tong

Chapter Twenty One

The Calling of the Third Pastor
David Tze Ming Chan and D.C.E. Allan Tong

Born in Hong Kong and baptized when 3 years old. In his early years he was greatly influenced by his Christian grandmother, who was a member of Rev. Wilbert Holt's church in Hong Kong.

He immigrated to the United States with his family in June 1969. He visited the church at 606 Jackson street with his grandmother but did not attend worship until the church moved to 1725 Washington street. He received his B/S degree from California State University in Hayward with a degree in Business Administration and Finance. For nine years he worked as a Financial Analyst at Bank of America.

In 1972 he joined a youth fellowship at Holy Spirit church. They were taught by Pastor Holt and Parish Worker Amy Mui to find their God given gifts and use them in outreach to others. Being influenced by Pastor Holt and Amy, he entered the Concordia Seminary at St. Louis in 1992. He served his vicarage at Mt. Olive Lutheran Church in Milpitas, California under the guidance of Rev. Mike Gibson.

He was ordained and installed as Pastor of the Lutheran Church of the Holy Spirit on June 30th, 1996. About this time he had emergency surgery for an Aortic Di-section. Later in 1997 he suffered a stroke which affected his speech and reading. During the many months of recuperation, God allowed the congregation to raise up new leaders from the congregation and many visiting Pastors filled the pulpit. God changed Pastor Chan's many plans. Pastor Chan knows God accomplishes what He has planned not according to our wishes. He was instrumental in the congregation's move from 1725 Washington Street to 2400 Noriega Street in the Sunset area of San Francisco.

In 2004 Pastor Chan received a call from Peninsula Asian Mission Society (PAMS) to begin the work of starting a Chinese mission at Bethany Lutheran church on the San Francisco peninsula. It was a hard decision—stay in comfort at Holy Spirit church or do something different—establish a new Chinese mission. God directed him to accept the challenge.

Today he sees the Gospel in action. He is Associate Pastor at Bethel Grace Lutheran Ministries. Over 550 Asian immigrants visit the food pantry weekly. They hear about the Gospel while visiting the pantry and in 2009 an average of 150 Chinese immigrants attended the weekly Bible class led by Pastor Chan.

One of Pastor Chan's favorite Bible Verses:
But the Lord said to me, "My grace is sufficient for you, for my power is made perfect in weakness. Therefore I will boast all the more gladly about my weaknesses, so that Christ's power may rest on me. " 2 Corinthians 12:9

D..E. C. Allan Tong

May 3, 1998 the Voters Assembly voted to call DCE Allan Tong as Director of Christian Evangelism for the English Ministry. On June 14, 1998 he accepted the call and was commissioned and installed at Holy Spirit congregation on July 5, 1998.

"It's in Christ that we find out who we are and what we are living for. Long before we first heard of Christ and got our hopes up, he had his eye on us, had designs on us for glorious living, part of the overall purpose he is working out in everything and everyone." Ephesians 1:11–12

I always knew there was a designer in my life. Finding myself bewildered in the midst of the vastness of space and the intricate details of small creatures, I was always drawn to the need to seek and the longing for the pursuit of a deeper meaning than what things simply appeared. What more intriguing were the phases of my life, from the moment my life started, learning the traits and treats of life, growing up and picking myself up from falling and failing; learning and gaining new knowledge in a media-saturated world; coping with people at different levels of temperament; and finally realizing I wasn't the center of the universe.

Being brought up as an "Overseas Born American," I was acculturated by pure Asian upbringing from my Hong Kong descent and academia on one side, and the gracious embrace of kindness and generosity of the American genre on the other side. I was seeking all right. Lost was the word that fits my upbringing as a young teenager trying to fit in and in need of a purpose. The more I try to find, the more I get lost. I knew the tricks of the game, but I have no strength to play. Until God found me!

I came to San Francisco when I was fourteen years old. Aunt Jenny was our only relative in the US. She had prepared an apartment for our family upon our arrival from Hong Kong, China. It was interesting to know many years later that this very place I stayed was only half a block away from Lutheran Church of the Holy Spirit on Washington Street. So close yet so far. Lost but yet in the process of being found.

Shortly after I moved to another neighborhood, God began his continual search for a servant at heart and whose heart held close to His. 1988 was the year I was assigned to Philip & Sala Burton Academic High, San Francisco. During my sophomore year, Jenny Szeto and Lisa Gin became my classmates. As much as they were compelled by the Spirit's call to share the Message of life and the story of what Christ Jesus did for the human race, I was lured by the genuine sincerity and kindness of two very unique people who care more than just telling me the three steps to eternal life and the ten reasons Jesus died on the cross. They established a genuine connection and friendship.

They had prepared God's truth. Moreover they displayed a friendship I had never seen or felt of. I remember the day we all came back from our Winter break, I saw pictures taken from their fellowship's winter retreat. Not only did I see photographs, I saw what I had lacked and longed for. From the pictures, I saw joy and happiness among the faces of young people. Accompanied by Lisa's and Jenny's genuine and sincere invitation,

I attended Hope Fellowships at Holy Spirit on Washington Street. God's word immersed Himself like fresh air being inhaled into a suffocating soul. Regeneration. Transformation. Director Amy Mui, who was then the spiritual facilitator for Hope Fellowship, was truly inspirational. She was faithful in sharing Christ with young people and their families. Her messages were so clear and simple, yet full of depth and insights. The Message of Christ, the redemption of the His sacrifice, and the clear work of the Trinity and their doctrine set the foundation of my faith. God's word built up my faith considerably. I couldn't but feel called and convicted to share this amazing truth with all my friends and family.

"It's in Christ that you, once you heard the and believed it (this Message of your salvation), found yourselves home free—signed, sealed, and delivered by the Holy Spirit." Ephesians 1:13

God's word nourished my roots. The amazing growing body of Christ at Hope Fellowship, Lutheran Church of the Holy Spirit watered and fertilized not only my faith, it provided me an environment that allowed me to serve and bear fruits. There was nothing except the pure teaching of Christ by Director Amy Mui and Pastor Wilbert Holt that motivated people to serve. Moreover they emulated Christ and taught Christ not in words, but Christ and the Holy Spirit through their actions and the overflowing personality of Christ Himself.

Leaders were devoted in prayers. People, like myself, who came to Lutheran Church of the Holy Spirit, heard Christ, believed the Message of His salvation, and were truly set free. We didn't serve Him because God needed us. We serve because we exist, we are, and we are here ONLY because of Him. Knowing my salvation is sure and the purpose why I'm here, I surrendered my life to Him. I realized becoming a follower of Christ isn't just trying to do what a follower of Christ ought to or should do. If we are regenerated as a child of God, we would have a transformed life naturally. Instead it is giving up everything we are and we have, and allowing the Holy Spirit Himself to lead without any of our own merit. I didn't decide at a defined moment of time to become and enter into full time ministry. It sounded very wrong for me to claim the volition to serve Him as if he needed me. He doesn't need me as if His work was depended on me.

My scrawny story compared to His larger-than-life epic is peerless, incomparable, and insanely absurd. It was my speechless and grateful response to Christ's amazing rescue and liberation from what could have been perpetual suffering and sin and death. There is nothing I rather do than to devote my life to Him, to do His will. Moreover, I know for a fact that I was secured and insured by Him by the promises of His Message. Though I will be under attack and will be faced with numerous challenges; persecuted and perplexed; I will never be abandoned by my Abba Father for I'm blessed by our Lord Jesus Christ, who signed, sealed, and delivered me from before Creation to the end of times.

May all Glory be to our Lord Jesus Christ!

Seminarian David Chan

Pastor David at Easter

Christmas 2003

Confirmation

DCE Allan Listening

Elders

Calling of the Third Pastor and D.C.E.   Chapter Twenty One

Allan and Friends

Pastor Iverson 2004

DCE Allan Tong and the Gang

Painting for Pastor Iverson

Music Session

Honoring Vets 2009

"Don't be impatient for the Lord to act. Keep traveling steadily along his pathway and in due season he will honor you with every blessing."
Ps 37:34 LB

The Lutheran church of the Holy Spirit 2012

Chapter Twenty Two

A New Century 2001-2010

January 2nd—a special Cantonese seekers worship was held at 1725 Washington street church. March 4th, a new church worker! Cindy Jeong became part time administrator assistant.

April - Easter Services—four persons were confirmed. Later in the month Pastor David was hospitalized for tests. Congregation continued to pray for his health and visiting pastors brought the Sunday messages.

May 27th Pastor Holt was hospitalized in serious condition with a perforated intestine. 24 hour prayer chain was activated. He returned home July 15th to recuperate.

July 5th—LWML held their District convention in San Jose, CA. Amy Mui was one of the featured speakers.

July 29th Seminarian Ryan Tietz was installed as Vicar—reception followed.

August 12th, members of AAL assembled 42 school back packs for HUL students
The fall session of HUL began on August 27th.

Another milestone in the church history! September 9th—At a Voters Assembly, 75% of the congregation voted to give permission to church officers to purchase the building at 2400 Noriega street and sell the church building at 1725 Washington street. September 16th our offer to purchase 2400 Noriega street building for 2.25 million dollars was accepted.

November 11th, 2001—the church celebrated Pastor Holt's 83rd birthday. 18 members of his family were present at the celebration. President Jerry Ma presented Pastor with a gift from the congregation.

December 15th the congregation celebrated Christmas at Patro Esponal restaurant. Christmas Day—22 persons baptized and 7 persons confirmed.

December 30th Pastor Holt returned and preached the Christmas message.

2002
January—Cantonese Worship was held monthly at Sunset extension.

February 10th—Elders hosted a "Prayer Power" meeting at Sunset extension and there was a kick-off of our Church's Building Project "Together We Build" with a building fund committee formed and pledge forms distributed.

March 10th an Open House was held at the New Church location—2400 Noriega street. The congregation rejoiced that Pledges from 152 members totaling $425,966 for the building fund was received as of April 14, 2002.

Help-U-Learn held a Summer Excel Program—June 25 to July 25th. A youth Summer Day Camp was held July 29—August 2nd with 47 student enrolled.

August 12—16 a Koinania Summer Adventure Camp was held with 50 young people enrolled.

Giving thanks for a successful start to remodel the new church building, a Praise Rally—"Togethr We Praise" was held at 2400 Noriega site—125 persons attended.

Cindy Jeong joined the staff as a full time worker!

July 13th a Congregational Picnic was held at Flood Park in Menlo Park.
July 21st Vicar Ryan and Jeanine returned to the seminary. 200 people attended a farewell party.

Its time to move! August 18th—"Together We Sort"— we sorted and packed as we anticipated moving to our new church. September 29th we finished packing, ready to move.

CNH President Tietjen preached the closing sermon "Mission is More Than Location" and the church at 1725 Washington Street was closed!

October 2, 2002 our new church at 2400 Noriega Street was dedicated by Pastor David T. Chan.

Thanksgiving worship—November 28th "Do Not Forget the Lord".
Christmas celebration was held on December 12th at West Portal Gym. The theme—"The Birth of Christ".

Christmas Day Worship—3 persons baptized and 25 person confirmed.

2003

January 26th—English Ministry held a winter retreat—40 persons attended.

February 6th the escrow and sale of 1725 Washington Street property was closed.

March 14th—Hope Fellowship had a retreat at South Lake Tahoe.
Pastor Holt and Parish Worker Amy Mui were both ill. Prayer teams activated.

April 14th Easter Faire—130 visitors attended the event.

April 29th Joy Fellowship held their 5th annual retreat with 53 persons attending.

May 25th—"Together We Build" has received $534,621.38 in pledges.

June 23rd—Youth Summer Life Saver Program held for four weeks—67 youth enrolled.

July 30th—a church picnic was held at Flood Park in Fremont—250 persons came, 90 were non-Christians.

August 12th—The church building project Phase #2 kick-off meeting was held. Pastor Iverson was the special speaker. He has assisted us in the discussion of the needs which were assessed for this project. Building committee members were Jerry Ma (chairman) Pastor David, DCE Allan Tong, Peter Ng, Sam Lam, Cindy Jeong, Winnie Lam, Martin Yuen, Vernice Louie, Jonathan Jeong.

Sad News! August 15, 2003! Pastor Holt has died! We have lost our beloved pastor, friend and father figure to many. He has entered into the Joy of the Lord he served with all his heart, mind and soul!

A New Century Chapter Twenty-Two

Memorial Service was held at St Cecilia's Catholic Church, 2555 - 17th Avenue, San Francisco. No Lutheran Church was large enough to contain the number of people who came to pay their respects to this great man.

On September 7th—a Memorial gift of $6,835 to the building fund was given in remembrance of Eddie J Lee, husband of Jean Lee.

Help-U-Learn After school Tutorial has 45 students enrolled for the Fall Semester, 12 of these are new students. There are 32 tutors (8 out of 11 graduates from Junior High returned as tutors). An average of 10 tutors a day helping 45 students.

September 21st—Director Amy Mui was granted an extended sick leave until end of the year.

October 5th—First Cantonese Contemporary Worship.

October 5th—Celebration of 1st Anniversary of the church at 2400 Noriega Street.
October 10th—Brothers in Christ held retreat—21 brothers attended.
October 19th—Memorial gift was received in remembrance of Wing You Louie—$3200, designated for church building fund.

October 31st—Family Fall Festival—Welcome bags were given to everyone who attended. There were Games, Booths, Ministry/church information, Goodie Bags and Costumes. Fun for all!

November 23rd—Thanksgiving Festival proceeds of $6359 were given to Building Fund and 429# of food donated to the SF Food Bank.

December 13th—Cantonese Gospel Outreach at West Portal Gym—Dr Abraham Law spoke—"Joy for Many, Sad for Some"—250 people attended—16 persons respond to the call to receive Jesus Christ.

December 21st—English Ministry Christmas was held at Hope Lutheran Church.
December 21st—English Contemporary Service –7 youths baptized, 1 confirmed.
December 25th Chinese Bilingual Traditional Service—"The Miracle of Christmas."

2004
January 1st - baptism of 3 infants. Help-U-Learn held a one day retreat for seekers, 30 people attended. Pastor Laurence Fung gave the message.

February 22nd LWML Zone One held a "Gospel Festival" at our church—112 women attended.

March 20th—Call committee interviewed Rev. Tim Leung for work as an English Ministry Parish Worker.

April 18th—Easter Festival—$2000 + $1300 matching funds from Thrivent for Lutherans.
Help-U-Learn —6th Annual Spring one day retreat for grades 2–7.

April 25th a short term Mission to Mexico was commissioned to build a home there and meet with young people.

May 2nd—80 people from our church attended "Support Traditional Marriage" event. Over 7,000 people attended from 200 churches.
May 2nd—Seminarian Warren Jow was ordained at Good Shepherd Lutheran Church in Hayward. He will be installed on 5/16/09 at First Lutheran Church in Dinuba. He is the 11th son of this congregation to become a Lutheran pastor.

May 16th—Voters Assembly voted to sell the Church Parsonage at 6th Avenue, San Francisco.

Bringing Christ to the Chinese

Pastor David Chan received a call from Bethany Lutheran Church in Menlo Park as Missionary Pastor to the Chinese in their area. He accepted the call.

June 6, 2004 - Help-U-Learn Family Picnic at San Pablo Recr Park -140 people attending.

June 27, 2004 Cantonese Evangelistic Event—180 people attended Rev. Yip was a well known radio D.J. in Hong Kong. 12 people came forward to accept Jesus as their Savior.

July 4th, 2004—two persons baptized and four persons confirmed. Help-U-Learn held a Summer Day Camp (Math Excel) with 30 youth counselors and 110 students attending.

July 28th—Farewell lunch for Pastor and Lucy Chan. Pastor Ted Zimmerman brought the message.
July 30th—Cafe Hope welcomed Christians and Seekers—Theme "Footprints in the Sand."

August 22, 2004—Congregational Retreat at Asilamar Conference Center in Pacific Grove—170 people attended.

September 5th—107 voting members attended Voters Assembly—Issue#1 Sale of parsonage on 6th Ave—99 yes, 7 no, 1 abstained. #2 issue—Proceeds of the sales of parsonage will be used to purchase additional property in the Sunset—33 yes, 73 no, 1 abstained.

Lutheran Doctrine retreat at Prince of Peace in Fremont—40 persons attended. Help-U-Learn began its 7th year with Fall Semester. Pastor David Chan was installed at Bethany Lutheran in Menlo Park.

September 19, 2004, President Daniel Lam reported that Pastor Iverson has agreed to serve as our Church's Advisor during the pastoral vacancy.

Pastor Iverson has been meeting with the Church Council and staff in preparation for the calling of a pastor.

October 1, 2004—Board of Elders begins Sunday Night Communion Service on 1st Monday of each month from 8 to 9:00 pm.

October 31, 2004—survey was taken (101 members replied) agreeing to supporting our church's building fund by prayer and pledges- "Together We Build".

2 food barrels were filled for the SF Food Bank. Shoe boxes of gifts for children were sent to Operation Christmas Child (a project of Samaritan's Purse) by Living Word Fellowship for children around the world.

November 7th—Pastor Iverson met with fellowship representatives to gain a better understanding of structure of each fellowship as well as their perception of a pastoral role.

Thanksgiving Food Fest raised $5555 - ½ given to Nehemiah Project and ½ to our Building Expansion Fund. Pastor David returned to confirm 4 persons on Thanksgiving Day.

November 21—Parsonage at 6th ave was sold for $830,000—a net amount of $781,630 was put in the Church General Reserves.

December 5—English Ministry Forum held by Pastor Iverson, our church advisor, to discuss the needs of the EM Ministry.

December 12th—Pastor Ted Iverson baptized eight persons and confirmed 15 persons.

English Ministry Christmas Celebration at Hope Lutheran Church—"The Greatest Gift of Christmas" speaker Rev. Lenny Szeto—260 young people attended.

A New Century   Chapter Twenty-Two

December 19th—Chinese Ministry Seekers Christmas celebration at Hope Church with 230 persons attending.

December 26th—Baptism of one adult.

2005

We begin another year without a pastor! This is the second year but God has provided for us—visiting pastors, officers from the congregation and a wonderful advisor, Rev. Ted Iverson!

January—$14,693.15 collected for victims of the Tsunami. Congregation gave Pastor Ihno Jannsen a special Bible verses picture for sharing of the Word many times during pastoral vacancy.

Peace Fellowship held a retreat at Zion Lutheran Church in Piedmont with DCE Allan—33 youth attended.

February –
Good News! The loan on the church property at 2400 Noriega has been paid in full.

March—Good Friday and Easter Services were held. 39 young people held a Prayer and Fasting meeting at the Extension church. They gave up 50% of their Chinese New Years red envelopes, and some gave up lunch every Wednesday during Lent. Some youth also gave up 20% of their allowance during Lent.
There was one baptism on Easter Sunday.

April—Emergency Voters Assembly on April 10th to discuss purchase of the church building at 34th and Noriega Streets. Congregation voted yes by 122 votes—1 abstained. A decision was made by present congregation to purchase the Church.

May—Celebration of Amy Mui's 38th Anniversary as a church worker at Holy Spirit. CNH District was in charge of the celebration with Pastor Ted Iverson as the MC.

June—During the English worship on June 5th, 32 adults and young people were commissioned on a Mission to Tijuana. The congregation raised $15,089.01 for this mission trip.

July—Call Committee invited Rev. R. Wong of Vancouver and his wife, Irene, to meet with our congregation. He preached July 31st at both worship services.

August—A nominating committee was appointed by the church council to find officers for the coming three years. Jean Lee, Mary Ma, Barbara Louie, Vernice Louie, Constant Suen and Andrew Fung served on the committee.

Rev. Shiu Ming Lau and his wife of St. Louis, visited our church November 4th–6th and met with members of the congregation

November 12th—Medicare Part D Workshop was held– Dr Tom Lee, speaker.

November 13th—Voters Assembly regarding 2006 budget and election of Church officers. Members wrote a thank you letter to God at Thanksgiving time.

Church officers elected—Peter Ng, Pres., Andrew Fung, VPres, Vernice Louie, Recording Secy, Keven Gong, Treas, Elaine Hung, Finance Secy, Ken Ye, Financial Analyst.
Baptism of baby girl by Rev. Ted Iverson.

December—Voters Assembly met to vote on calling of Rev. Shiu Ming Lau as our new pastor.
Rev. Ted Iverson baptized 15 persons and confirmed 14 persons.

2006—A New Year!

January—Commissioning of 2006-2009 Church officers.

February 26 - Chinese Lutheran Hour celebration

April 9th—Congregational meeting re Phase II Building Fund.

April 16th—Easter—3 babies baptized

April 23rd—New altar candles and candle holders given by Yun Deen LWML.

Help-U-Learn reports enrollment for "One Way" Summer Day Camp is full.

May 7th—Yun Deen LWML presents Rev. Chris Benson with 3 pastoral stoles in thanks for the many Sundays in which he served as visiting pastor.

May 21st—Rev. Shiu Ming Lau of St Louis visited with us.
May Festival held after Bilingual service. Proceeds $2982 plus $1300 matching funds from Thrivent for Lutherans.

June 4th—Good News! Rev. Shiu Ming Lau has accepted our call to become our new pastor. He will be installed June 25th.
June 11th—Informal reception for Rev. Lau and his family.

June 25th—Installation of Rev. Shiu Ming Lau as our new pastor! 235 persons attended the ceremony including 14 pastors who took part in the installation.

Sept 3rd—Our new church website is now "alive"—www.lcholyspirit.org.
Sept 24th—Baptism of five persons by Pastor Lau.

Nov 19th—Voters Assembly—1) Changed work status of Cindy Jeong to Pastorial Assistant. 2) Approved 2007 Church Budget. 3) Report on church building expansion. 4) Affirmation of Daniel Lam (CM) and Ricky Chan (EM) as elders. We now have six elders on the board.

Nov 26th—Distributed first version of booklet "A Great Cloud of Witnesses" which was collection of testimonies of many members.

Dec 17th—Congregational Christmas celebration at Empress of China
Dec. 24th—Pastor Lau baptized 15 persons and confirmed 15 persons.

"Learning Together—Growing in Christ" Theme for 2007!

Jan 7th—Installation of Elders Danel Lam (CM) and Ricky Chan (EM).

April 8th—Easter Services—2 baptisms and 12 persons confirmed

May 20th—May Fest—Proceeds $4125 plus $1300 from Thrivent for Lutherans

June 10th—Commissioned 18 persons on Short Term Mission Team to China.

July 2nd—August 10th—Help-U-Learn Summer Day Camp—170 youth enrolled.

August 12th—Mission Sunday—sharing by Missionary Deaconess Carol Lee Halter

September 15th—Gala Mid Autumn Event—Crown Plaza Hotel Ballroom. An Awesome Event! $65,028 was raised for the Building Expansion Fund!

September 23rd—Reorganized Call Committee for Calling Associate Pastor.

November 22nd—Thanksgiving Day—special presentation to Dir Amy Mui for her 40 years of Service to the Lord.
November 22nd—Third edition of "Clouds of Witnesses" booklet containing testimonies of church members.

A New Century   Chapter Twenty-Two

Dec 16th—Chinese Ministry celebration at Empress of China
Dec 23rd—Special service—7 persons baptized, 12 persons confirmed
Dec 30th—Installed Jerry Ma as Head Elder

"To Worship in Spirit—To Serve with Heart" 2008 Theme!

Jan 14th—Cantonese Communion Service, Monday night, 3 persons were confirmed.

Feb. 17th—Congregational Reports and Vision sharing.

March 23rd—Easter Sunday—three persons baptized, seven persons confirmed.
June 15th—Father's Day—Baptism of infant child.

June 29th—Congregation gave $6120 to World Relief for Burma, $21,450 to Sichuan Earthquake relief.

July 17th—Public Hearing at City Hall for Permit to build our new church building.
July 19th—Congregational Picnic at Coyote Point Park

August 10th—Installation of Vicar John Genter.

August 17, 2008 - Observed the 5th Anniversary of Pastor Holt's death with special video.
Aug 24th—Affordability report on building a new church by Advisor Rev. Ted Iverson. September 5th–10th Anniversary of Help-U-Learn and DCE Allan's work with us

October 26th—Visit and report by Missionary Deaconess Carol Lee Halter.

November 16th—Voters Assembly approved budget.

Nov. 27th—Thanksgiving Day—EM service—baptism of twin babies Bilingual service—5 persons baptized.

December 13th—English Ministry Christmas celebration

December 14th—Chinese Ministry Christmas celebration.

December 21st—Baptized 18 persons and confirmed 18 persons.

It is 2009! "The Spirit our Strength—Christ our Bond!"

January 4th—Installed Church Officers and Elders

February 22nd—Voters Assembly met regarding an Associate Pastor. Confirmed Tom Lee as an Elder.

March 1st—Commissioning of China Short Term Mission Team—ten persons.
March 15th—Building Fund Drive Ends 4-30-09! 80% of $699,845 pledged has been paid.

April 19th—Mission Team returned and shared about the trip—showing video.

May 24th—Help-U-Learn Family Camp held in Petaluma. 19 Agape/Unity members attend with Pastor Lau and DCE Allan Tong.
May 31st—Pentecost Sunday—3 persons baptized—8 persons confirmed.

June 29–August 7th—Summer Day Camp (HUL) "Big God—Big Plan—Big Impact!

July 19th—We Celebrated! Rev. Christopher Ng is installed at Associate Pastor! He is the 12th "son" of Holy Spirit church to become a Lutheran pastor. The church was full and overflowing—many pastors came to celebrate.

August 1st—Walk A Thon—$5933 raised for Building Fund.

August 2nd—Farewell to Vicar John Genter and wife Teddie as they returned to the Seminary.
August 15th—DCE Allan Tong and Jennifer Chow were married at Hope Lutheran Church.

September 11th—Mission Workshop - "The Last Baton" - Rev. Lawrence Fung.
September 27th—2 "Parenting workshops" given by Elizabeth Lau

October 18th—Food Fest held to support Sports Ministry—proceeds $3,034 and matching funds from Thrivent for Lutherans of $1020 = $4054.

November 15th—Voters Assembly—to approve budget for 2010. Members filled 2 barrels of food for the SF Food Pantry.

November 29th—Welcome home for 3 servicemen just returned from Iraq.

December 12th—English Ministry Celebration at Municipal Service Building in South San Francisco. Theme is "More". 3 service opportunities for congregation to give back to the community: Habitat for Humanity & Operation Christmas child. 2) Laguna Honda visitation, 3) Brown Bag lunch for the Homeless. Due to the poor economy this year, there was no Chinese Christmas celebration.

December 20th—At Bilingual service 4 persons baptized, 4 persons confirmed.

It is 2010!

We leave this New Year to posterity and in the hands of our Gracious Heavenly Father. All Praise and Glory be to Him alone!

Our plan is to build a 3 story new church at 2400 Noriega Street in 2010 and extend our work among people living in the Sunset area.

"Oh, what a wonderful God we have! How great are His works and knowledge and riches! How impossible it is for us to understand His decisions and His methods! " Romans 11: 30 (TLB).

Baptism December 2004

A New Century   Chapter Twenty-Two

Living Spirit

Brothers in Christ 2003

Choir 2002

Easter 2003

Fellowhip Easter 2003

Confirmation June 2004

Elders 2004

Faithfulness

2006 Yun Deen Ladies

Faithfulness Retreat

A New Century   Chapter Twenty-Two

Easter Time

Food Fest

LWML in Action

Leaders of SDC

Agape Unity

Young men at Extension

Senior Project

Praise Team

Bringing Christ to the Chinese

Picnic Time

LIA President Cindy Jeong

Winner

Help U Learn

Rev. and Mrs Ted Iverson

A New Century   Chapter Twenty-Two

Pastor amd Mrs Jannsen with Amy

Worship at Noriega

Pastor Lau and Betty Ng

Tai Chi

2007 Council

Walk-A-thon

AU-Truth LS- Ladies

Bringing Christ to the Chinese

Truth Fellowship Dinner

Seniors 2008

Youth at Extension

Nursery

Picnic

LIA Making Banners

Preparing Food At the Picnic

A New Century   Chapter Twenty-Two

LWML 2008

HUL Trinity

ACM Training

President Peter and Vicar John

Elders March 2009

Peace JR 2009

Summer Day Camp

Amy and Daniel Lam

Bringing Christ to the Chinese

Seniors 2009

Living Water

Amy, Jason and family

New Officers 2010

Welcoming Associate
Pastor Chris

A New Century   Chapter Twenty-Two

Family Sunday

Farewell To Vicar John

Bringing Christ to the Chinese

Cindy Jeong, Pastoral Assistant

Gospel Fellowship

Youth Fellowship at Extension

A New Century   Chapter Twenty-Two

Allen and Rebecca Lin

Calvin and Joyce Phui

Chris and Cheryl Ng

Constant and Cindy Suen

Denise and Daniel Brown

Janet and Mathew Jung

Jennifer and Allan Tong

Mr & Mrs. Jon Jeong

Ron & Stella Lok

Vernice & Robby Leung

Wendy and Dennis Lin

Mr. and Mrs. Chris Ng

Barbara Lee's Wedding

Mr. and Mrs Allan Tong' Wedding Party

"Behold, on the mountains, the feet of him who brings good tidings, who proclaims peace"

Nah. 1:15 RSV

12 Lutheran Pastors equipped to share the Good News!

Holy Bible, Baptismal Shell, Pastoral Stoles

Holy Communion Wine and Wafers

Chapter Twenty Three

These Are Her Sons Now 12 Lutheran Pastors!

Rev. Paul V. Holt
Son #1 Ordained 12/30/1979

Rev. Holt was born in 1947 in Enshish, Hupeh, China to Wilbert and Geraldine Holt who were missionaries to China. He grew up and lived in Hong Kong until the age of 16 when the family returned to the United States.

He attended the Lutheran Church of the Holy Spirit, which his father founded in 1964 at 606 Jackson Street in San Francisco. He served as Sunday School teacher and youth leader while attending school at Concordia Junior College in Oakland.

Rev. Holt attended Concordia Jr. College in Oakland and Concordia Senior College in Fort Wayne, Ind. It was here that he met his wife Linda. They were married in 1969. Paul and Linda were blessed with six children, Michael, Amy, Anne, Jonathan, Matthew and Amanda. They became foster parents in 1991, and have adopted six children of various ethnic backgrounds, Brian, Leland, Benjamin, Joshua, Noah and Ashley. Additionally they have fostered more than 35 children and currently are fostering 3 sisters.

In 2004, Pastor Holt and Linda received the National Angels of Adoption Award. He is also a proud grandfather to Sequoia and William.

Rev. Holt graduated from Pacific Lutheran Theological Seminary in Berkeley and Concordia Lutheran Seminary in Springfield, Illinois with dual Masters of Divinity Degrees. He was ordained by his father, Rev. Wilbert V. Holt, in 1979 at the Lutheran Church of the Holy Spirit at 1725 Washington Street, San Francisco, CA. He is the first "son" of this congregation to become a Lutheran pastor.

In 1975 he was called to his first church, St. Thomas Lutheran Church in Gardena, California, a church started by the Nisei during World War II. There he also had a ministry to Spastic Children's Foundation serving people with cerebral palsy.

He became the pastor of Pilgrim Lutheran Church in Oakland in 1980. He attended Holy Names College's Marriage and Family Counseling Program. At Pilgrim he has overseen a Chinese Ministry outreach and started a Preschool and Daycare program in 1989, with his wife serving as Director. He serves in an active capacity leading devotions, teaching and driving the church bus for weekly field trips in the summer. He has lead disadvantaged and culturally diverse youth group retreats through out Northern California. He served as chaplain in California State Park Chaplain Program for more than ten years.

He has served on the boards of Lutheran Social Services and Mount Cross Lutheran Camp. He served for 10 years as chaplain to Highland Hospital, John George Psychiatric Hospital and Villa Fairmount. Most recently, Pastor Holt has become active with the 100 Black Men Association through the Tommy Smith Tract Teams. He serves as an assistant coach while his 3 youngest children and foster children participate in the tract events. He also has a kayak ministry overseeing day trips in the beautiful waters of our bay.

Rev. Timothy K Yip
Son # 2 Ordained 1/16/1983

He came from Hong Kong to study at Simpson College, a Christian and Missionary Alliance Bible college in 1974 and there met Pastor Holt. He still remembers the day Pastor Holt took him to Simpson College, and many people nodded at Pastor Holt because he wore a clerical shirt. At that time, he was strong and he walked fast.

He joined Lutheran Church of the Holy Spirit. Pastor Holt talked to him a number of times about the Lutheran teachings. He was not convinced about the Lutheran teaching of monergism, that Christians are converted to believe in Jesus only by the work of God, without human cooperation. Finally Pastor Holt sent him to talk with a Lutheran pastor who used to be a Christian and Missionary Alliance pastor. After he studied through a Greek-English interlinear New Testament and found that the Bible does support monergism. Then he went to the Lutheran seminary in Fort Wayne, Indiana, and became a Lutheran pastor.

What impressed him most about Pastor Holt was his humility, his gentleness, his heart for evangelism, his conviction of the Lutheran teachings, his acceptance of people of all backgrounds and spiritual condition, including homeless people, and his faith in prayer. He told me he had a Pentecostal mother who prayed much. Pastor Holt prayed for me many times no matter where we were and I saw him pray for people countless times. He said that he believes in the power of the Holy Spirit, and that is why he named the church "Lutheran Church of the Holy Spirit."

I visited Pastor Holt a number of times in his last days. We prayed together every time. He told me some of his deep feelings. I told him how I experienced the supernatural power and the overwhelming love of the Holy Spirit when an evangelist laid hand on me in Hong Kong, and that is why I serve God in the Assemblies of God now. I still hold on to and teach the Lutheran teachings. At the same time, I have prayed for tens of thousands of people to experience the life-transformation and supernatural power of the Holy Spirit. I saw supernatural miracles and healing in front of my eyes many times. I saw people transformed spiritually totally through prayer.

I am very blessed to have known Pastor Holt. His personality, his Lutheran conviction and his faith in prayer have influenced me greatly. Like him, I have prayed for many people right on the spot many times- on the street, in hospitals, in a car, in a shopping center, and in countless Spirit-filled revival meetings.

Pastor Holt had been a missionary to China and Hong Kong for 16 years. When he knew I was going back to Hong Kong, he said, "I admire you going to Hong Kong." I will leave the U.S. in January, 2011, to be a missionary serving on the mission fields. I will carry the heart of Pastor Holt with me: believing in the power of prayer and the power of the Holy Spirit, carrying the compassion to save souls and to revive the spiritual life of Christians, and the heart to bring spiritual revival to churches and nations.

Rev. Patrick Jow
Son # 3 Ordained 6/22/1986

I am my parents' only son, but I am also proud to be "a son of the Lutheran Church of the Holy Spirit." I am the "third" son to go out as a Lutheran Pastor.

The year was 1975. In God's providence and all within a short span of time I was approached by several Christian friends — three of them were Baptists, and one of them was a Lutheran — who evangelized me with the Gospel of Jesus Christ. I followed the Lutheran to the Lutheran Church of the Holy Spirit (hereafter referred to as LCHS), and that began the process of my eventually becoming a "son" of this congregation.

My first encounter with LCHS was being invited by a Lutheran friend to a concert presented by the youths from the different fellowships. I enjoyed the songs they sang (one of them was "Top of the World" originally sung by the Carpenters) and the joy-filled atmosphere. At the conclusion of the concert it was announced that the pastor would like to say a few words to the audience. I did not expect to see a Caucasian man as the pastor of a predominately Chinese congregation. But that surprise made a deep impression on me, as this told me that this man in clerical collar had a special love for the Chinese people.

Having had a positive, first experience with LCHS I began to attend one of the Chinese youth fellowships held on Saturday mornings at 9:00. In the fellowship I got to know Mrs. Amy Mui, my teacher, and learned from her the way of salvation and many practical lessons for the Christian life. She impressed me as a person with excellent speaking ability and a teacher who had a genuine concern for the welfare of the youths. An example of the latter was a phone call I received from her one night shortly after I began attending the fellowship. She called to welcome me, to introduce herself to me, and to learn something about me. Just as I did not expect the pastor of LCHS to be a Caucasian man, neither did I expect the teacher of the fellowship to take the initiative to call one of her students.

I actually attended the youth fellowship for quite an extended period of time before I joined in the Sunday worship services. Out of necessity to meet the different language needs of the members, everything in the service was done bilingually in English and Chinese. This, of course, would entail translating the sermon from one language to another. (In this case the translation was from English to Chinese, as Pastor Holt would preach in English and Amy would translate the message into Chinese.) Even though this way of doing things would cause minor inconveniences for both the preacher (I know, I am a preacher!) and the hearers, three possible benefits which might result from that were: Chinese speaking folks might be able to learn some English, English-speaking members might be able to pick up some Chinese, and those who understood both languages would hear the sermon twice to ensure that the message would become ingrained in their hearts and minds! As I learned to serve God in different areas at LCHS, I also had opportunities to translate the Sunday sermon for Pastor Holt. This experience had the effect of drawing me closer to this devoted servant of God.

I do not remember how long after I came to know Pastor Holt when I learned that he had been a missionary to China and also had a fruitful ministry among the Chinese people in Hong Kong. But I thought that with such background and experiences, he must have learned the Chinese language and dialect(s). Sure enough, on one occasion some Chinese-speaking middle age women from the congregation went to visit him at his office and brought him some Chinese herbal medicine soup. (Pastor Holt was recovering from a minor illness at that time.) As soon as they stepped into his office, they started talking to him and inquiring about his health — in Chinese! But Pastor Holt had no difficulty understanding what they were saying to him, nor did he have any trouble responding to them in Chinese.

I would not attribute my desire to enter the ministry to either Pastor Holt or Amy, although both of them had been very supportive of my aspiration and played an important role in affirming my decision. Three factors caused my young heart and mind to consider the Holy Ministry as a possible life long service: a strong interest in Bible study, a fascination for theology, and a burden to share the saving Gospel with those who don't know the Savior. But I knew that wanting to become a pastor should not be an impulsive or self-willed decision on my part, so I spent two years (my last year in high school and my first year in college) praying, waiting on God, discovering my spiritual gifts by trying out various avenues of service in the church, and consulting with my spiritual elders (Pastor Holt and Amy) and peers (the brothers and sisters in the youth fellowship) until God led me to the conviction that my original desire to enter the ministry conformed to His will.

Having received the green light from God I immediately applied to the pre-ministerial program at Christ College Irvine. I graduated in 1981 with a major in theology. After that I spent six months at Holy Spirit serving as a Lay Worker, and another ten months at Pilgrim Lutheran Church in Oakland serving as a Director of Christian Education (DCE), although I was not really trained in that field. In November, 1982, my wife Esther and I drove to Concordia Seminary in St. Louis where I would be trained to become a pastor.

After my vicarage. I returned to St. Louis for my final year of classroom learning. Then in 1986 I graduated from the seminary and was assigned to Emmaus Lutheran Church in Alhambra (about 11 miles from downtown Los Angeles), California, to start a Chinese ministry from scratch, working in conjunction with the existing predominately Anglo congregation. And I am still serving the Mandarin speaking congregation I founded more than twenty years ago.

Before my wife and I permanently moved to Southern California, I came back to San Francisco to be ordained at Holy Spirit. Pastor Holt, my beloved spiritual father, who baptized me on December 25, 1976, and pronounced Esther and I, husband and wife on July 24, 1982, ordained me into the Holy Ministry on June 22, 1986.

I am proud to be "a son of Holy Spirit Church". I know that there are other such "sons" our beloved congregation has produced in these many years. I think I know who is the "baby brother" among us, but will someone please tell us who is the "elder son"?

Rev. Patrick Jow
Emmaus Lutheran Church
Alhambra, California

**Rev. Terrence C. Chan
Son #4 Ordained 10/25/1987**

As a young child I slept in a bunk bed. I had the lower bunk while my younger brother slept above. It was situated in the corner of the room surrounded by two walls and a large desk on the end. It had a sheet draped over the side to block out the early morning sunlight. One night as I laid in bed staring at my dark, tight enclosed space I thought to myself, "This is like a coffin, I wonder what it would be like to die?" So I held my breath for while to see what would happen. Nothing. After a few moments I thought to myself, "Gee, is this all there is to life? What happens when a person dies? What a shame to die and have nothing to look forward to."

That was my first recollection of asking the question about life and death and I had no answers. My family never talked about death. They never talked about religion or God or anything spiritual. I was filled with a sense of emptiness and a nagging question that needed an answer.

As a teenager I was confronted with the realities of death as several of my friends and acquaintances got caught up in the gang wars of the 1970's and were killed or murdered. Again the questions about life and death came to mind and still I had no answers. I had been on the fringe of involvement with gangs but I knew that I didn't want the same fate and needed to get out of that violent environment. I turned to sports and spent the majority of my time playing basketball, baseball and football at the Spring Valley school yard, Helen Wills Playground and Chinese Recreation Center. That saved me from further serious trouble but I was still mostly an unfocused, undisciplined and unruly youth; a streetwise kid that had no real direction or purpose in life. What I did have was that nagging question about life ... and death. And it was still unanswered.

One day I met a new friend at the school yard and we began to hang out together all the time. We played ball and did a few other activities together mostly after school and on Saturdays. The few times I asked him to go out on Friday nights I was told that he had other plans. When I asked him to join me for Sunday morning softball games he was never available but most any other time he was free. I figured my friend was out with his family for Friday night dinners and Sunday morning Dim Sum. I finally asked him what he did during those times. He nervously told me he went to church. "Church?" I thought that was interesting. I had never gone to church before except for a few times when I was about 4 years old. I remember walking two blocks with my older brother to a corner church. We would walk up the hill from our one room cottage, pass the corner grocery store, turn right, cross two streets and we were there. Our dad gave us a coin and told us to give it to the people at the church. That seemed okay to do but the third time I passed the grocery store I decided to use the coin for some candy instead. I never made it back to that church again.

A few months went by and out of nowhere my friend asked me to join him and some of his church friends for an outing at old Broadway Bowl. I wasn't much into bowling but decided to drop by and check out some of his other friends. It was during Christmas vacation and since I had nothing better to do that Saturday afternoon I went. I also met Carol their youth leader. After a while we struck up a conversation. She asked me if I knew the real meaning of Christmas. I stuttered and stammered some incoherent answer and she proceeded to tell me the Christmas story about Jesus' birth. "Oh, okay" I thought. "Well, nice meeting you all, time for me to go." Afterwards, my friend never asked me what I thought about his other friends. He didn't mention anything about church. The question about life and death continued to nag me though it was being buried deeper and deeper within my heart.

April came around and it was now spring break. The nice weather must have had a good effect on my friend because out of the blue he asked me to join him for the Good Friday afternoon worship service at his church. I said yes immediately. Never mind that I had no idea what Good Friday meant. I was finally invited to church and I was going! I remember that day very well. It was a bright sunny day and my friend and I made sandwiches and ate lunch up at Lafayette Park. Then my friend went to Woolworth's on Polk Street to buy some flowers for the church. Before I knew it we were walking up several steep concrete steps and I entered The Lutheran Church of the Holy Spirit for the first time ever.

My friend asked me to wait in the lobby by myself as he took the flowers into the sanctuary. There I was all alone in a strange place, uncertain and uncomfortable with my surroundings when someone from behind said, "Terry, welcome to our church." Now who could that be? I didn't know anyone who went to church except my one friend and I certainly didn't know anyone in this church. As I turned around I was warmly greeted by Carol the youth leader, the one I had met briefly over five months earlier. I was impressed that she could recognize me on sight—even with my back to her—and she even remembered my name! I was very, very impressed. I discovered soon thereafter that Carol Halter was a Deaconess at the church. I later discovered that she had been praying for me all these months and it was no wonder that she knew me on sight. She had actually been encouraging my friend to invite me to church!

During my first Good Friday service I heard a sermon by Pastor Wilbert Holt that talked about life and death and eternal life. I heard about Jesus' life and death and resurrection on the third day—all for a sinner like me. I heard the Gospel of Jesus Christ and I liked what I heard. It began to answer the nagging questions I had. After the Good Friday service I was invited to come back to their Friday night fellowship group meeting. Then I was invited to come back on Saturday night for a sleep over so that we could all go to an Easter Sun Rise service at Golden Gate Park—a spectacular re-enactment of Good Friday and Easter, with the performers in full costume including a centurion riding on a horse. Then I was invited to my first Easter breakfast, my first Sunday school class and my first Easter Day worship service. It was an intense, life changing weekend but that was just the beginning. Forty five days later I prayed and asked Jesus into my heart to be my Savior, to forgive me for all my sins and to be the Lord of my life. (At the time I was sitting at a table in the upstairs room—the exact spot which years later turned out to be the exact center of my office). Fifty three days after I was invited to church and first time I entered The Lutheran Church of the Holy Spirit, I was baptized into the Christian faith, on Pentecost Day, June 6, 1976.

Jesus and the church became the center of my life and all my activities. The one constant desire God had given me was to serve the Lord. But I was a very young Christian, full of energy and enthusiasm but lacking leadership, experience and maturity. I was never a leader among my peers. I was never a church officer or even a fellowship group officer, or usher or communion assistant. I was quiet and shy and not a very good speaker. So it was quite a surprise to many including my family, fellowship friends, Deaconess Halter and Pastor Holt that I wanted to become a pastor after being a Christian for only two years.

Thank goodness my parents said NO! Why would my parents deny my request?

Why didn't God answer my prayer? Isn't serving the Lord a good thing, a noble task? But I had learned in my brief time in Sunday school that we must honor and obey our parents. So I didn't pursue being a pastor. But I didn't give up wanting to serve the Lord either. Perhaps I was just stubborn and determined to get my way so I researched and found that there was a program to train to be a Director of Christian Education (DCE). When I presented this alternative to my then unchurched parents they asked, "What's a DCE?" I told them it was like a teacher but instead of teaching in a school they teach in a church. Becoming a teacher sounded good to them so they consented for me to attend Concordia College in Portland, Oregon.

After completing a fifth year internship and graduating and receiving my first call as a DCE my parents were pleasantly pleased. I was able to work my way through college, be the first in the family to receive a college degree and I was now employed and living on my own and supporting myself. Like most parents mine asked how far I could go in my profession. I told them that maybe some day I could serve in a larger church or teach at a college or study some more and become a pastor and lead my own church. When they heard that I could lead my own church they told me to go and be a pastor. They finally consented and gave me their blessing. But then I didn't want to be a pastor—I liked being a DCE!

It wasn't until after serving five years as a DCE, eight years since I first asked my parents, and ten years after I became a Christian that I finally went to study at the seminary to become a pastor. But that was all in God's plan and preparations for me because I was still too new a Christian and still too young in the faith when I first received the desire to serve. I needed time to learn from my mistakes, to mature as a child of God and to discover that no matter what happens in my life God is always there, always present, always reliable, always loving and forgiving and gracious and merciful. And always there with the answer: Jesus Christ!

"For I know the plans I have for you," declares the LORD, "plans to prosper you and not to harm you, plans to give you hope and a future. Then you will call upon me and come and pray to me, and I will listen to you. You will seek me and find me when you seek me with all your heart".
Jeramiah 29:11-13 + To God be the glory! +

Reverend Terrence Chan
Senior Pastor/Lead Missionary
Bethel Grace Lutheran Ministries
San Francisco

**Rev. Henry H.S. Lai
Son #5 Ordained 12/31/1987**

There is so much I could write about Pastor Holt, but I will focus on my relationship with him and saying good bye. In our Chinese language good-bye means see you again.

When I was asked to write an article about Pastor Wilbert Holt, my heart flowed with vibrant memories about this great man. I feel that Pastor Holt is still in my heart. Why do I say that? If feels just like yesterday that he asked me to walk him around the block.

On one occasion, my son David and I were visiting Pastor Holt. Pastor asked, "Henry would you please walk me around the block?" With David on one side of him, and me on the other, the three of us strolled from 6th Avenue, around Geary Boulevard. After one round, Pastor requested, "Henry, how about just one more time?" We went around again!

During our walk, Pastor asked me about First Trinity in Oakland, and he encouraged me to work hard and to remain patient in the ministry.

Looking back, I recall a time when Pastor Holt came to watch a play called "Luther's Life." The play was performed by our Young People's Society at Kowloon Savior Lutheran Church. After Pastor Holt enjoyed the play, he told me that I had great talents. Imagine how that felt to a 14 year-old boy. He had kind words to say. That was first time I met Pastor Holt. Pastor Holt would often invite me to have lunch at his home at 19 Oxford Road, and would also often ask me to babysit all his boys on Saturdays, so that he and Mrs Holt could go out. Sometimes I took the boys to Lai Chi Kook to swim. During those times in Hong Kong, he often visited my family because he wanted to win my parents to believe in Jesus.

I will never forget that it was Pastor Holt who buried my father, who was a Rattan furniture worker's Union Counselor, with a 1,000 membership. At my dad's funeral, there were more than 600 workers who came to pay their respects. Pastor Holt preached the Gospel at the funeral service. As a result of Pastor Holt's preaching at this funeral, a son of a Rattan furniture Union worker came to be Christian. Later, he became the Hong Kong Lutheran Synod president.

Pastor Holt was a soul winner who loved Chinese people. When I turned 21 years old, Pastor left for America for furlough, and he took my school credentials to Valparaiso University, in Indiana. There, he convinced Coach Walt Reiner to offer me a tuition scholarship. The Lutheran Laymen's League was interested in my studies, and through Pastor's efforts, the LLL Club directors paid for my room and board.

In 1963, Pastor Holt started a mission at 606 Jackson Street in SF Chinatown. At that time, my wife and I were still teaching at a Honolulu parochial school. Pastor invited me to San Francisco, requesting my assistance. It was a wonderful experience to work with Pastor. As a missionary, Pastor Holt has performed miracles; one of them was a sack containing a sandwich that was always in his pocket. Once, a hungry homeless man was begging nearby while we walked down Washington Street. He asked (as if to a priest), "Father, could you give me some money to buy food? I haven't had food for two days." Pastor Holt reached into his front suit pocket and took out a ham sandwich. I will never forget the look on the face of the man, and the attitude of awe he showed. Afterwards, Pastor Holt and I joked a little bit, "That is the greatest and speediest miracle that ever happened."

Pastor Holt was a faithful leader who planted spiritual seeds. Soon Amy (nee Hau) Mui appeared on the scene. Pastor Holt hired Amy to help as interpreter for the worship services. Pastor Holt's prayers and interests influenced me to prepare for an ordained ministry. Pastor and I constantly communicated; he was my mentor. I became a seminarian at the age of 40 at Concordia Seminary in St. Louis. I was ordained at 45.

Pastor Holt endured a lot for friends and he even suffered for the Gospel. His advice to me when I was ordained as a Missionary-at-Large for the CNH District was, "Work hard in the field, pray for a harvest, and ignore outside worthless arguments." He was right. He always said he was called to do a job, and he would not quit that easy. He also was known to say, "I will die with my boots on."

"Dear Pastor, I am not saying goodbye, because I will see you in heaven someday when the Lord Jesus calls. I still have a lot to do in Oakland. Today I am 75 years old. The Lord blessed me! I hope I will do exactly as you did, that I would die with my boots on, but until the Lord calls, I will say again—"see you again."

Rev. Henry H.S. Lai
First Trinity Lutheran Church
Oakland, California

**Rev. Marty Reed
Son #6 Ordained 7/25/1993**

Pastor Holt and I first met one Sunday in the early 1980s. He wasn't, however, the first person to greet me at Holy Spirit. I was hesitant when I walked in and I almost left. But a young man warmly welcomed me. He introduced me to others, sat with me during the Sunday school opening, brought me down to Bible class, and introduced me to Pastor Holt. And Pastor Holt introduced me to the Gospel of peace. I am thankful that the Lord used his faithful Gospel ministry in my life, and that the Lord used that young man and many others at Holy Spirit to aid and assist their pastor in this eternally significant work!

Pastor Holt was an excellent example of what a pastor should be, and I remember especially the way he visited with me privately. Again, this didn't happen immediately, but after a time I found myself sitting in his office. The thought of talking privately with a called minister of Christ is intimidating, but Pastor put me at ease. And over the course of a number of visits, in a personal and direct way, Pastor Holt spoke the Gospel to me and applied it to my life.

At first, though, he used the Law. He showed me my sinfulness and what I deserved from God due to sin. When I heard this truth from his lips, the truth declared by God Himself in the Bible, I was shocked! Up to this point in my life I thought of myself as a good guy, not as a sinner deserving God's eternal punishment. Amazingly, I didn't get up and leave. Praise God, I didn't! The Holy Spirit kept me there, and Pastor Holt went on to tell me, to bring to me, the forgiveness of sins won by Jesus through His life, death and resurrection.

The time I spent under the care of Pastor Holt was short. But through his ministry, I learned the basics of the Christian faith, received the Sacrament of Holy Baptism, was confirmed and admitted to the Sacrament of the Altar. This was a wonderful time in my life. Pastor Holt was there to counsel me through this transition in my life from fulltime employment, to college, and finally the seminary.

Now, by God's grace, I serve in a congregation in Southeast Missouri, in a place and among a people much different from Pastor Holt's ministry. Still, the people I meet need the same thing I needed when the Lord led me to Holy Spirit Lutheran Church and brought me under Pastor Holt's care some 25 years ago. That's what the Holy Christian Church on earth has the privilege of doing. Pastors and God's people— in San Francisco, Missouri or in other parts of the world— have excellent examples of individuals to emulate, like Pastor Holt. And, through Word and Sacrament, God's forgiveness in Christ Jesus, pastors and God's people have the honor and strength to work together to tell the good news about Jesus! "You are a chosen generation, a royal priesthood, a holy nation, His own special people, that you may proclaim the praises of Him who called you out of darkness into His marvelous light" (1Peter 2:9). To God alone be all glory!

Rev. Marty E. Reed,
Zion Lutheran Church
Poplar Bluffs, Mo.

Rev. David T.M. Chan
Son #7 Ordained 6/30/1996

I visited the church at 606 Jackson street with my grandmother but did not attend worship until the church moved to 1725 Washington street. I attended Berkeley University and received my B/S degree from California State College in Hayward with a degree in Business Administration and Finance. For nine years I worked as a Financial Analyst at Bank of America.

In 1962 I joined a young people's fellowship at Holy Spirit church. We were taught by Pastor Holt and Parish Worker Amy Mui to find our God given gifts and use them in outreach to others. Under the influence of Pastor Holt and Amy, I entered the Concordia Theological Seminary at St. Louis in 1992.

I served my vicarage at Mt. Olive Lutheran Church in Milpitas under the guidance of Rev. Gibson. Later Pastor Gibson accepted another call, half way through my vicarage. God sent Rev. Ihno Jannsen to be my supervisor, father-like figure and life long friend.

I was ordained and installed as Pastor of the Lutheran Church of the Holy Spirit in 1996. About this time I had surgery for an Aortic Disection. Later in 1997, I suffered a stroke which affected my speech and reading. God changed my many plans. God accomplishes what He has planned not according to our wishes.

The community around the church at 1725 Washington Street began to change. Members of the church purchased homes in the Richmond and Sunset district. Parking around the church was a serious problem. The church could no longer serve the community. People came to worship on Sundays only. I firmly believed a church cannot be separated from the community. An extension church had been opened in the Sunset area but it was impossible to serve both locations. The problem was brought to the congregation for a vote, should they purchase a building in the Sunset for a new church? There was a vast mission field in the sunset area among the Chinese families and youth. The congregation voted to sell Washington street property and purchase a building at 2400 Noriega street. The new church was dedicated Oct 2, 2002. The congregation continued to outreach and grow.

We were all shocked to learn that our beloved Pastor Holt had died suddenly on August 15, 2003. He was the spiritual father to many in the congregation.

In 2004 I received a call from Peninsula Asian Mission Society (PAMS) to begin the work of starting a Chinese congregation at Bethany Lutheran Church on the San Francisco Peninsula. It was a hard decision—stay in comfort at Holy Spirit church or do something different—establish a new Chinese mission. God directed him to accept the challenge.

Today I see the Gospel in action as Associate Pastor at Bethel/Grace Ministries in San Francisco. Over 550 Chinese immigrants visit the food pantry weekly. They hear about the church at the pantry and in 2009 an average of 150 Chinese immigrants attended the weekly Bible class.

Today I use the ideas learned from Pastor Holt to serve the community. He talked to people, learned their needs, like jobs, housing, doctors, schools and then he shared the Gospel. We have weekly Bible Studies at 8:30 a.m. each Saturday, to bring the Gospel of hope and assurance to them. The goal is to begin Chinese young peoples' fellowships and other children's ministries in the near future. There is a great need for God to raise up co-workers who are accountable, speak Chinese and can share the Gospel.

Rev. David T. M. Chan
Associate Pastor
Bethel/Grace Ministries
San Francisco, California

Rev. Bill S. Chu
Son #8 Ordained 8/18/1996

I can say much about my years at Holy Spirit Lutheran Church, particularly about being part of the fellowship of young people dedicated to what the first Christians devoted themselves to: God's Word, fellowship, the Sacrament, and prayer (Acts 2:42). Through that formative experience rooted in and centered around the means of grace and God's gift of Christian fellowship, the Holy Spirit fostered in us a love for the Word and a zeal for the Gospel of Jesus Christ which planted in me the seed of desire to serve the Lord in full-time pastoral ministry. Though mine was a circuitous path to the ministry, that seed finally bore fruit when I was ordained by the Reverend Wilbert Holt into the Office of the Public Ministry in 1996.

I thank God for the blessings I received from Him through the Sunday school teachers and brothers and sisters in Christ at Holy Spirit Lutheran Church. I especially thank Him for His blessings through Pastor Holt. While I was not certain — not even while I was studying at Concordia Seminary, and not until I received my first call — that it was God's will that I serve Him in the pastoral ministry, I was certain that Pastor Holt was a god-pleasing model for how a pastor ought to be: he loved and served the Lord with all his heart, soul, mind, and strength (Mark 12:30).

"He always had time for you" is often no more than a cliché when speaking about most people, but when referring to Pastor Holt, it was true: he made time for anyone who needed pastoral care. He was a man of prayer; few were the conversations we had that did not end with prayer. His compassion for the unsaved was Christ-like and his faithful and humble devotion to the Word of God and in particular, to the Gospel, beyond reproach. He had a servant's heart: he served, helped, and reached out even to those whom most of us — Christian or unbeliever, clergy or laity — would walk by on the street with nary a glance, just like the priest and the Levite did to the injured Jew in Jesus' parable. He fought tirelessly to protect the life of the unborn.

Pastor Holt would have been perturbed by such accolades as I, and no doubt others, heap on him in this book because he would have wanted all glory to be given to God who saved him from sin and death by grace through faith in the Christ crucified for him; like St. Paul, he resolved to know nothing.. except Jesus Christ and him crucified (1Corinthians 2:2). St. Paul's words in Acts 20 spoke for Pastor Holt in life and in death. "But I do not account my life of any value nor as precious to myself, if only I may finish my course and the ministry that I received from the Lord Jesus, to testify to the gospel of the grace of God" (verse 24). His life and ministry answered Christ's call to deny self, take up the cross, and follow Him (Matthew 16:24).

Though Pastor Holt was easily identified as clergy by his clerical collar (most who knew Pastor Holt know that rare was the occasion when he did not wear his clerical collar), what left no doubt that his was a pastoral heart that burned with love for the Gospel of the cross of Jesus Christ as the power of God to save (Romans 1:16-17) and that he loved not just the Chinese people but all people and desired that all come to know Christ as Savior was his zeal to preach the word, be ready in season and out of season, reprove, rebuke, and exhort with complete patience and teaching (2Timothy 4:2).

I thank God for Pastor Holt's pastoral care during my time at Holy Spirit Lutheran Church. I thank God for the privilege of learning the Catechism from Pastor Holt who not only taught the Word of God but, knowing that he was at the same time "saint and sinner," lived that Word in and by the forgiving love of God in Jesus Christ. I thank God for my conversations with Pastor Holt about the joys and challenges of pastoral ministry. I thank God for the blessing of knowing Pastor Holt as Pastor, father-in-the-faith, and friend.

I have fought the good fight, I have finished the race, I have kept the faith. Henceforth there is laid up for me the crown of righteousness, which the Lord, the righteous judge, will award to me on that Day, and not only to me but also to all who have loved his appearing. (2Timothy 4:7-8). Well done, good and faithful servant (Matthew 25:21). To our God and Father be glory forever and ever!

Rev. Bill Chu
Holy Cross Lutheran Church
Concord, California

Daniel K. Woo
Son #9 Ordained 7/26/1998

I am grateful for the Christian brothers and sisters in Christ who encouraged me along the way in my walk with the Lord Jesus. When I was still in high school, Robert Schnitzer, a dear friend and teacher, challenged me to do mission work. When I expressed doubt about my worthiness and ability, he reassured me of his confidence in me and encouraged me to get involved in shot-term mission projects and works. It was in those mission opportunities that I experienced the joy of giving, the need of loving for the sake of Jesus Christ.

While I was in college, the Rev. Tom and Denise Allen, staff members of InterVarsity, took the time one day to advise me, to help me see that the university setting was a great mission field and opportunity for the proclamation of the Good News of Jesus Christ. It was there, on a college campus, where I experienced the power of God, the power of the Gospel working through His servants to bring forth conversion. The seed of salvation was planted. Needs of students were met. Lonely hearts were heard and comforted. The Word of God was studied in small groups with hunger and fervor. The love of Christ was communicated and shared. Souls, by the power of the Holy Spirit, were saved. Their faith was nurtured and strengthened. The Kingdom of God was advanced on this college campus.

When I returned to my home church, the Lutheran Church of the Holy Spirit, during those summers of my college years, Amy Mui, a dear sister and teacher, challenged me to consider full-time ministry. I still recall those very words from her sincere heart: "Daniel, you don't look like a lawyer. You look like a pastor. You have the gifts of a pastor." It was that challenge with those words that led to two years of intensive prayer, seeking the Lord's will in my life.

Whenever a question on the subject of God's calling was raised, I turned to Pastor Holt, a humble pastor and friend, who took the time and interest to explain and expound on the biblical teaching of vocation. I recall him saying, "Those who are called to public ministry (that's a noble task) have an inner conviction that God has called them to the work of being a spiritual leader, teacher, and undershepherd for His people. When that call is confirmed by the church, they will be ordained for lifelong ministry of Word and Sacraments, usually in a congregational setting."

God, in His perfect timing, opened the door to Concordia Seminary, St. Louis, where I was trained and further equipped as a servant in the Lord. Now, I seriously doubt that any of these men and women in the Lord realized how important they were in my spiritual and educational development. As I reflect on their counsel, I thank God for each one of them. And I realize anew the importance of giving a word of encouragement to God's people—especially the young—along the way of their Christian formation.

If you have not been informed, let me tell you. "The harvest is plentiful, but the workers are few." Let's pray to God that He send forth more workers to His harvest field. The Christian church is in need of faithful church workers. We need more candidates going into full-time ministry to be trained as pastors, missionaries, teachers, DCE's, and the like. You can be instrumental in the life of a future pastor or DCE now as you speak words of encouragement to the next generation. God will use you when you make yourself available. All praise and glory be to our Lord!

Rev. Daniel K. Woo
Hope Lutheran Church
Daly City, CA

**Rev. Lenny Szeto
Son# 10 Ordained 7/11/1999**

My journey with LCHS began at the age of 11. My family had been invited many times by Eugene and Gail Wong to celebrate Christmas and attend other activities at the church. On some occasions we would attend, but we were we never committed.

Then one day, our television broke and we did not know who to turn to or how to have it repaired. So Gail and Eugene introduced my family to Tony Ma who was working for Zenith at the time. Tony came over, repaired our television, got permission from my parents, and came to pick my sister and me up for Sunday School. That's when we started attending Sunday School every week.

It was during those years, that I met Pastor Holt and Director Amy. A few years later Amy decided to start a new fellowship group, "Hope" and invited me to join. Through the fellowship group, Amy taught me the Bible, cared for me and guided me through my teenage years.

By the summer of 1987, the love of Jesus and His forgiveness became so real to me that I realized that I was a terrible sinner. I was wasting time living a life that did not bring glory to God or help others in anyway. During the Summer Retreat of 1987, overwhelmed by the love and forgiveness of Jesus, I told Him that I wanted to live for Him and serve Him, but I don't want to be a pastor. But God had other plans. Gradually, He began to change my heart and attitude about that.

About that time, I began attending the 11am Worship Service regularly. God began to speak to me through Pastor Holt's sermons. One thing I remember most about Pastor was that he often taught us to pray, "Lord, what do you want me to do today." Gradually, I got to know Pastor Holt. We began a journey of passing out gospel tracts, gathering signatures, and standing up for the rights of unborn children.

Slowly God began to put a burden on my heart and a passion for the lost. I had this love and desire to serve God. Through Pastor Holt, Amy, and the church, I was given many opportunities to serve, to gain experience from, and be a part of a ministry that brought the gospel message to our parents and friends. Because of Pastor Holt's example and Amy's passion for the lost, they made a huge impact in my life. I knew God was using them to prepare me for the ministry.

By the time I reached 20 years of age, I wanted to be a pastor and also knew that God was calling me into the ministry. So, I finished my undergraduate degree at San Francisco State and graduated with a B.A. in clinical psychology in 1994 with the hope of preparing for pastoral ministry right away.

On a family vacation trip to L.A., I shared with my parents about my desire to serve God as a pastor. At the same time, my friend Daniel Woo was entering the seminary in the summer of 1994 and it would have been nice if we could go through the training together. But my parents were unhappy about my desire. And I prayed, "Lord, I can't go to the seminary like this. Lord, if this is You please open a door."

From that day, God began to change my parents' perspective about pastoral ministry. A year later they said to me, "If this is what you want to do in life, go do it." Praise God! It was His time that I would begin preparing for pastoral ministry in 1995.

It was about that time my friendship with my Julie began to develop into a companionship. I had known Julie at our fellowship group for years and always admired her love and passion for the Lord. Julie was studying to be a D.C.E at the time, while I was studying at the seminary. We both did not know where God would lead us.

In the spring of 1997, I was assigned to Hope Lutheran Church in Daly City for my vicarage. Julie had graduated at the time and was awaiting placement. Then she received a phone call from Pastor Hedstrom of Hope Lutheran Church in Daly City and asked if she would serve the church as a Youth Worker. We both served at Hope Lutheran in Daly City together. How can something like this happen? Only God can put things together this way. Then in the summer of 1998 we got married and returned to the seminary for the final year of studies.

I graduated from the seminary in 1999. I was ordained at Holy Spirit during the summer of 1999 and was called to serve at Redeemer Lutheran Church in Shawnee, Oklahoma. We served there for two years and God blessed us with a son, Kean. After that, we were called to True Light Lutheran Church in New York, New York. We served there 2 ½ years and God blessed us with a daughter, Meagan. Then we were called to serve at Our Savior Lutheran Church in Fremont in 2004. Julie is serving here with me as the Director of Family Ministries. All Glory be to our Lord Jesus!
Rev. Lenny Szeto
Our Savior Lutheran Church
Fremont, CA.

Rev. Warren Jow
Son # 11 Ordained 4/7/2004

Ours was the typical, first generation traditional Chinese immigrant family: frugal, hardworking; where respect for elders was expected and an education was highly esteemed. These were the fundamental building blocks for wealth, honor, and a better life. Born in San Francisco, I also grew up with the religious traditions my folks brought over as well. And yet life took a different direction for me—one that saw those valued things in a different light; not as ends in themselves, but as means to a greater end; one that also led to the one true God.
My sister, who was older than me by 12 years, was a Sunday school teacher when I was still a child. It was she who started me going to church the same time I started grade school. But being an introvert by nature, my fears overpowered even my desire to know about God. Consequently, I stopped going to church altogether, being too timid to seek out another church on my own. But after a year of running on empty, hunger pains to know more about God began to gnaw at me. One day, as I was walking to the neighborhood playground, I suddenly looked up to heaven and said, "God, if you're real, find me a church to go to; a church that really teaches about You." I didn't expect that anything would come from that outburst of longing. But two weeks later, outside that very same playground not more than fifty feet away from where I prayed that prayer,

I happened to be sitting and chatting with a schoolmate, when Pastor Holt happened by. What I didn't know at the time, was that my classmate had been to his church. Pastor Holt apparently saw him and took the opportunity to invite me to come as well. Unbeknownst to him, the prayer I had spoken only a couple of weeks earlier was still echoing in my head. His invitation was like a light bulb turning on. "Could this be the answer to my prayer?" Hearing the truths of God's Word taught reassured me that it was; and a year later, I was baptized and became a member of the Lutheran Church of the Holy Spirit for the next 35 years.

Graduating from high school, I narrowed my career choices down to three possibilities. I studied architectural drafting at the local city college as the default mode. But opportunities for a teaching career and ministry presented themselves as well. God, however, redirected me away from them, and I found myself considering the last of my options —a job interview for a drafting position. By the time I was walking away from that interview, though, I considered that I had failed miserably. So it was that once again I prayed, "God, just find me a regular job. Any ol' job; one that'll provide enough for me and a family maybe; and I'll just serve you like everyone else in the church—as a layperson." God, however, prompted me to follow through with sending in a sample of my drawings to supplement my disastrous interview. Despite having done everything wrong, to my utter astonishment, I landed the job! What began as a long shot turned out not only becoming a twenty-one year career, but one that perfectly fit the talents and aptitude that God had blessed me with as well. Marriage and children came along soon enough. Meanwhile, the thought of ever being in full-time ministry faded as I started to see myself retiring with the company. But God had other plans.

Having learned from an earlier incident in my faith walk to learn to let go when God says to let go, and after He had prepared me by using a situation that lasted two years to sever my emotional attachments to the firm, God's Spirit one day indicated to me, that it was "time to go." Despite the timing of it all not seeming to make any sense, I knew the implications of the call, in four months time, my whole life and that of my family's as well, was turned around. The numerous "miracles" that saw us through seminary and to the parish I now serve, despite the many inadequacies I had felt and still feel, only confirms for me what should be true for every believer: that one's life's calling is not so much about what they do for God, but about what He is able to do through them; for "we are not adequate in ourselves to think of anything as being from ourselves; but our adequacy is from God." (2 Corinthians 3:5) Serving Him, is simply a matter of being available. All Glory be to God!

Rev. Warren Jow
First Lutheran Church
Dinuba, CA

Rev. Christopher H.W. Ng
Son #12 7/19/2009

My family immigrated to San Francisco, Ca from Hong Kong, China back in the late 1960's. I was born in San Francisco. The maternal side of the family was Christian for several generations; apparently, my great-great grandfather was a bishop in China. I cannot trace a direct influence of that towards my pastoral vocation. Nonetheless, I was baptized as an infant at True Sunshine Episcopal Church and my family worshiped there as I grew up.

My first impression of Christianity was that it was a Sunday family activity with a short walk to Chinatown for lunch. I went to private school for the first half of my elementary education, so I was also exposed to Catholicism. After transferring to the public school system, I was relieved that I could finally wear my weekend clothes to school. I also had friends who didn't go to church on Sundays. This was the beginning of how I learned to appreciate certain dualities of life, especially being raised as an American-born Chinese person.

My family was introduced to The Lutheran Church of the Holy Spirit through a family friend. My parents wanted a good foundation for my cultural heritage and language skills, so the Chinese School program was suitable. I had a good time and at the same time, I noticed that other students had a strong negative reaction. This was one example which showed me that things never are as perfect as they seem. Another was that we stopped attending True Sunshine Episcopal Church due to their church conflict at the time.

From the Chinese program, I experienced the love and devotion of Director Amy Mui and many teachers throughout the years. They had a heart for sharing the Gospel with youth and I appreciated the positive influence. My family started to worship at Lutheran Church of the Holy Spirit and we were confirmed together in 1995.

During my teenage and college years, I've been blessed to know the leaders at that time. If I had one word to describe each, it would be as follows: Pastor Wilbert Holt - shepherd, Director Amy Mui - truth, Pastor David Chan - perseverance. Pastor Holt loved his flock and those outside his flock. Director Amy knew how to speak God's Word to young and old. Pastor David modeled how to live with quiet strength from God.

Things are never as perfect as they seem, but God can still use those moments to show us His love and grace. That being said, it's not easy being the poster child of a Chinese family. It's not easy being the poster child of a church either, especially within a Chinese church. I understand what several of my Chinese School classmates had experienced. While I did enjoy being a "good Chinese kid" at home and at church, I admit that it bothered me while growing up. If academic and character excellences were encouraged and rewarded, then what is there for those who don't achieve that? The challenge for Chinese youth who "succeed" is not so much developing a haughty pride but living under the pressure to keep up the good work. This was a major influence how I understood what it meant to live under the grace of God. I'd like to draw parallels to Martin Luther's experiences of angfechtungen—despair over one's limitations and brokenness. Can we bring all of that to God or do we anguish, expecting His wrath at our failures? Martin Luther used the phrase "Simultaneously Saint and Sinner" to describe our relationship to God and others. God sees us as saints because of Jesus' forgiveness and grace to us. Yet, we still break things as sinners when we live apart from Jesus. Reflecting on my life to date, I think Luther was right. He'd hit " the nail on the head".

All this got played out during college. I knew college would be a spiritual battlefield and I'm glad I had the support of brothers and sisters in Christ from Hope Fellowship. The challenge was integrating my weekday and weekend life. It was difficult to share with family and friends how different my life was while I was away in college. When it was time to graduate, I reflected that the best thing that happened to me wasn't getting a diploma but that God had never forsaken me throughout my wanderings. Only He can break my cycle of meaningless pursuits. His mercy and His steadfast love continues to cover my shortcomings.

I'm glad I settled back into Lutheran Church of the Holy Spirit after college. I thank my first class of Sunday School students (Emmaus Fellowship) for allowing me to grow up with them. My greatest joy was to go from teaching them to serving with them on a mission trip before I went to the Seminary. It is also my joy to see some of them serve in greater roles in church today. I also thank my brothers and sisters in Tweeners Fellowship for letting me experience the small group dynamics and learning together about life after college. And of course, I thank Cheryl Suen for being my friend through college, a sister in Christ through fellowship, and eventually, my wife through an interesting courtship.

The path to the Seminary was not an easy decision. I am glad for that because I treat the call of God very seriously. A pastor once said, °The call is the need". I heard that there was a shortage of Lutheran pastors available for congregations and I had the desire to say, "°God, here I am, if you see fit." It was humbling to be examined by people at church and at the Seminary yet also reassuring that this is not finalized by my will. I believe God was merciful to work with me step by step through His plan. God opened doors through the Seminary years. I studied and served by His strength and love. I've went through sorrow and joy, like my wife's miscarriage then the birth of our child, Zoe. It means "life" in the Biblical Greek language. And I've learned to live according to what God provides.

There is more to be shared about how God leads me, but for now, simultaneously saint and sinner. That is why one of my favorite Bible verses is from Philippians 3:12 "Not that I have already obtained all this or already have been made perfect, but I press on to take hold of that for which Christ Jesus took hold of me." To conclude with my favorite of the Four Gospels, "But these are written that you may believe that Jesus is the Christ, the Son of God, and that by believing you may have life in His name." I John 20:31.

Christopher Ng
Associate Pastor
Lutheran Church of the Holy Spirit
San Francisco, California

Bringing Christ to the Chinese
The Sons and Their Families

Pastor Paul Holt and Family

Pastor Yip and Rita

Pastor Patrick Jow and Esther

Pastor Terrence Chan and Daughters

Pastor Marty Reed and Family

Pastor Henry Lai and Family

Pastor David Chan and Family

Pastor Daniel Woo and Family

Pastor Bill Chu and Family

These Are Her Sons   Chapter Twenty-Three

Pastor Lenny Szeto and Family

Pastor Chris Ng and Family

Pastor Warren Jow and Family

"I have fought the good fight, I have finished the race, I have kept the faith. Henceforth there is laid up for me the crown of righteousness, which the Lord, the righteous judge, will award to me on that Day, and not only to me but also to all who have loved his appearing."

2 Tim. 4:7–8 RSV

Chapter Twenty Four

A Tribute to
Rev. Wilbert Victor Holt
November 11, 1918 to August 15, 2003

Rev. Wilbert Victor Holt was known for his love for spreading the Gospel to each person he encountered regardless of the time, place, or situation. He had a special gift for conveying a deep and genuine love for each person he met as he considered each person a special child of God.

Pastor Holt was born in Oak Park, Illinois. He was the second of six siblings (3 boys and 3 girls) born to Walter and Lydia Hoeltje. He was greatly influenced by his mother who was from a strong religious family. Her kind treatment of the traveling hobos that came by their house during the Great Depression along with the abject poverty Pastor Holt witnessed as a missionary to China and Hong Kong, instilled in him a deep-rooted and life-long concern for the destitute. Pastor Holt also was influenced by a cousin studying for the ministry as well as an elderly pastor from his mother's church. After one of this pastor's evening services, while alone waiting to take the train home, Wilbert decided at the age of 17 that he would serve the Lord fulltime. Despite the difficult financial times, his mother encouraged him to go to the Seminary. The following items are a list of some of his ministries and main events in his life: 2 year vicarage — Year one: Dean of Boys at the Lutheran Welfare Association in Addison, Illinois. — Year two: organized a Lutheran congregation in Colton, California.

1945
Graduated and ordained into Holy ministry and married Geraldine Bierworth.

1945–1962
Missionary to China (Enshiah, Hupeh), Geri worked as a nurse at the hospital.

Co-founder of the Hong Kong Lutheran Synod, a partner church of Missouri's Synod and the Seminary in Hong Kong where he was its first President.

Geri & Pastor Holt along with other missionary families became advocates for the deaf and blind in Hong Kong.

Upon his departure from Hong Kong in 1962 there were 20 Lutheran congregations, 7 primary schools, a secondary school, and a seminary.

1964–1997
Accepted a call to the Chinese people of San Francisco.

1964
Founder of Lutheran Church of the Holy Spirit, a storefront mission on Jackson Street.

1969
Thriving congregation moved to the Washington Street site. Late 1980's he received honorary Doctorate degree from Concordia Theological Seminary (now located in Fort Wayne, Indiana).

Before his retirement in 1997, many Chinese Lutheran ministries were started throughout the Bay Area and many young men and women from Holy Spirit congregation went into various Church ministries.

He was grateful to his loving congregations and parishioners for sponsoring his and Geri's trips to the Holy Land and Germany.

Other Ministries

Pastor Holt was a member of both the board of the Interfaith Committee for Life and United For Life and was given the Human Life Award by the latter group.

Until a few months before his death, he continued to have weekly Bible studies at his home. He continued to conduct baptisms, funerals, and counseling phone calls even up to the day before his death on August 15, 2003.

Pastor Holt was pre-deceased by his wife Geri in March of 2000 and is survived by six sons and five daughter-in-laws: Paul & Linda, John & Janet, Joel & Rhonda, Daniel & Angela, James, and David & Sandy, and 19 grandchildren.

**My Father
Rev. Paul V. Holt**
(Spoken at the memorial service)

The Reverend Wilbert Holt is my father and my pastor. His faith, love, and ministry have been largely responsible for the person I am and the way I do ministry. He still inspires, comforts, and encourages me. He baptized me and gave me a lifetime internship in what it means to be a man of God, the people of God in his world. He planted and nourished my fate, prayed for me, financially supported my studies and ministry, counseled me in difficulties and found others to help me in my ministry. His example and zeal has been the foundation in many of the things I rejoice the most in and have fought the hardest for. His missionary zeal for the people of China worldwide has given me also a missionary heart for all people. I rejoice to have been a part of establishing a Chinese Lutheran Church in Oakland. I rejoice to have been part of building a mixed Japanese American Church in Gardena, California. I rejoice to have been part of the civil rights movement, and to have formed an integrated church in Oakland, California that serves many races, nationalities, and social-economic groups, as well as, starting a multi ethnic Christian preschool and daycare, so that all could have a new opportunity for salvation and education. My father's concern for orphans in Addison, Illinois and Enshiah, and Hong Kong, his enthusiasm for the rights of the unborn as God's children were part of the reason my wife, Linda, and I took on over 45 foster children, and adopted six.

My father's concern for the sick and suffering in Enshiah's hospital, Hong Kong's refugee hospitals, and San Francisco's Laguna Honda hospitals, are part of the reason I spent eight years as a chaplain to Alameda County's Highland Hospital. John George Psychiatric Hospital, and Fairmont Hospital--serving some of Oakland's poorest people.

Above all, my father gave himself to his Savior, body, soul, mind, and spirit. He worked for God everyday, all day. He wore his clerical to say he was on duty to be the voice, the heart, the arms, legs, hands, and feet of God. If you were part of the body you were invited, respected, and expected to help with your best talents, cooperation, and energy. He was there to remind people of God's presence, to pray, to help, to baptize, to share God's word, God's plan of salvation and labor in his kingdom. He was there to save you from your sins and hell and move you into the kingdom of heaven. It was the same if you were a stranger, a doctor, a refugee, a student, a member of his family. a person with psychiatric illness, or a professional church worker. Every conversation, phone call, chance meeting was a God given opportunity to pray and share the faith. Some of my friends called him "Dial-a-prayer" because they knew if he answered the phone, when they called me, they would have to pray before they talked to me. His spirit was in this: he had not put on his collar, left his homeland, family, worldly comforts behind, not to take the opportunity to speak of God. He had not survived the Great Depression, World War II, the communist takeover of his church twice, he had not survived strokes, cancer, his wife's illness, raising six boys, car accidents, sinking boats, crashing planes, the loss of all personal goods, not to share the peace and assurance of God.

He would be late, he would be busy because there was no one lost, no task too small that he could not do what was necessary.

This spirit especially, I pray for, and it has helped with the small struggling congregations I have served. I remember at one time Holy Spirit's small storefront church also needed me to haul debris to the dump, to take Sunday school teachers, students, translators to church, to usher, to teach Sunday School, count offering, clean floors, set up chairs among other tasks. I saw God's miracles with students that met with my father in our home becoming Hong Kong's first seminary, and pastors that could lead a church body of strong Christian Churches through Hong Kong's poverty, economic boom, and change of government. Sick, orphans, refugees, immigrants, became powerful, generous Christian, storefronts becoming loving, serving churches with hospitals, schools, food and clothing distribution centers. Christian workers around the world were inspired, helped in Enshiah, China, in Hong Kong, in San Francisco. God's people were a great body. This spirit and blessing has always given me hope in a faithful God, the God of my Father and me.

Remembering My Father!
Daniel V. Holt
(Spoken at the memorial service)

I'm embarrassed to speak after such distinguished speakers, and my own older brother speaking so well about my father. I think I should be up here singing the solo "Chief of sinners though I be"

Distinguished pastors, priests, parishioners from Holy Spirit Congregation, parishioners from other congregations and friends:
On behalf of my whole family, I'd like to thank you all for all the kindness and comfort you have shown our family and the help of so many of you in the past years of my father's illness. This helped him to be able to live at home during his final years. Many of the comments that I have heard during this past two weeks are consistent with the words of that prayer throughout his life.

I'd like to begin by reading a thank-you note written by my father after June third, 2001 operation. This letter captures his thankful heart, his prayerful trust in the Lord for all things, and his spirit of evangelizing at any time and place. A portion of the note reads as follows, "Thank you for your prayers, the very night of my operation on June third. That Sunday I was scheduled to preach, but instead that Sunday, the surgeon preached to me and my family. He said, 'Pastor Holt, if you allow me to operate on you today, you have 50% chance you will live. You can expect a long convalescence.' We agreed to go ahead with the operation though I added with a smile, 'You don't mind if we pray with more optimism than your prognosis.'

"That operation on June third saved my life from a perforated intestine. The doctor said that the operation was successful. Thank you Lord Jesus.

"Before the operation, I had the opportunity to say a fond farewell to each of my sons, individually. Never before did I sleep not knowing before I woke whether I would see Jesus or my family. Never was the Word of God so deeply impressed in mind as those words of St. Paul, 'I have a desire to depart and be with Christ which is far better. Yet is beneficial for you that I remain.' How wonderful it is that you and I are Christians and have such a good way to answer as we face death. It is not eventually heaven or hell, but rather, will I see Jesus, or my family and friends?"

This attitude is not unlike his attitude when for a cancer operation more than a decade preceding the operation stated. I remember visiting him that time in his hospital bed with my father doing the comforting. He assured me that he did not fear death as his life was in God's hands. He did mention he hoped the operation would be worth it. He wanted all his time to count, and be a beautiful service to God.

Upon first visiting him after the June, 2001 operation in a somewhat weakened and delirious state, he immediately wanted to finish the Pentecost sermon that he had been writing shortly before he came to the hospital. During his three week convalescence, he came to the realization that he had been given extra time. He immediately sent notes. He wanted to establish a nation's ministry building, which could be used by various ethnic ministries. He wanted to highlight in his words what he called, "Lived in moments." These are the special moments in his life where he felt God's presence close to him.

Another calling that was to die a poor man. He took seriously the Scripture verse that was just read, which states, "Don't turn anyone away that wants to borrow something from you." He once told me, "If someone has more need of something that I have, I will give it to him." All this he did and at times he would give the coat off his back and ask others to give their coats as well. But his chief goal was to be available to minister to others and use every ministry opportunity given to him to share God's love with others.

What ministry did God gave him to do in the last two years? He was able to conduct Friday night Bible classes in his own home up until January this year. He counseled and prayed with one who had been advised by his doctor to terminate his wife's pregnancy due to a potential unhealthy child. He conducted funerals of former parishioners and spent the rest of the day with the family in Christian witness. He visited the sick and dying. He baptized a few people in their last days. He witnessed to the Muslim para-transport driver who drove him to his radiation treatments. Last September my wife volunteered my father to an impromptu outdoor memorial service for a man who had no relatives but an elderly aunt. Of course, my father did it gladly. It's told me he did it in the context of God's promise of eternal life and the Christian hope and joy of the resurrection.

Through his last year of ministry he got all involved in the Scripture words of a previous sentence - "My kindness is all that you need. My power is strongest when you are weak. So I will brag more about my weakness in order that Christ's power will live in me."

I often thought about his ongoing faithfulness during these trials. The words of St. Paul come to my mind found in Romans 8:38–39, St. Paul states, "For I am sure that neither death nor life, nor principalities, nor things present, nor things to come, nor powers, nor heights, nor depths, nor anything else of all creation, will be able to separate us from the love of Christ."

If I were to read it applied to my father, it might read, "Neither tuberculosis nor malaria, nor strokes, nor heart attacks, nor a colonostomy, nor a loss of sight and hearing, nor cancer, can separate me from a love of God in Christ Jesus our Lord."

I'm sure he shared the same strength of faith that St. Paul had when St. Paul wrote in Romans 8:15, "I consider that the sufferings of this present time are not worthy to compare to the glory that will be with Christ."

So what did Dan learn at the end of my father's life? His genuine passion for others. His contentment with varied ills. He never complained about his illness, rather seeing what he could do for others. His thankfulness in all things including the health he still had. His love for his family, his incurable appreciation for all the help, his humility. For example, when my mother passed away, he gathered his sons in the hospital and confessed to his family what he perceived as his shortcomings as a husband to his wife and our mother. His devoted prayer life. He told me he learned to pray in the year he was in a Denver sanatorium recovering from TB in the early 1950s. It also stood out that he needed to pray as his memory began to fail him. He would pray with pictures in his hands to remind him of family, friends, and parishioners.

His prayers have sustained him throughout his whole life and were his clearest communications in this. One of his last prayers was with his brother, the day before my father died. Two days later his brother also went to his heavenly rest. To summarize this point, one could simply say he was faithful to the end. His dream of multi-ethnic buildings is left for someone else to do. His book may yet be written for the end of the service bulletin will tell you how. He was a joyful servant of God, rejoicing in emergency to the end of her life. He was overjoyed yet humble in responsibility from that couple that he previously counseled about keeping their unborn child. Thankful for the word from them of a healthy child. However he was wrong about one thing, from the comments I have heard today and in the other places, in addition to the fact that all you people are here today in a common purpose.

I would say my father died a rich man. Let me read to you this Bible verse in James 5:16, it appeared in simple regards in a home, "Pray for one another that you may be healed. However, prayer of a righteous person has a great power in its effects."

We thank God for my father's life today and all the glory be to Christ, He is our creator and sustainer. He is our witness, faithful to the end.

Faithful Servant of Christ
Amy Hau Mui

Pastor Holt and I worked together for over thirty years. I knew him and admired him! I am deeply touched by his love for the Chinese people and the experiences he encountered in his life long dedication as a missionary. He was committed to learning the Chinese language, culture and tradition.

He loved Chinese food, especially rice and a few homemade dishes. He was everyone's good friend and a model pastor. He loved his wife and family. His six sons are all grown and have their individual families. The eldest son is also a pastor. Pastor Holt's love for the Chinese people and his life long passion to win them for Christ never diminished. Pastor Holt, Mrs. Holt, and their family sacrificed much so that many Chinese people could receive the Gospel.

Once he spoke of his experience in sharing the Gospel among the farmers in a poor village in China; I then realized what a huge sacrifice it was for him to preach in China during that generation fifty years ago. If it were not out of a pure love for God, a dedicated heart to serve the Lord, and a zealous love for Chinese people, he would never have sacrificed his all for the Chinese people's sake.

After the political power shifted in China, Pastor Holt left China for Hong Kong. There he continued to share the Gospel with the Chinese people. He mobilized the Chinese ministry in Hong Kong. At that time thousands of refugees fled daily from China to Hong Kong, his spiritual foresight told him that this was a golden opportunity to spread the Gospel and to train the next generation of Chinese church leaders. He spread the Gospel among the refugees, set up training courses, Bible study classes, and brought seekers to Christ. Countless Chinese received Jesus as their Savior, experienced revival and dedicated their lives to serve the Lord.

Now, in Hong Kong, there are over thirty Chinese Lutheran Churches. God remembered Pastor Holt, His faithful servant's love in telling the Gospel to the Chinese people; He blessed the Hong Kong churches and advanced the Gospel.

God continued to use Pastor Holt. In 1963, He led the Holt family to San Francisco. In 1964, Pastor Holt founded the Lutheran Church of the Holy Spirit in the heart of Chinatown, Jackson Street. Three years later, in 1966, while I was fund raising in California for the refugee services in Hong Kong I met Pastor Holt during one of these functions. My first impression of him was his genuine faith toward God and his sincere love for men, and his deep belief in he power of the Holy Spirit. In all situations, He always sought God's will and shepherded the church according to God's word.

Through God's wondrous plan, I started to work with Pastor Holt at Lutheran Church of the Holy Spirit in August of 1967. For over thirty years, I was his interpreter, secretary, parish worker and Gospel partner. He trained, taught, encouraged, and appreciated me. He gave me many opportunities to learn. He was my good teacher and I gained much in his friendship. He treated people with humility, never with a trace of arrogant attitude. He lived a simple life, untiringly visiting neighborhood Chinese families. He never refused anyone's request for help. When people rejected the Gospel, he never grumbled or showed any signs of dissatisfaction. He always had a smile on his face, always lived out the joy of Christ. He was very approachable, a man of prayer quietly sowing the Gospel seeds.

He lifted high the cross of salvation wherever he went. He interceded for the church, various ministries, and personal needs of people without ceasing. Pastor Holt served at Lutheran Church of the Holy Spirit for almost forty years.

During these years, he guided eight members into the pastoral ministries and over ten members into the church worker field. They are now serving the Lord throughout the state in various churches.

He led close to 900 Chinese believers to the Lord and baptized them. He was truly God's faithful servant.

At the age of 84, Pastor Holt departed from this world in peace. Indeed, this is God's grace and blessing upon this servant, "that they will rest from their labors, for their deeds will follow them!" Revelations 14:13. What Pastor Holt and Mrs. Holt have done on earth for the Lord and their contribution to the Chinese Lutheran churches are tremendous. My deepest regret is that due to my illness, I was not able to have a last visit with him. Pastor Holt, you are the one I admired and you are my model. The gate of heaven opened wide for you, and God Himself with all the saints welcomed you. Now you are with the Lord, which is the best!

Your Partner in the Gospel
Amy Mui
With tears of gratitude!

~~~~~~~~~~

Memories of Pastor Holt
Mary Ma
(Spoken at the memorial service)

I have known Pastor Holt for the past 37 years. Pastor Holt first saw me playing in my uncle's front door, which was the back alley behind our Jackson Street church. Pastor tried to share the love of God with me, but I avoided him. The only time I accepted his invitation to church was for a scoop of ice-cream. It took him almost one year before I finally accepted his invitation to church. I was then 12 years old. I made friends at church, and when Amy Mui joined our church as our parish worker, she started our first fellowship group which was called "Bible Club".

We had a lot of fun with Pastor. He took us to the circus, picnics, hiking, camping, and even fishing.

As the church grew, Pastor Holt and Amy made many home visits. When Pastor found out my father wanted to apply for a kitchen helpers job but he couldn't lift 100 lbs, Pastor Holt advocated for my father. He wrote a letter to the department head and my father was exempt from that requirement. For this, my father was forever grateful, and Pastor Holt gained the trust of my parents and they permitted me to join the church.

Pastor Holt often said that the secret to his success was he knew how to select co-workers that made him look good. To me, I think the truth was, he knew how to be effective as an administrator and as a supervisor. He gave his staff a lot of support and a lot of autonomy to strive and thrive and to excel in their God given talents. Whenever there was conflict or challenge among the youth, Pastor Holt would be there, to do counseling when he could, support the staff, and set limits for us. He did it in a non-judgmental way, in a very loving and encouraging way. He had a Bible verse for everything. And I was under the impression that he memorized the whole Bible. He was a very humorous person. Every situation was a win-win situation. There was no way to be angry with him, nor challenge his authority.

As our church thrived and moved to Washington Street, he began the Lutheran Hour and we had fund raising dinners. We served Chinese food and performed Chinese folk dance during the fund raising event. All the proceeds went to the Lutheran Hour. Pastor Holt never, never kept any money, he refused to accept any percentage of the proceeds for our church. He always said to us, "Other churches have been very kind and generous to us, it is our privilege to serve."

Pastor Holt also during the 80s got involved in Community Social Welfare issues.

Once when Agnos was mayor of San Francisco, he came to our church to thank Pastor Holt for his contribution to the city. I'm sure the mayor got a surprise. After his short words of appreciation, the mayor proceeded down our church aisle and Pastor Holt said, "Let us all rise to say a prayer for the mayor." And the mayor stopped in the middle of our aisle, bowed his head and waited for Pastor Holt to finish his long prayer. That was an unforgettable moment for me. I was so proud of Pastor Holt.

He was never ashamed of the Gospel. Later I found out he literally gave away all his money to the homeless drug addicts. I was so angry. But when I got over it, I became very judgmental. I began to see Pastor as a kind, old, gullible creature who wasnot above letting people take advantage of him. I set up a conversation with him, trying to convince him to wise up, and stop allowing people to take advantage of his kindness. After each conversation, he always said to me, "I surely need you to remind me, and he loves me so much". The next day, of course, Pastor Holt continued on his old way.

Two years ago, I knew he was terminally ill. I wanted to spend more time with him. I let go of my desire to change him. I visited him more regularly, and oh how I enjoyed those visits. Once he told me, he knew they were hounding him, but he still had to believe their stories and respond to their needs. I asked him, "How come?" He said, "What else can I do?" It was not his job to change people, it was his job to love them. Once they believe in Jesus, they will change. In the meantime, his job was to love them as Christ loved them. This was paradigm shift for me. I realized Pastor was preaching and practicing "for God so loved the world" Jesus came to serve, not to be served.

Pastor Holt took his ministry of reconciliation very seriously.. like St Paul, he shared the Gospel wherever he went.. And repeatedly he would say to people, "God wants to be reconciled with you, would you please be reconciled with God"

Three months ago, Pastor told me, he heard the bells on the other side waiting for him. He said, "So little time left, so much left undone. What am I going to do?" In tears he asked,

"What will God say?" and in tears I said to him, "I know what God will say. He will say, "Well done, my good and faithful servant. Come and enjoy the blessings I have prepared for you."

Two weeks before his departure, he drew, what he envisioned the bells at the gates of heaven might look like. He said, the gates are opening, soon it will be, "Welcome home." There were no tears in his eyes, just longing!

Today we give thanks to God for he has welcomed our spiritual father home, my beloved Pastor Holt. We are here to give glory to God for Pastor Holt's legacy of service.

A Great Person Forever Remembered: Rev. Dr. Wilbert V. Holt

Martin Luther's birthday is November 10, while Sun Yat-Sen was born on November 12. In between these two great persons, Rev. Dr. Wilbert V. Holt (who was born on November 11), is the greatest person I will forever remember because of how he has so deeply affected my life.

At the end of 1949, since the American Lutheran missionaries were unable to evangelize in the mainland China, Pastor Wilbert Holt along with three female missionaries, Gertrude Simon, Martha Boss, and Lorraine Behling came to Hong Kong from Szechwan to wait for transportation for their return to America. During the time in Hong Kong, they discovered many refugees spoke the common language (Mandarin) that they knew, so they stayed to share the gospel with them. In January of 1950, I also took refuge in Hong Kong. Through the guidance of Missionary Simon, I received Jesus in the refugee camp. In the same year during Pentecost, Pastor Holt baptized me, along with 25 other people. These people eventually formed the beginning of the Lutheran Church in Hong Kong.

In June of 1950, the Hong Kong government moved the refugee camp to Tiu Keng Leng.

The Lutheran Church also built tents there to invite the refugees to worship. In addition, they began the Concordia Bible College and Gertrude Simon was its president. After I was baptized, I was immediately hired to do literary work for Missionary Simon while studying at the College. Unfortunately Pastor Holt developed tuberculosis as a result of his heavy workload so he had to return the United States to recuperate following doctor's orders. Due to the tradition of the Lutheran Church at the time, female missionaries were not allowed to preach at the pulpit. After Pastor Holt and his family left Hong Kong, I started to preach at Sunday worships and teach Sunday school. Upon graduating from the College, I was sent to Macau and started the two churches, St. Paul and St. Peter.

After Pastor Holt recovered and returned to Hong Kong, he not only taught me at the College, he also taught at our Workers Advance Study class. In 1956, while I was processing my application in Hong Kong's U.S. Consulate for immigration to New York in accordance of the Refugee Relief Act, Pastor Holt met up with me. He told me that the Hong Kong's Workers Advance Study class had been granted seminary status from the Synod and he was appointed as its first president. He hoped that I would not immigrate but to stay in Hong Kong, studying in the seminary while working. He told me after being installed as pastor for two years, the church would then send me to St. Louis's Concordia Seminary for further study, and then I could return to teach in the seminary. I was touched by his sincerity, and this became the road of no return for my service to the Lord.

I graduated from the seminary in 1961, in February of the next year I was installed as the pastor for Concordia Lutheran Church. Due to Mrs. Holt's mal-adjustment of Hong Kong's climate, Pastor Holt and his family left Hong Kong in May 5, 1962 following the doctor's advice. Later on he began the Lutheran Church of the Holy Spirit in San Francisco. In the spring of 1964, since there were no words from the Hong Kong Synod to send me to America for further studies, I then personally applied and was accepted to several universities for a master degree in counseling. I chose San Francisco State University and immediately applied for a 2 year sabbatical from the Hong Kong Synod, but the synod hastily decided to send me to St. Louis instead.

Originally I was suppose to start school in United States in the fall of 1964, but because the secretary of the Board of Directors of the Hong Kong Concordia Seminary was a Mandarin speaking missionary, on his meeting minutes he wrote sending Andrew Chiu to United States to study Master in Divinity, while the secretary for the Hong Kong Synod was a Cantonese speaking missionary, on his record he recorded sending Andrew Yau to United States to study. The Lutheran mission board from United States replied in July of that year: Who are you sending? Andrew Chiu, or Andrew Yau? As a result, I was not able to go until 1965. In January of that year, I arrived in San Francisco and stayed at Pastor Holt's home. However, he told me, "The St. Louis seminary won't start the spring semester registration until March 6, why don't you stay at Holy Spirit and be the assistant pastor for a couple months before going there, in the meantime you can live at my home." I accepted this fine arrangement. This is also the reason that I am able to speak a few words in the Toi Shan dialect!

When going to St. Louis for advance studies, or passing through San Francisco on other businesses, when preaching and worshiping at Holy Spirit, I have always stayed at Pastor Holt's home. I will never forget this teacher - friend relationship. Pastor Holt not only showed his care in every possible way to me, but also extended this type of care to everyone who was in need whether physically or mentally. Besides being a loving pastor, he was also a very humble person. His alma mater, Concordia Seminary in Springfield, Illinois, commended him with an honorary degree of Doctor in Divinity (D.D.) for the ministry work he did for the Chinese. As far as I know, he has never proclaimed this honor in any occasions or on business cards. And for this reason, as the title for this article, I specifically use "A Great Person Forever Remembered—Rev. Dr. Wilbert V. Holt".

In addition to remembering Pastor Holt,

I also remember my dear Mrs. Holt. Mrs. Holt took extra care of me while I was a guest in her home. In Hong Kong, besides busy taking care of her six sons, she spent much time and energy with the ladies' ministry, especially the ministry with the blind. In particular, one occasion I will never forget is when I was younger, I always coughed and blood would come up. After I was diagnosed with bronchiectasis in the 1950's, Mrs. Holt, who was a nurse, taught me to lower my head and use the "body positional flow" technique to ease the elimination of the phlegm, this way, the illness will not progress due to the phlegm accumulation. From that time on, I go through this same technique everyday. The reason I am still alive today in my 80's is because of what she had taught me! I truly thank, respect and love Dr. and Mrs. Holt, I will never forget them!

Rev. Dr. Andrew Chiu (Former President of Hong Kong Synod Lutheran Church)

~~~~~~~~~~

Pastor Holt The Good Shepherd
Henry Chan

Jesus said to Peter: "You feed my lambs." It is just like Jesus had said the same to Pastor Holt. Pastor Holt was really a good shepherd who took good care of his sheep. He knew his sheep by their names, and always kept his eye on them.

Each time I talked with Pastor Holt he always asked about the fellowship and the members. Particularly those who had not been seen for sometime. He was very much concerned about whether they were still going to church and He always talked about them to the Lord in his prayers. My brother had stopped coming to church for a long time. Each time we saw Pastor Holt he asked me about him and his family. My mother passed away a long time ago but each time I talked to Pastor Holt he would say to me how nice she was and how she had served at the church.

While Pastor Holt was in the hospital in his life's last days, I visited him a couple of times. He told me about a man that he wanted to help very much and hoped to win for Christ. Many times he helped this man with money. People told Pastor that this man was a drug addict and only interested in his money but that did not stop Pastor or cause him to give up on this man.

Pastor Holt was very persistent in helping people who needed help, particularly spiritual needs. He will not give up, just like a good shepherd will not give up until he finds the lost lamb.

(Henry Chan was one of the first interpreters for Pastor Holt at the 606 Jackson street church and also interpreted for him many times at the 1725 Washington Street church—he is now an active member at Cannan Chinese Church.

~~~~~~~~~~

He Worked for Social Justice for Prolife
Beatrice Klein Smalley

Pastor Holt was active in two Prolife groups in the early 1970's. It was some decades ago, before the West Coast Walk for Life, before Operation Rescue, before prayer vigils were held and the big demonstrations. The infamous date of January 22, 1973 is not forgotten by the real Prolife members and Pastor Holt was one committed to the Prolife cause as the greatest issue of our time.

In those days Planned Parenthood was located on Bush street, between Franklin and Van Ness, next door to St Gregory Episcopal Church. Pastor Holt joined the small group on January 22nd with a most creative and effective message. He pushed an empty baby carriage that had a pair of baby booties hanging from it. That said it all! Very simply! Later when we had prayer protests, he was there too!

We had many good Prolife mutual friends. We remember Felton Howe, a Lutheran parishioner, who lived around the corner form the Holts. Felton was a Catholic but he went to church in both faiths. He was very devoted to get out the Prolife message. Nowadays

Planned Parenthood is located on Eddy Street and Prolife still carries on its prayer witness across the street. We feel Pastor Holt's spirit joins our efforts.

Pastor Holt was a longtime member of our United for Life Board and always brought thoughtful views to our meetings. He was such an understanding pastor. One time there was a difficult person who insisted on "crashing" our meetings. He was a "idiot type" whom nobody could manage but Pastor Holt would counsel this man with social advice that would help him become more acceptable and Pastor Holt always gave him a ride home. Pastor Holt was a very unique person who loved people.
Pastor Holt was presented a special award by United for Life!

The Mission, Not The Place!
Rev. Ted Iverson

(Former President of the Church Extension Fund (CEF) which financed the purchase of buildings over the years as the Lutheran Church of the Holy Spirit expanded.)

The Lutheran Church of the Holy Spirit was founded by Pastor Wilbert Holt to bring Chinese people to Christ. He was a furloughed missionary from China, offered by the Synodical Mission Department in St Louis to the District because there was no hope of his returning to China.

In March of 1964 the District found a storefront to lease at 606 Jackson in China town for $450.00 per month and, with the support of the many volunteers, remodeled and operated ministries (especially ESL classes and children's activities) as outreach to the community.

In 1968 the lease expired and the rent was increased to $550.00 per month. The facility was proving to be too small and the location too impacted with traffic. For Pastor Holt the mission and not the place was what was important. He found a closed theater at 1725 Washington Street and proposed that the District buy it for the ministry. That caused a certain amount of controversy since the location was not in the heart of Chinatown where many of the District leaders thought they should stay.

The LWML came up with $100,000 to purchase the property, and the District agreed to make $150,000 available to remodel the building.

Once there the ministry was never confined to the building. If there was money, they spent it on adding staff --- Amy Mui, and Henry Lai, Carol Halter. They used a park nearby to meet the neighborhood children and draw them into the ministries. They also used locations like Christ Lutheran Church and a West Portal Lutheran facility for language schools. Pastor Holt offered support for a Chinese outreach at the Good Shepherd Lutheran Church in the Sunset when that Anglo congregation closed.

The youth of the Congregation did outreach at Laguna Honda and also supported the ministry at Diamond Heights when the District wanted to restart a mission there. Pastor Holt, working with the District, conducted a lay training institute for adults at the Sunset Extension church of the Lutheran Church of the Holy Spirit. The Chinese language school at Greenhaven Lutheran Church in Sacramento was begun by one of these lay trained graduates.

So focused was Holy Spirit on ministry that at one time in the 1970's, Holy Spirit had ten young people studying to be DCEs and church workers at Christ (now "Concordia") College in Irvine.

The emphasis was always upon outreach and service. A small remodeling project at Washington did add some additional space for ministry but the kitchen and fellowship space were inadequate for the growing congregation. Parking was always a problem.

The Chinese population changed as the children of the immigrants that flooded into San Francisco in the '50s and '60s grew up, married and began their own families. Many, if not most of the members joined the rest of the Chinatown population in relocating to other parts the City, especially the Richmond and the Sunset. Pastor Holt felt that they needed another location, especially in the Sunset, to continue the language schools for which he was losing the sites he had been using.

However, he wasn't totally happy with the building that he found on Noriega. It had housed a plumbing business and a dry cleaners. As we stood across the street, Pastor Holt exclaimed, "But $476,000 is a lot of money!"

I was concerned about more than the cost. It wasn't as centrally located as I would have liked. But, as with Washington Street, Wil was not concerned about the location. He was not concerned---as I was---about the building's remodeling challenges. There were drums of potentially toxic waste in the dry cleaners. There was a huge roll-up door that admitted trucks into the building which had to be replaced. There was no kitchen, a questionable bathroom, and a tiny over-grown back lot.

I was amazed when I first saw the remodeling that they had done with what came to be called the "Extension".

The building was relatively small but tall. From the beginning there was a desire to expand the building. Chuck Brophy studied the structure of the building and the zoning to see if a second (or even a third) floor could be added. Unfortunately, he discovered that an additional floor would require either a completely new inside or outside frame to support it. In addition, building code requirements, potential problems with height limitations, and possible neighborhood opposition were insurmountable obstacles.

So, for over a year we cultivated the owner of the little (old) house next to the Extension and of the vacant lot that abutted it on the corner. These would provide a more economical way to expand the ministry space if they could be acquired. Unfortunately, the owner of those sites did not want to part with them because of his plans to develop a multi-story condo building on the sites.

Unlike Holy Spirit which continued at Washington and added an "extension" in the Sunset, many of the Chinese congregations were relocating their entire ministries and following their membership out to other areas of the City. Church buildings were becoming available as Anglo congregations in these areas were closing up. Holy Spirit was using the Extension for more and more activities because it was convenient for most members who no longer lived in or near Chinatown. However, because they had never limited their ministries to their building on Washington, Holy Spirit did not feel the same urgency to move.

Meanwhile, the District became very interested in the 1980's and 90's in beginning new Chinese congregations in many locations in the City. Among the sites that began or were considered outreach to Chinese were Zion, Diamond Heights, Grace, and Daly City. Holy Spirit released its pastor and a number of members for one such attempt in the Sunset. The plan was to start by beginning a preschool in a defunct bowling alley as the community outreach tool. That mission languished when the original plan could not be implemented and it searched fruitlessly for a suitable location in which to settle.

It became apparent to those of us on the outside that the Washington Street property could not provide the location or space for Holy Spirit to grow. Efforts to begin new missions were both expensive and were not succeeding. Meanwhile, Anglo congregations were shrinking or closing as the demographics of the City changed.

The feeling within Holy Spirit that it should itself relocate to the Sunset prompted several congregational meetings over a period of time. I listened in on one such meeting after worship one Sunday and I could see it was not going to be an easy decision to make. After all, location had never seemed to be that important.

In time I found myself standing at 2400 Noriega looking at a recently-vacated Bank building which was being considered as the site for a relocated Holy Spirit. It was an attractive location, not far from the Extension, but it appeared to me to be too small. It was hard to imagine how adequate space for worship could be created where there was a lobby and teller windows. It presented interesting challenges, like how to use the vault or what to do with the space where the ATM machine was. There was very limited space upstairs and expanding the building appeared to be very problematical.

Yet, this building had one thing going for it---it was not a traditional church building. I had learned from my experience with Wil, Amy, Allen, and the Holy Spirit leadership that its about the bringing people to Christ not about creating "sacred" spaces. After all, it had been a storefront, an old theater, and a plumbing shop that had served them so well over the years. Now it would be a former bank.

Like the Extension, it was clear from the start that the bank building would have to be expanded or replaced to accommodate their growth but Holy Spirit had always found other places for weddings, funerals, and large special events. They were prepared to adapt this building as they had done at their previous locations.

There were issues with neighbors and building codes that were dealt with and the remodeling was even able to produce an office were the ATM machine had been. They were able to accommodate classes and fellowship in the limited space available upstairs. The worship space became very attractive and by using the lobby area for additional seating they were able to provide enough seating for worshippers.

A building committee and fund raising efforts were undertaken to lay the ground work for expanding or replacing the building. It was difficult to discuss designing a building because they had always looked for available buildings that could be adapted to their use. They were averse to having debt and wanted the maximum amount of money devoted to ministries. This was Holy Spirit's history and culture. So it was not surprising that the process of providing expanded facilities took longer and with many twists and turns.

These efforts to provide plan and raise money for more space on Noriega did not deter the staff and the Congregation from helping start a new Chinese outreach ministry in locations on the Peninsula and at Grace Lutheran Church.

It was only fitting that the San Francisco city staff, upon review of the proposed drawings submitted for the building permit, commented that it did not look enough "like a Church". Holy Spirit, true to its history, isn't interested in what buildings look like. They are just places to reach out and draw people into that new life which only Christ can give to our faulty human nature.

Today the Holy Spirit congregation has moved to temporary locations while a new three story building will be built on the lot at 2400 Noriega Street, San Francisco. They look forward to 2012! Praise the Lord!

A Prayer of Thanksgiving!

Dear Heavenly Father,

We praise and thank You for guiding our Lutheran Church of the Holy Spirit over the past almost 50 years. Each time we think about our church, our hearts are filled with gratitude and thanksgiving to you.

Oh, Heavenly Father! Workers may pass, surroundings and situations may change, but your work will not cease. It will continue to move forward, for You are the Lord of our church, Lord of the harvest, and Lord of the threshing field. Thank you for giving us co-workers and believers who are faithful and who love the Lord with all their hearts.

You have been the head of our church from the very beginning until now. Ever since the day you called Rev. Wilbert Holt to establish our church, our brothers and sisters have been committed to share the gospel, and today your power strengthens us as we continue to proclaim your gospel. May our hearts be filled with your word as our foundation, and a sacrificial love that is rich in giving.

You are the same yesterday, today and forever. You, who began a good work in the hearts of the brothers and sisters in our church, will surely complete this work, until the day of Jesus Christ. Guide us so we may continue to conduct ourselves in a manner worthy of the Gospel of Christ, united in one mind, standing firm, and working hard together to proclaim your gospel and not compromising with the ways of the world..

We pray the Holy Spirit will fill our hearts with unity, sincere love and passion, making us pure and trustworthy persons, seeking to give encouragement, comfort and fellowship to one another. Help us use our days on this earth, bearing good fruits for you. Always seeking to please only you!

May our attitude be the same as that of Christ Jesus, humble in learning, respectful and loving, good examples as children of God in this sinful generation. May we shine like stars in the universe as we proclaim your words of life. Help us to lift high the Cross of Jesus Christ. May His name be glorified and His kingdom return soon.

In Jesus name we pray. Amen.
Your people

"Preach the Word of God urgently at all times, whenever you get the chance, in season or out, when it is convenient and when it is not. Correct and rebuke your people when they need it, encourage them to do right, and all the time be feeding them patiently with God's word."

2 Tim. 4:2 LB

Chapter 25

The Church 2012

Rev. Shiu Ming Lau, Senior Pastor
Rev. Christopher Ng, Associate Pastor

Staff:
Allan Tong, Director of Christian Education
Amy Mui, Director of Evangelism
Cindy Jeong, Pastoral Assistant

Officers:
Peter Ng, President
Andrew Fung, Vice President
Vernice Louie, Recording Secretary
Gavin Yuen, Treasurer
Elaine Hung, Financial Secretary
Terry Wu, Financial Analyst

Elders:
Barron Fong, Head Elder; Daniel Lam, Tom Lee, Robert Leung

Rev. Shiu Ming Lau
Senior Pastor

Rev. Shiu Ming Lau was born in Hong Kong in 1962. He became a Christian when in high school and was baptized on December 3, 1979. He graduated from the Lutheran Theological Seminary in Hong Kong in May, 1991 with a Master of Divinity Degree. After coming to the United States for study, he received his MA degree, in 1993, at the Assemblies of God Theological Seminary in Springfield, Missouri. In 1995 he was ordained at the Assemblies of God in Springfield.

In 1999 he received his Master of Scared Theology degree from Concordia Lutheran Seminary in St Louis. He is now working towards his PhD degree. Rev. Lau is fluent in Cantonese, Mandarin and English.

In 1990 he married his wife, Janice. They have a son, Josiah and a daughter, Jessica. The children were born in Springfield, Missouri.

Over the past twenty years, Rev. Lau has served as Distribution Officer of the Hong Kong Bible Society and ministered at churches in Hong Kong and Springfield, Missouri. In 2000, the Lord Called Rev. Lau. through the Missouri District of the Lutheran Church, to plant a Chinese Mission in St Louis, MO, the Light of Christ Lutheran Chinese Mission. He was recently elected chairman of CliMB (Chinese Lutherans in Mission Building).

Rev. Lau is very mission minded. Before receiving the call from the Lutheran Church of the Holy Spirit in San Francisco, Rev. Lau applied to serve as a Missionary to the Chinese in China; however, the Lord chose to give him the call from the Lutheran Church of the Holy Spirit where the mission field among the Chinese in the Sunset area was ripe unto harvest. He accepted the call to be pastor of the predominately Chinese congregation, The Lutheran Church of the Holy Spirit and was installed on June 25, 2006 as the fifth pastor of this congregation.

Rev. Lau believes the new ministry will be a challenge but a joyful and fruitful one for him. God will lead and richly provide mission opportunities when he teams with members of the Holy Spirit congregation as God multiplies His kingdom and blesses the Chinese people in San Francisco and around the world.

"But you will receive power when the Holy Spirit comes on you; you will be my witnesses in Jerusalem, and in all Judea and Samaria, and to the ends of the earth" (Acts 1:8).

To God be the Glory!

~~~~~~~~~~~~~~~~~~~~~~~~~~

Rev. Christopher H.W. Ng
Associate Pastor

Rev. Christopher Ng was born in San Francisco, Ca. He was baptized as an infant in 1977 at True Sunshine Episcopal Church and was confirmed as a member of Lutheran Church of the Holy Spirit in 1995. He married Cheryl Suen in 2006. They have a daughter, Zoe Ng, born February 2009 in Saint Louis, Mo. Rev. Ng is fluent in English and Cantonese.

Rev. Ng graduated from the University of California, Davis, with a Bachelor of Science degree in Microbial Biotechnology and a Minor in Dramatic Arts in 2000. After five years of working in the biotechnology field, he answered the Lord's call to the seminary. In 2005, he began his internship at Light of Christ Chinese Mission in Saint Louis, Mo. In 2007, he served as a vicar at Mount Olive Lutheran Church in Milpitas, Ca. In May 2009, Rev. Ng received a Master of Divinity degree from Concordia Seminary St. Louis. He was also the 2009 recipient of The Rev. Dr. Victor C. Rickman Scholarship.

In July 2009, Rev. Ng was ordained and installed as Associate Pastor of the Lutheran Church of the Holy Spirit. As an American-born Chinese, he is excited to be part of a team ministry in a diverse community of many languages, generations, and cultures. Rev. Ng believes the Lord has blessed the congregation with the gifts and talents to reach people for Christ in such contexts. Aside from parish ministry, he currently serves as vice-chairman of Chinese Lutherans in Mission Building (CLiMB).

"Not that I have already obtained all this, or have already been made perfect, but I press on to take hold of that for which Christ Jesus took hold of me." (Philippians 3:12 NIV)
"For we do not preach ourselves, but Jesus Christ as Lord, and ourselves as your servants for Jesus' sake." (2 Corinthians 4:5 NIV)

~~~~~~~~~~~~~~~~~~~~~~~~~~

Christian Education Committee

The goal of this committee shall be to teach the Good News to children, youth and adults and equip them for mature Christian living. The committee is chaired by the Director of

Christian Education, and a member of the Pastoral Staff or an Elder. Their responsibilities include Children's Worship, Day Camp, Nursery, Sunday School and Fellowship Groups.

Church Building Expansion Committee:

The Building Committee worked with the architect to create a functional and aesthetic design for the new church building at 2400 Noriega Street. The detailed design drawings were completed and submitted to the City and County of San Francisco for permit review on December 30, 2009. Ground will be broken to begin building this new three story church in Fall 2010! Please view the building on our web site—www.lcholyspirit.org

Church Expansion Building Fund

We began our ll phase Building Fund drive in April 2006.

Caring Committee

The purpose of this committee is to be sensitive to the health and welfare of the congregational members, providing the comfort of God's Word and appropriate care in times of illness, bereavement and shut-in situations.

Evangelism Committee:

This committee promotes the work of winning souls for Jesus Christ in our community and concerns itself with work of child, youth and adult evangelism. They assemble "gospel envelopes" to seekers and new comers to the church.

Team members join in home visitation of the Summer Camp youth and welcome them to our worship services and fellowships. They also visit and welcome members of Tai Chi classes to worship and attend other seeker events.

Maintenance Committee:

The purpose of this committee is to provide a well maintained facility for worship and fellowship of it members.

Mission Task Force:

This committee plans short term mission trips to China and Mexico. In 2010 there will be two trips to China to Canton and Sichuan respectively. We will join Club Dust for a mission trip to Mexico. There is a Mission Rally planned for each year with a special mission speaker. We have become a Partner Church with SOBEM (Showers of Blessings Evangelistic Ministry) by which we support them financially yearly and in return we receive their quarterly reports and the copyright to reproduce their 1000+ gospel DVDs. We are presently supporting several overseas missionaries in their work in Hong Kong and China.

Worship Committee:

The purpose of this committee is to create an atmosphere that enables the congregation to worship in spirit and truth so each member will be blessed and strengthened with the Word of God and the Sacraments. There are two chairmen, one for the Bilingual Service and one for the English Service. The choir director is also a member of this committee.

Other Ministries

Chinese Lutheran Hour—This ministry was established in 1969 as a radio broadcast. In 2006 it initiated a Website and radio programs are broadcast known as "God Knows My Heart" as a radio outreach to the Chinese in San Francisco on Station KUSF, FM90.3, each Wednesday evening at 6:30 p.m. You can listen to each program by logging on to our website www.chineselutheranhour.org.
Chinese Lutheran Hour has a link to our Church Website. where Sunday Sermons, messages of

special speakers, church news and opportunity items are available.

Church Web Site

This ministry's mission is to bring the Good News of Jesus Christ and our church to the people of the congregation and community at large. Church information is updated weekly including the announcements at worship services, copies of both English and Chinese sermons and any other speakers or workshops that have taken place at the church. Opportunity pages contain upcoming events. The News pages show pictures and articles of special happenings at church events or fellowships. Website is www.lcholyspirit.org.

Help-U-Learn Ministry

After School Tutorial (1st Grade–8th Grade) Weekdays 2–7 pm The Lord is exalted, for He dwells on high; he will fill Zion with justice and righteousness. He will be the sure foundation for your times, a rich store of salvation and wisdom and knowledge; the fear of the Lord is the Lord is the key to this treasure." Isaiah 33:5–6. Mission: to establish a long term relationship with the students through meeting their needs; assisting them academically; providing them with resources to face the many life challenges; to share the good news of Jesus Christ with them and their families so they can have a personal relationship with Him.

Help-U-Learn After School Tutorial started August 1999. Fall Semester begins in the end of August and Spring Semester ends in early June of the following year. It's a daily program for students who attend both public schools and private school, from 2 pm to 7 pm at Sunset Extension. Students are under disciplinary guidance and are expect to develop healthy habits in their own individual academic pursuit. Many students return and become tutors.

Vision for the Help-U-Learn Ministry. After-school tutoring during the weekdays is an ever-growing need in our Sunset community. Our "Help-U-Learn" (HUL) After-School Tutorial Ministry started in 1998 and is ongoing into our twelfth year. More than 170 students have been enrolled in the HUL program. Students who graduated were willing to come back to serve as tutors and also invite their high-school & college age friends to join in this experience. From this "tutor referral", new high school age and college friends can come to hear the gospel when they are invited to attend our high-school and young adults fellowships.

Through the youth leaders training and service evolved from this amazing ministry, many new and gifted young members are given the opportunity to serve in many outreach programs.

At the same time, the students' families are being invited to fellowships and church outreach events. Some are willing to really seek to know the one true God and we have members to follow up on their faith. They can see the love of God through brothers and sisters who really care about their lives and not just tutoring their children's school work. Parents who are baptized and growing in their faith in turn encourage and witness to their friends and relative and they in turn play an important role in our evangelism and follow up work.

In the future with more space, we may expand this ministry to pre-school age children, special education, private tutoring, and hold various cultural interest classes to meet the various needs of the families in our community. Our ultimate goal, of course, is to draw people to come and to know Christ.

"Be happy! Grow in Christ! Pay attention to what I have said. Live in harmony and peace and may the God of love and peace be with you" 2 Cor 13:11 LB

The Church 2012 — Chapter Twenty Five

Written by Lorraine Ma, Assistent Director

Fellowships Under Help-U-Learn Ministry
DCE Allan Tong:

PEACE Fellowship (College & Career)
1st & 3rd Sat 7–9 pm.
"The crucible for silver and the furnace for gold, but the Lord tests the heart" Proverbs 17:3

Mission: To incorporate a group of young adults into a family where they can be known and challenged through God's Word, cared for as a close knitted community of support, held accountable in spiritual maturity and encouraged by one another.

TRINITY Fellowship (High School)

1st & 3rd Friday 7–9 pm
"Trust the Lord with all your heart; do not depend on your own understanding. Seek his will in all you do; and he will direct your paths." Proverbs 3:5–6

Mission: To celebrate God's presence and honoring God with our lifestyle; to meet each other's need with God's love; to invite new friends to fellowship through building long lasting friendship; to care, held accountable and encourage each other as God's people; and to learn God's truth and His message to build a foundation on Jesus Christ.

PEACE JR Fellowship (Middle School)

2nd & 4th Friday 6:30–9 pm
"My grace is sufficient for you, for my power is made perfect in weakness. Therefore I will boast all the more gladly about my weaknesses, so that Christ's power may rent on me. That is why, for Christ's sake, I delight in weaknesses, in insults, in hardships, in persecutions, in difficulties. For when I am weak, then I am strong." 2 Corinthians 12:9–10

Mission: To celebrate God's presence and honoring God with worship & praise; to meet each others need with God's love; to invite new friends to fellowships; to care for, held accountable and encourage each other as God's people and to prepare for a solid foundation by studying God's word; prepare to serve God and become a servant of God by serving each other.

Youth Lock-In (1st–6th Graders & SDC students) 2nd Sat. monthly from Sep–April
"His divine power has given us everything we need for life and godliness through our knowledge of him who called us by his own glory and goodness" 2 Peter 1:3

Mission: To continue to invite and follow up on the students who had attended Summer Day Camp and to incorporate young people into a family where they can be known, cared for, held accountable, and encouraged. To establish a long term relationship with the students through friendship building and ultimately to share the good news of Jesus Christ with them and their families so they can have a personal relationship with Him.

Summer Day Camp Ministry
(Summer Math Excel/Outdoor Activities Camp (1st Grade–8th Grade) 6 weeks.
"We loved you so much that we were delighted to share with you not only the gospel of God but our lives as well, because you had become so dear to us." 1 Thessalonians 2:8

Mission: To establish a long term relationship with the students through meeting their needs; assisting them academically; providing them with resources to face the many life challenges; empowering them with tools to become responsible adults in facing the future; and ultimately to share the good news of Jesus Christ with them and their families so they can have a personal relationship with Him.

Summer Sports Ministry
(Inter-church Summer Basketball, Softball, Volleyball)

"They then do it to receive a perishable wreath, but we an imperishable" 1 Corinthians 9:25

Mission: This unified sports league has many goals. It's foremost goal is to spread the

Gospel to everyone. Through the support of the participants from churches and organizations, CCU strives to provide a quality fellowship experience for all, Christians and non-Christians. These goals will be achieved if we put Jesus Christ first in our individual lives. In the process of achieving these primary goals, effect outreach, unity, spiritual growth, and developing Christian examples will also occur.

Other Ministries

Tai Chi Classes!—Tai Chi Master Carmen Wong

Classes are held every Saturday morning, beginning at 8:30am for Intermediate class and 9:30am for Beginners class. It is open to all persons.

"A cheerful heart is good medicine, but a crushed spirit dries up the bones." (Proverbs 17:22)

This bible verse is a motto that the Tai Chi class uses frequently. Looking back on the purpose of the Tai Chi classes, we wanted this to be an outreach ministry and an opportunity to proclaim the Gospel. Besides getting acquainted with our neighbors in this community, we want to be able to share the Gospel with them. We are like a patient farmer who is sowing the Gospel seeds and waiting for the harvest. Every time we have the class, we have a short message and sharing so the students can get to know Jesus Christ, the only true God, our Savior.

I thank God because many brothers and sisters have joined this ministry. They have a common mind and goal to bring people before our Lord. In addition, thanks to the pastors, the church staff, the elders, and the brothers and sisters in Christ, for their prayers and participation. Proclaiming the Gospel is our mission.

We hope to understand the needs of the students more and to build a deeper relationship with them. After each class, everyone stays and talks. We also have gatherings at some sisters' homes for fellowship and sharing during special holidays.

The Tai Chi Class team plans to have different activities each year. These include the Gospel Tea House, Seminar on Life, songs, testimony sharing, short videos, etc. We become friends through personal follow up. We pray that more people will be able to teach Tai Chi and be part of the follow up work. We ask God to give us strength in this ministry and through His grace people will be benefited both physically and spiritually.

"For physical training is of some value, but godliness has value for all things, holding promise for both the present life and the life to come." (1 Tim 4:8)

This Bible verse is another verse the class uses as a motto for the Tai Chi Class. It reminds us that only through Jesus we have the true joy and peace, and the assurance of the everlasting life. Let us sow and water together, knowing God is the one who makes them grow. We trust in the coming days, the Holy Spirit will lead the Lutheran Church of the Holy Spirit to open the door of the Gospel; so many more people will come to know the Lord through the Tai Chi classes. All Glory be to God!

Auxiliary of The Lutheran Church Missouri Synod Yun Deen Society —A LWML Society

This is a group of Chinese speaking senior ladies who "Serve the Lord with Gladness" in many ways. They are chartered by District CNH—LWML Some ladies serve on the Altar Guild, preparing the sacraments for Holy Communion and Baptism. Candles and altar supplies are provided. Others provide flowers to be arranged for use on the altar. The ladies regularly prepare meals for the monthly congregational prayer meetings.

Since our society is comprised of mostly senior ladies, much time is spent on the telephone encouraging and sharing the concerns of our sisters and families.

Prayer is one of our strongest points. We also support the LWML mite projects with our monthly mites. We join with our sisters in Love in Action in making "Tools for Missions" and other service projects. We continue to "Serve the Lord whenever and wherever He has need of us"

Love in Action ——A LWML Society

This is an English speaking society which was Chartered by District CNH-LWML in June 1987. The ladies serve in the Altar Guild to prepare the sacraments and care for the altar area, changing the paraments during the church year. Some ladies are talented in flower arranging so the church chancel always has beautiful floral arrangements.

Ladies of this society support the Mite projects of LWML. Each second Sunday of the month mites are poured into a silver bowl and pastor prayers for the use of the mites.

The ladies are busy making "Tools for Missions" crosses are cut out from used greeting cards and a Chinese Bible verse is attached to the reverse side.

Other ladies use colored beads to make beaded crosses. These tools are sent to our Missionary Deaconess Carol Halter to give to people on the Mission field. A new project, began in 2009, is crocheting and knitting Love Blankets which are given to shut ins and persons in the hospitals, to share the Love of Jesus when visited by the Care committee.

These ladies continue to Serve the Lord with Gladness, whenever and wherever He has need of them!

LWML Altar Guild

It is a privilege to "Serve the Lord with Gladness" through the LWML Altar Guild.

Our Altar Guild is divided into two groups, with ladies from each of our LWML Society divided into two groups: Altar Flower Arrangers and Holy Communion & Baptism servers.

We are thankful for the many faithful members of our congregation who provide flowers to beautify the altar each Sunday. Members provide $20 per Sunday to purchase the flowers. Six ladies of the Altar Guild purchase and prepare the flower arrangements.

Another team serves in preparing the Holy Communion Sacraments and the Baptismal font for the English Service, Bilingual and Cantonese Worships. All ladies serve the Lord and His church wherever and whenever He has need of them.

Fellowship Groups

Agape Unity (AU) Fellowship
Bilingual—Adults—Age 40+

EM Adult Fellowship
English Speaking Adults

Faithfulness Fellowship
Bilingual—Young Professionals—Age 20s–35s

Gospel Fellowship
Cantonese & Mandarin —Age 25–50
Seekers & New Believers

Hope Fellowship
Bilingual—Adults—late 20's–30'—Career

Living Spirit Fellowship
English and Cantonese—College Career

Living Water Felllowship
Bilingual —High School Students

Living Word Fellowship
English & Cantonese—College & Career

Praise Fellowship
Cantonese—HUL Parents

Senior Fellowship
Cantonese—Seniors

Truth Fellowship
Cantonese—Adults

Young Couples—Bilingual
Young Married Couples

Help–U–Learn
(After School Tutorial—English speaking)

Peace Fellowship (College and Career)

Trinity Fellowship (High School)

Peace JR Fellowship (Middle School)

Youth Lock In
(1ST–6TH Graders & SDC students)

Summer Daycamp (Math Excel—Outdoor Camp)

Summer Sports Ministry
(Inter-church Basketball)

The Church 2012   Chapter Twenty Five

The Vision! – Pastor Shiu Ming Lau

Reading this book, I have seen how God blessed Pastor Holt's ministry during his life. Also, He has lead the ministry of the Lutheran Church of the Holy Spirit throughout the years. God's hand has been blessings us from the beginning until now.

Ten years ago, when I was still in St. Louis, I was assigned to plant a Chinese mission in a place where the Chinese population was less than 3%. I really sat down and asked myself why is a new mission needed. My struggle was: How could I tell the people the importance of this ministry and its goal for the future? After praying, I had two affirmations in my mind: the first affirmation is that Chinese people, like other ethnic group, would need to worship the One true God with their mother tongue. Since so many new immigrants were settled down in the US, they might want to share their faith with the language they were familiar with. As long as the new immigrants keep coming to this land of freedom to pursue their new life, they may like someone to understand their struggles and help them solve their problems. It is good for us to serve them in this moment. Generally, the services that we provided for them are a step before evangelism. We are showing them the love of Christ. The goal of a Church planter is to mobilize many other Christians, including those who are from other Caucasian Churches, to reach out and evangelize the Chinese people. After praying, I know that I am on the right track!

Another affirmation is that the Chinese Christians in the US are prepared for sending many more workers into the big harvest in the mission field in Asia. When a Chinese Church grows strong and mature, they may be able to send Asian missionaries out. These people are more-likely bi-cultural, and bilingual; some of them may even be tri-lingual. They are able to help build a bridge between the world mission office and local church bodies in Asia. Perhaps they have better understanding of the local culture in order to share the gospel with the local people in Asia. With the burden to spread the good news to the people of same race, like Paul's burden to the Jews, many Chinese Christians have been working hard to achieve the goal. Because they are fluent in their Asian language, which they have been learning from the parents, they may be starting the mission work right away. They don't need to spend a lot of time to learn the Asian language. The cost of the mission will be less and the turn out and result will be obvious.

I think these two affirmations still apply to the Church of the Holy Spirit. The congregation members in this Church have a great burden to share the gospel with the Chinese community. They want more people from the same race to join the family of the heavenly kingdom. They are praying for their relatives in Hong Kong, China, and be Taiwan to hear the good gospel.

God has richly blessed the Church. Several years ago, I challenged them to try joining the mission team for the world mission. That means we will not just focus on evangelism in the local area, but also look for the opportunity to work with missionaries in Asia.

I remembered the first year when I took the call to serve in this Church, someone approached me and asked my advice how she and her husband could celebrate their 25th year wedding anniversary. I casually told them that it would be a great memory if they are able to join the short mission trip on their 25th wedding anniversary. Then they asked me to organize one in the church. I promised. This is the humble beginning but also the beautiful beginning of the mission task force. Now, we are not just giving financial support to the world mission, we are also sending out people in the mission field. The first mission team had a good enrollment. Since then, we have at least one team sent out every year. The next year, someone told me, "Pastor, doing the world mission is the heart of Pastor Holt. Now, God achieved Pastor Holt's prayer through you!" I appreciated Pastor Holt, who as a Caucasian loved the Chinese so much. Now is the time we continue his burden.

I pray that our church is a missional church. We will continually spread the gospel in the US and share the good news all over the world to accomplish the Great Commission. I pray that our church is a training center of mission and evangelism for the glory of God, Amen!

"But you will receive power when the Holy Spirit comes on you; and you will be my witness in Jerusalem, and in all Judea and Samaria, and to the ends of the earth." (Acts 1:8)

From a very humble beginning, built by the Power of the Holy Spirit, the many prayers of her people and the sheer will power and strength of its leadership which never faltered, today the Lutheran Church of the Holy Spirit is a shining beacon holding up the banner "God Is Love—Christ Died for Sinners". May God richly bless their vision as they strive to build a larger church building to extend their outreach to the Chinese people in the Sunset area and beyond!

Benediction

"To Him who is able to keep you from falling and to present you before his glorious presence without fault and with great joy—to the only God our Savior be glory, majesty, power and authority, through Jesus Christ our Lord, before all ages, now and forevermore! Amen." Jude 1:24–25

The Church 2012   Chapter Twenty Five

Installation of Pastor Ng September 2009

Installation of Pastor Lau June 2006

Pastor Lau's Family

Pastor Ng's Family

About the Author

The author, Vangina E. Lee comes from Norwegian ancestry. Early in life she had a keen desire to learn the Chinese culture, language and its people. The Lord led her to marry a wonderful Chinese Christian husband, and gave her the privilege to speak fluently the Toy Shan dialect of Cantonese. All praise be to our Lord Jesus! She is a senior member of the Lutheran Church of the Holy Spirit.

Colophon

Text in Hiroshige
Titles in Hiroshige ATT
Set using Adobe InDesign 5

Printed in USA

ww.onespiritpress.com
onespiritpress@gmail.com

www.ingramcontent.com/pod-product-compliance
Lightning Source LLC
Chambersburg PA
CBHW082111230426
43671CB00015B/2666